30,95N

D1074729

Economic Theory

VOLUME ONE

The elementary relations of economic life

By the same author

Economic Studies: Contributions to the Critique of Economic Theory
(Routledge & Kegan Paul, 1977)

Economic Theory

VOLUME ONE

The elementary relations of economic life

DAVID P. LEVINE

ROUTLEDGE & KEGAN PAUL
LONDON, HENLEY AND BOSTON

First published in 1978
by Routledge & Kegan Paul Ltd
39 Store Street,
London WC1E 7DD,
Broadway House,
Newtown Road,
Henley-on-Thames,
Oxon RG9 1EN and
9 Park Street,
Boston, Mass. 02108, USA
Set in 11 on 12-point Imprint
and printed and bound in Great Britain by
Morrison & Gibb Ltd, London and Edinburgh
Copyright David P. Levine 1978
No part of this book may be reproduced in
any form without permission from the
publisher, except for the quotation of brief
passages in criticism

British Library Cataloguing in Publication Data

Levine, David P.

Economic theory.
Vol. 1: The elementary relations of economic life.
I. Economics
1. Title
330.1   HB171   78–40277

ISBN 0 7100 8837 X

For Lynn

Contents

Contents

Contents

Contents

Acknowledgments

Once a science is established by an original act of systemization, such as that of Marx particularly in his treatment of capital in general, the further clarification and development of the ideas, however necessary, will inevitably appear as a pale reflection of the original. It need hardly be said that there is nothing of importance which is original in the present volume. Indeed, it is precisely in the compulsive search for something 'new' that the social sciences reveal most vividly that loss of direction and failure of purpose which makes each flash of originality quickly reveal itself to be nothing more than the tired repetition of the same dogmas. The debt which the present volume owes to classical political economy, and above all to Marx, will be obvious. To encumber the argument with specific references to the relevant texts would only serve to trivialize their contribution, while forcing the positive exposition of the science to adopt the form of a compendium of *ad hoc* insights.

The theoretical treatment of value and exchange, of labor and social production, all find their first clear and compelling statement in the work of Marx. It needs particularly to be emphasized that the absence, in the following, of any assertion regarding the proportionality between ratios of exchange and of 'embodied labor time' constitutes a repudiation of the so-called 'labor theory of value' only in a formal sense. The idea of commodity production has been fully retained without the least accession to the notion of the transformation of 'scarce factors of production.' What has been left aside is the idea that the commodity and its value are fully determined within the immediate production process; that false idea of Ricardo's that, as Marx puts it, 'the production of the commodity is directly equivalent to its real realization.' This idea, as it presents itself in classical political economy, has been fully criticized in the volume *Economic Studies*. In the present, positive, treatment of economic relations, every effort has been made to purge the argument of even those elements of the reductionism of the classical value theory retained by Marx.

The ideas presented here were originally formulated in lectures delivered at Yale University. I would like to acknowledge the contribution made by participants in those courses, and especially to thank them for their critical reception of the argument in the various stages of its development. In a period during which the recalcitrance of the disciplines in defending orthodox modes of thinking remains undiminished, the possibilities for a sustained discussion of the fundamental premises of the theoretical investigation of economic life, within the scientific community, are sharply restricted. Universities have not encouraged, and, indeed, in many instances have actively opposed, the serious confrontation with alternatives to the prevailing methodology of the social sciences. Given the virtually unquestioned hegemony of the prevailing logic of the sciences, it is both remarkable and encouraging that students are able to see clearly that to which their teachers remain blind: the necessity for a sustained critical investigation of the fundamental structure of ideas, and of the logic of their development.

I would like also to thank Betsy Aron, whose editorial work on the manuscript of this volume has contributed greatly to the clarity of the exposition, and Carol Heim for preparation of the index.

Prologue

This book is the second in a three-part investigation of the system of economic relations and of the development of its conception. In the previous book,[1] we considered the logical structures of the different conceptions of economic life as the basis for an evaluation of their adequacy to the object of establishing economic analysis on a scientific footing. In the present and the subsequent volume the attempt is made to overcome the deficiencies of these conceptions and to put forward a comprehensive theoretical treatment of economic life.

The critique already presented makes possible the work of reconstruction so far as it succeeds in eliminating not only false ideas, but the whole of the logical structure which makes those false ideas necessary. Only where the ideas which present themselves as scientific are made to repudiate their own foundations and necessary presuppositions is the further development of the theory possible. The immanent critique of the logical structure of the theoretical argument provides the only definitive basis for a scientific judgment of its adequacy. This is the method employed by Marx in his critique of classical political economy. There can be no question whatever as to the immediate preconditions for the advance in the science marked by the preparation of the three volumes of *Capital*. The work which was involved in this reconstruction of economics as a science is now a matter of public record,[2] a record of Marx's unrelenting critique of the inner logical structure of classical political economy. And it is precisely this same method, applied to Marx's own work, which will alone make possible the final completion of the project first begun by classical political economy and first placed upon a systematic footing by Marx.

Subsequent to Marx, the failure of his followers to apply his own method has succeeded in bringing economic theory to a virtual standstill. The essential reason for this impasse is connected to the repudiation of the dialectical logic first firmly established by Hegel, and first employed in the treatment of economic relations by Marx. This repudiation is connected both to the hegemony of various forms of empiricism within the social sciences, and to the ever-intensified effort on the part of Marxian economists and social scientists to sever the fundamental link between Marx's theoretical work and the Hegelian philosophy. This effort was encouraged by Marx himself, and provides the starting point for the degeneration of his contribution into a series of theoretically problematic claims regarding, in particular, the 'material' determination of social life, and therefore the relation which is sustained between the 'social relations of production,' and the relations of exchange and distribution which, taken in their concretely determined forms, constitute the system of market interactions. That the method which underlies these claims plays a central role in the Marxian conception of economic life could hardly be denied. Indeed, the 'materialist' conception finds a peculiarly congenial subject-matter in the system of economic relations, especially as that system is conceptualized in classical political economy.[3] The determination of commodity exchange in labor-time roots the social relation of exchange in the solid ground of 'material life,' thereby providing a theoretical account for the relation of reciprocity in accordance with the material subsistence of the species.

What is characteristic of the classical method is precisely this effort to ground commodity exchange in a condition – labor considered as a material relation – determined outside of the relations of commodities and commodity owners. Methodologically, determination is identified by classical political economy with reduction to an independently fixed condition. It is this independence which allows the material relations to exert a casual, therefore determining, influence over the social relation of exchange. The

characteristic project of classical economics is that of establishing
the consistency of the substantively economic relations of exchange
and distribution with the theoretically primordial relations of the
material reproduction of the species.

Thus, for Ricardo, the problem of the theory of value is that of
establishing the consistency of the determination of exchange-
value in labor time with the conditions sustained within the system
of economic relations taken as a whole. Ricardo grasps that the
system of economic relations entails a distinctive determination
not immediately equivalent to the material conditions. Value is
labor time. Yet, value is also the market price which sustains the
system of competing capitals by bringing about an equalization of
profit rates. Indeed, value is immediately a purely economic
relation (exchange-value or price). It is the economic analysis
which shows that the economically determined value is necessarily
the life-form of a material condition. The determination of commodity exchange in labor time is the first step in this theoretical
work. Here, it is necessary to establish that the concrete mechanisms of price determination within a system of market relations
only serve to make effective the material conditions of commodity
production. Thus the general average brought about by fluctuations in market price is the cost determined value fixed prior to
the market existence of the commodity, in its material production.
The real cost which governs market price is also independent of
the market; it is market determining and not market determined.
This cost is represented by Ricardo as a quantity of labor time
fixed strictly by the conditions of production, especially the
fertility of the earth.

It is upon this basis that Ricardo proceeds to argue that the
economic relations of distribution (wages, profit, rent) are determined by the prior condition of material productivity. The wage
is immediately determined by the material requirements of the
reproduction of the worker. The fulfilment of these requirements
through the purchase and sale of commodities (including the
commodity labor-power) is essentially accidental. Indeed, since
the money wage simply represents ideally the economic form
adopted by the material subsistence, Ricardo considers it analytically necessary to dispense with those aspects of the wage-
contract irrevocably connected to its monetary form. The purchase
and sale of the commodity labor-power becomes the material

transfer of labor for the means of subsistence required in its reproduction.

Similarly, when Ricardo considers the determination of rent, he takes for his starting point the 'original and indestructible powers of the soil.' These powers are fixed naturally and are measured, as a schedule of diminishing productivity, independently of the relevant economic relations – rent and profit. The category of rent gives economic form to this material condition; it is the representative within economic life of the natural fertility of the earth. As in the case of the wage, the economic relation has no independent determination; it is the economic reflection of the material life of the species.

For Ricardo it is, however, insufficient to merely assert the determination of price in labor time or of rent in fertility. It is also necessary to establish concretely that the real conditions of economic life conform, especially quantitatively, to their prior material determination. Market determination of prices in the context of the competition of capitals must establish the economic force of the prior determination of value within production. Similarly, the measurement of the 'original and indestructible powers of the soil' must remain a material measurement, independent of the economic life of the product, in the face of the concrete conditions of capitalist production on the land. It is at this point that the weaknesses of the classical method make themselves felt most acutely. The quantitative determination of price in accordance with the inner logic of economic life does not correspond with the material determination of value in production. Production for profit, and the competition among producers which it implies, obliterates any immediate equivalence between the rates at which commodities exchange and the proportions of labor time required for their production. The schedule of the diminishing productivity of the soil, which establishes the determination of rent in fertility, is effectively obliterated by the subordination of production to capital, particularly by the investment of capital on the land.* In the light of this failure to establish the full determination of the

---

* The intelligibility (including measurability) of the 'original and indestructible powers' can only be sustained when capital investment leaves unaffected the relative productivities of the different units of land, and alters only the absolute productivity of each; see *The Principles of Political Economy and Taxation*, ed. P. Sraffa (Cambridge: Cambridge University Press, 1951) pp. 80–3.

economic relations in the material life of the species, the admission of a distinctively economic determination of the economic relations becomes inevitable.

If any economist can lay claim to overthrowing the classical conception by asserting a distinct mode of determination of economic relations, it is Marx, whose object is to theorize the social determination of economic life. What for Ricardo always remains the attempt to root the economic forms in the natural condition of fertility, becomes for Marx the attempt to establish the direct relations of social production as the determinants of the economic forms of exchange and distribution. Marx establishes relations of production as social relations, and thereby makes the determination of exchange and distribution in production their social determination.

Marx retains the classical idea that exchange is determined by relations of production. The method of determination is in this respect common to Ricardo and Marx. Marx also considers market price to be the socially contingent form of a conceptually primordial productive act. The original determination of price in labor-value is retained. Profit is constituted as a form (indeed a 'mystified form') of the surplus-value fully determined in magnitude by the immediate relation of the owners of the conditions of production to the direct producers. Given the system of values (labor time), including the 'value of labor-power,' it only remains to be shown that prices and profits are fully determined as transformations of value and of the rate of surplus-value (the ratio of surplus to necessary labor time). To be sure, there need be no implication of any quantitative equivalence of labor-value and price or of surplus-value and profit. It only needs to be established that (1) the system of values is originally fixed in production, and (2) the system of prices bears a quantitatively determinate relation to labor-values.

This is the essential point. The full determination of value and surplus-value within the immediate production process leaves for the analysis of circulation, competition, price formation and accumulation only the task of reconciling the 'apparent,' and therefore superficial, forms with an already fully developed essence. This idea has the most profound implications for the conception of economic life. It excludes any substantive market determination of capitalist expansion by making the constitution of capital in the form of a system of interacting particular units inessential to the deduction of the laws of economic development. In all respects the conception of the economy as a living totality, determined within its own process of self-development, dissipates into a wholly abstract conception of the immediate production process viewed as a material interchange.

For Marx, the Ricardian contradiction between labor-value and price is replaced by the 'transformation of values into prices.' It is through this 'transformation' that Marx seeks to establish the price system as a 'phenomenal form.' Indeed, it is precisely by transforming labor-value into price that Marx finally consummates the classical project of constituting the determination of the system of market relations upon the basis of production considered as a theoretically primordial condition. What distinguishes the Marxian project is the attempt to constitute production as the materializing process of a social relation. Marx attempts to complete the classical theory by establishing the social determination of production as the logical basis for the material determination of commodity exchange. The contradictions within the Marxian reformulation of the essentially classical idea of material determination all derive from the attempt to constitute the material determination of social life upon the basis of the social determination of the presumed material relations of economic life.

By asserting the primacy of social determination in the logical investigation of economic relations, Marx seeks to break with the reductionism of the classical theory. Classical theory accounts for social relations by equating them with natural conditions, thereby reducing them to the external effects of a natural principle. This method excludes any substantively economic determination. As regards the relations of economic life, the object of the theory is to discover their mode of determination not within economic life, but outside. For Marx, economic determination refers to a substantive reality irreducible to externally fixed natural relations. And yet, the import of social determination remains ambiguous. Marx asserts that the labor which produces, and thereby determines, value is social labor. This constitution of labor as a social relation is made, by Marx, conceptually independent of the system of economic relations. In particular, the social determination of labor is made effectively independent of the social relation of exchange. That the[4] necessity of distributing social labor in definite proportions cannot be done away with by the *particular form* of social production, but can only change the *form it assumes*, is self-evident. No natural laws can be done away with. What can change, in changing historical circumstances, is the *form* in which these laws operate. And the form in which this proportional division of labor operates, in a state of society where the interconnection of social labor is manifested in *private exchange*, is precisely the *exchange-value* of these products.

The sociality of the labor is not intrinsically connected either to the system of property rights, or to the specificity of the exchange relation. That labor is in this sense primordial is connected by classical political economy to its natural determination. Marx, however, seeks to constitute labor as the primordial social relation, primordial in that its social determination is unconnected to any specification of a system of social relations. In so doing Marx strikes a precarious balance. He partakes of the reductionism of the classical theory by establishing the determination of market interaction in a relation fixed outside of the system of market relations. In this respect, the method employed by Marx is that of Smith and Ricardo. It claims to provide a theoretical account for specific economic phenomena (e.g. price) by reducing them to a primordial condition which is asserted to be the essence of the socially contingent form. Theory penetrates the forms of appearance by showing those forms to be, in actuality, the mere expressions of a substantive condition – social labor – which provides for them an account. Yet, the implication of this method is also that the specific economic relations (e.g. exchange) are excluded from entering into the social determination of the 'real relations' which produce and determine them. Thus, in establishing the sociality of the labor, no reference can be made to exchange, since, so far as social determination is concerned, the exchange relation is inessential.

What, then, accounts for that social determination of production which provides the logical basis for the social determination of the forms of economic interaction? On this question Marx is effectively silent. Yet silence on this question speaks more loudly than all protestations regarding the social relations of production, the sequence of 'modes of production,' and the material conditions of social life. After a century of Marxian theory, the idea of social production, once shorn of that rich content provided for it by Marx in the specification of *capitalist* production, remains an empty shell. That this conception remains deficient is the result not of a failure of Marx's followers to seek out a concrete content for the idea of social production made independent of its bourgeois 'form,' but of their failure to discover any positive quality which continues to adhere to the idea of labor when its specification to capital is left aside. Yet, only so long as it is possible to remove the 'bourgeois form of labor' without obliterating altogether the idea of labor as a social relation, can the laboring which works for capital be considered as a form of labor.

The attempt to theorize economic relations by the method of reduction to primordial conditions, engaged in both by classical political economy and Marx, condemns social theory to an endless fluctuation between two opposed and yet mutually dependent conceptions of social determination: that by which laboring is socially determined prior to the system of economic relations; and that by which the system of economic relations is socially determined by its reduction to the form of appearance of social labor. The second method of determination makes all concrete economic relations essentially contingent. As forms of appearance they remain historically accidental. The necessity of the distribution of social labor is that of a 'natural law'; that this distribution proceed via the exchange of commodities is at best an historical accident. This method of determination is incapable of accounting for the system of commodity relations upon the basis of a conception of their necessity.

At the same time, that mode of determination by which labor is established as a social relation, since devoid of content, is no real social determination of labor, but the mere abstract assertion of the sociality of labor. Since social labor is made to account for the relation of reciprocity, the social determination of labor must be given independently of the relations of reciprocal recognition of individuals, especially exchange. It is precisely this *a priori* constitution of labor as a social relation which deprives social labor of any determinable content. This indeterminacy is fully exposed when the supposedly social labor is described concretely either as the immediate natural relation of man to nature ('work'), or as the purely subjective relation of individual purposive activity.

These two methods of social determination form a unit. And yet, when merged together they provide nothing more than the empty assertions of which they are each separately composed. They provide only the semblance of a social determination of economic life, and not its systematic account. For the theoretical treatment of the system of economic relations it is necessary to leave behind that logic which proceeds via the reduction of social relations to primordial conditions, however those conditions may be conceived. This requires a break with certain of the most strongly held claims of the Marxian method. It is not, however, implied by this that an equally sharp break is necessary from the logical structure of Marx's argument. The latter is by no means the direct realization of the method of material determination adapted by Marx from classical political economy. To be sure, the idea of a primordial material determination does play a central role in providing methodological support for certain of Marx's most forcefully argued propositions: the equation of value with labor time, the determination of the rate of exploitation within the immediate production process, the determination of the rate of profit by conditions of production (especially the organic composition of capital), etc. None the less, the idea of a primordial determination fails utterly to account for the fundamental logical structure of the text. It is wholly unable to establish the necessity of the order and method of presentation of the system of relations of capital. Here, a radically distinct method makes its greater theoretical force known.

Once we leave behind Marx's explicit methodological strictures, together with the abstract assertions with which his theory has been falsely identified, in order to consider instead his actual theoretical practice as it presents itself in the form of a sustained argument, we leave behind as well the reductionism of his 'material' determination and find in its place the living form of an essentially different method. To be sure, this distinctive logic presents itself as a part of the material determination, and can only be separated from that determination by a sustained critique. None the less, the force of the logic by which the social relations of economic life are developed by Marx in accordance with their inner logic and self-determination is sufficient to dominate the structure of the argument as a whole.

What is this alternative method which provides the force of

9

Marx's argument, and yet is more frequently suppressed than articulated in Marx's own methodological writings? How does the Marxian theory propose to provide a theoretical account for the system of economic relations which does not impose upon them a primordial determination in an externally fixed 'material' condition?

To give an account, within orthodox social science, for the emergence of a particular phenomenon (e.g. a price, or a system of prices) is to reduce that phenomenon to a premise, thereby showing how it expresses in a relation the force of an externally fixed condition. The analysis proceeds through a series of reductions (price is reduced to a relation of supply and demand, supply and demand are constituted as manifestations of preferences and endowments) until the point is reached at which the bedrock conditions which determine economic interaction are fully exposed. To establish the origin and determination of exchange is to constitute exchange as the form of manifestation of naturally determined resource availability and individual whim. The theory has completed its work when it reaches such boundaries as are defined by the necessity of uncovering the external determinants of economic interaction. The real account for the object of the theory is always across those boundaries, and is therefore not provided by the theoretical argument. In this respect, the dominant methodology of the social sciences bears a strong affinity to the method employed by classical political economy, and to a lesser extent by Marx. The relations of reciprocity do not sustain themselves of their own inner force, but are sustained by analytically primordial conditions. While the differences which separate the 'allocation of resources,' with which modern economics identifies market interaction, from the 'allocation of social labor' of Marxian economics are by no means trivial, the two conceptions share in common an essential methodological premise. So long as the distribution of labor, even of social labor, is determined independently of the market, the market must eventually be seen to constitute itself as an 'allocative mechanism.' Thus the specification of the needs fulfilled may be considered differently in classical and in modern economics, but the logic of the market provides a common ground. And it must be so, as long as the market is constrained to 'execute' laws (e.g. of production) determined outside of, and logically prior to, exchange. The ideas of fixed premises, causal determination, and social relations as phenomenal forms, are all methodologically linked. So long as the determining conditions (whether the distribution of social labor, or the supply of scarce resources) are taken to be fixed independently, the social and economic relations, which provide for those conditions a form of existence, must remain arbitrary. They can be nothing more than the external and inessential forms. As such they cannot be accounted for by any inner necessity and can provide, at best, a limited subject-matter for a theoretical investigation. Economic theory cannot establish the necessity of exchange, since exchange is the inessential form. Indeed, it becomes the task of economic analysis to show that exchange is unnecessary either by establishing it to be a purely contingent form of a material relation, or by showing it to be the accidental result of a configuration of individual whim and resource availability.

Is it possible to move beyond this conception and destabilize the apparently fixed premises which provide an external determination for the system of economic interactions? In order to do so it is necessary to find the determination of the premises of economic life within the system of economic relations itself. The idea of external determination by reduction to primordial conditions must give way to the idea of intrinsic determination within a process; and this process must be constituted not as the external form of manifestation of a prior material reality, but as the process of the self-determination of the system of relations taken as a whole. The relations of economic life are made accountable not to materially given 'facts,' but to their own process of self-constitution.

This necessity of transforming fixed conditions into moments of a process is generally recognized within Marxian analysis, but only in the special form of the historicizing of the conception of economic relations. The categories of economic analysis (exchange, money, capital, etc.) are considered to be historically relative, limited to a fixed stage in the sequence of development of 'modes of production.' Apparently given conditions can be established as results when they are considered in the context of the historical process and, in particular, when their historical limitations, their origins and their eventual transcendence, are specified. To recognize that the relations of economic life have a history is necessarily to deny to those relations any purely natural deter-

mination, and to establish, at least implicitly, their social determination. None the less, the attempt to ground the analysis
historically runs up against serious obstacles when it is required
to take the form of a truly theoretical argument. To know the
history of the relations of bourgeois economy, it is first necessary
to grasp its analytic specificity. Such a determination cannot be
made from the historical 'facts,' since taken on their own, in the
form of isolated instances, events or data, they must remain mute
with respect to their inner connection to the process by which
wealth is constituted as a self-determining structure. It is only
possible to write the history of capital (of exchange, social production, etc.) from the vantage point of the systematic analysis
of capital.

Ultimately, history taken as a point of departure must either
make the logical conception essentially contingent upon geo-
graphic, climatic, demographic or cultural accidents; or it must
constitute capital as a particular *form* of economic life. The idea
that the object of analysis is a specific 'mode of production' makes
the relations of capital contingent forms of generalized relations of
production and appropriation. It is precisely this generalization
which, however, deprives the conception of the 'social relations of
production' of any rigorously determinable content. Unless it is
accepted that, within the system of bourgeois economic relations,
there can be found a universality not restricted to a fixed historical
epoch, the logical investigation of wealth becomes impossible. For
the consummation of a theoretical conception of production and
exchange, it must be admitted that the idea of social labor is not
logically independent of the relations of private property and
exchange; that, in general, the significance of the concept of capital
for the conception of labor as a social relation extends to all
constitution of production as a social relation; and that, in Marx's
words, 'bourgeois economy holds the key to ancient economy.'[5]

In general it is impossible to ground the conception of capital
by considering it immediately within the process of its emergence:[6]

> The conditions and presuppositions of the *becoming*, of the
> *arising*, of capital presuppose precisely that it is not yet in
> being but merely in *becoming*; they therefore disappear as real
> capital arises, capital which itself, on the basis of its own
> reality, posits conditions of its realization.

The conditions which define the historical emergence of capital are, by that fact, fetters to the full constitution of capital. They deny, rather than affirm, the process of capital's self-constitution, so that their retention must fundamentally impede the logical investigation of the system of economic relations. The idea of history can provide no immediate basis for a conception of the process within which the relations of wealth are intrinsically determined. The history concerns itself with the manner in which the economic relations shed those natural determining conditions within which they originally present themselves. Economic theory constructs a conception of the inner determination of wealth as a process of its self-constitution not in accordance with externally given natural laws, but in accordance with its own inner nature and with the requirements of its characteristic life-process.

The idea of self-determination is the methodological foundation upon which it is possible to construct a theoretical conception of economic life which overcomes the deep structural weaknesses of the idea of a primordial material determination. It is the constitution of economic relations within the ongoing process of their self-determination and self-development that makes possible the elimination of all extrinsically fixed determinants of the life-cycle of wealth.

The logic of causal determination is intrinsically incapable of grasping a system within a process of self-development. Where premises are considered as moments of a continuing process which is substantively self-contained, the logic of the process must also be self-contained. All premises can be simultaneously results only when the logic within which the relations subsist shares the circularity implied by the idea of self-constitution.

While such a logic may appear to be necessarily both tautological and empty, this is by no means the case. The force of the idea of self-determination is already evident in one of the most common-place, and yet significant, ideas of economic science, that of the 'circular flow of economic life.' In the course of its circular flow, the economic process succeeds, from one period to the next, in *renewing itself*. This process of self-renewal incorporates the whole of the system of economic relations as its own product. The circularity of the flow of economic life is only really established where the elements of the flow originate within the movement itself. Otherwise circularity becomes nothing more than a false form for a movement the substantive reality of which is linear. This linearity is characteristic of neo-classical economics which views the motion of commodities as determinable in accordance with a fixed starting point (resources) and a given end (individual consumption). This construction conflicts essentially with the idea of self-renewal which is deeply embedded in the idea of a circular flow. A truly self-determining system *replaces itself*, and can only do so by producing itself from period to period. Self-renewal or self-replacement is therefore reproduction.

In the reproduction cycle, all preconditions of production (e.g. commodity inputs) are themselves produced. It is for this reason that the concept of reproduction plays an essential role in economic theory. The economic process as depicted in any period is the premise for production in the next period, and it is the result of production in the previous period. Reproduction is the positing within a process of the conditions for its repetition and continuation. It is a process of self-generation and regeneration. Now it is necessary to grasp the system as a whole, the interconnected and interdependent manifold of economic relations, as self-conditioning. Each particular relation (e.g. an individual price) is determined by its participation in the system of relations as a whole considered as a self-sustaining process.

The methodological import of the idea of self-renewal is manifest. It is upon the basis of this conception that economic relations can be made determinate not in accordance with the causal force of an externally given material condition, but in accordance with their situation within the ongoing process of reproduction. Determination is no longer the equilibration of given conditions, the adjustment of resources according to need or the distribution of social labor in accordance with its relative productivities and technical interdependence. Determination is now the ongoing process of the self-regeneration of a system of relations.

The object of economic science is to construct a conception of the system of economic relations established within its generative cycle. In this way, the theory provides a systematic account for the determination of prices, profits, etc., in accordance with the exigencies of the reproduction and growth of wealth. In effect, the condition of self-renewal can be made to replace that of equilibration in characterizing the process within which the system of economic relations is determined.

This is, indeed, the starting point, for example, of Piero Sraffa, who takes a system of price relations based upon a complex of technical relations considered under conditions of self-renewal as the starting point for the investigation of price determination.[7] It is readily established that the condition of self-replacement fixes the system of prices quantitatively, and in that sense establishes their determinacy. The individual price is thereby determined not by the allocation of a given substance in accordance with externally fixed needs, as in the method of equilibration, but by the exigencies of the reproduction of the system as a whole. Methodologically this idea is most forcefully established under conditions of expanded reproduction, where both the abstract condition of self-renewal, and its rate, contribute to the determination of the system of structural relations through which self-renewal transpires.

It would seem logical, then, to begin the analysis directly with the idea of reproduction, establishing the self-renewal of the system of economic relations as the immediate basis upon which to develop a theoretical account for particular relations of the whole (e.g. particular prices). However, since it is only the system as a whole that, within its cycle of self-renewal, establishes its self-determination, to posit that process of self-renewal at the outset would be tantamount to positing the system of economic relations as a whole prior to the analytic specification of that system. This amounts, as Marx puts it, to giving the science before the science. To simply posit reproduction at the outset is to posit at once the totality of the system of economic relations, since reproduction is nothing other than that system considered as a moving process.

Reproduction, taken in the abstract, can in no way be supposed to account for the complex of economic relations undergoing the cycle of renewal. Taken outside of the context of the concrete specification of the nature of the system undergoing the cycle of self-replacement, that cycle cannot be made to account for the specificity of its relations as economic (in opposition, for example, to natural) relations. In the so-called 'corn model' of Ricardo, it is nature which renews itself from period to period. Corn provides the substance consumed in its own renewal. The labor required for the reproduction of corn is provided by the consumption of corn, and the seeds required for the planting of corn come directly out of the corn product of the preceding cycle. For Ricardo, the economic system is a constituent of the natural or ecological system.

A natural system can be as readily grasped in terms of the idea of reproduction and self-development as can the system of economic relations. Indeed, in the period of classical political economy, the idea of a 'natural law' entailed precisely this element of self-determination. In this respect the philosophical basis for the emergence of economics as a science was the constitution of nature as a self-ordering totality. Where the laws of nature are considered mere expressions of the arbitrary will of a primordial being, they cannot be considered scientifically, but only descriptively or theologically. Nature becomes the object of scientific investigation (therefore science emerges as a distinct mode of grasping the determinacy of nature) only when nature ceases to be determined externally, and is instead considered upon the basis of its intrinsic laws. This constitution of the idea of a natural law requires the conception of natural relations not as mere forms of some primordial substance, but as the relations of a self-ordering system. This result is made manifest with the idea of evolution, which represents the natural world within its process of self-development. The object of economic theory is no less that of establishing its subject-matter – wealth – as a self-ordering totality within its characteristic process of self-development. In this respect, economic theory considers the 'natural laws' of economic life. These 'natural laws' are not, however, laws of nature. And it is this distinction which cannot be fully established where the reproduction of the system of economic relations as a whole is taken as the starting point for its conception. There must be a prior conceptual specification of the economic character of the relations sustained within a process of self-renewal.

The standpoint of economic science is not simply that of the economic system taken as a whole, and therefore in process; it is also that of accounting for the richness of content of the whole. In order to do so, it is not sufficient to assert a series of *ad hoc* properties (commodity exchange, equalization of profit rates, steady-state growth, etc.) which specify arbitrarily the relations reproduced and the mode of their renewal. What is required is a specifically conceptual analysis aimed at constructing the totality of relations (1) upon the basis of a rigorous argumentation, which (2) specifies the system of reproduction to economic life both by endowing the particular relations with a specific determination, and endowing their totality with an inner law of motion. The system of reproduction mediated by commodity exchange must be constituted as the reproduction of the system of commodity exchange. This requires a rigorous analytic specification of the exchange relation and of the commodity. Prior to any investigation of the self-development of wealth as a complex structure of relations, there must be a conception of wealth considered in general, therefore, upon the basis of the defining qualities of its elementary unit. Before the full determination of price (including its quantitative determination) can be considered, it is necessary to investigate the most general defining feature of the price relation.

Where the inner nature of price is taken to be its function as an allocative mechanism or scarcity index, the theoretical determination of price (as in the general equilibrium conception) proceeds upon the basis of a specification of resource supply and preference. Where the price relation is taken to signify a relative productivity of labor, the concrete determination of the system of prices proceeds upon the basis of a conception of labor-value. Where price is considered to express the relative dynamism of particular producers and industries, the determination of the price system proceeds upon the basis of a conception of accumulation. Which conception best grasps the inner nature of exchange can only be established by determining which conception is consistent with the development of a price system and with the full determination of that system. Still, in the case of each alternative conception, the idea of price determination within a system of relations depends essentially upon a prior judgment, developed on a highly abstract plane, of the inner nature of the price relation. This judgment is in all cases purely conceptual, and rests not at all upon the empirical study of the phenomena. At such a level of investigation, it would be just as absurd to request 'empirical proof' for the idea that value is 'intrinsic' as it would be for the idea that price is a 'scarcity index.'

The necessity for a prior conceptual investigation holds also for the determination of the mode of renewal and development of the system of economic relations. The abstract idea of self-development may be concretized into a number of distinct forms of movement. Reproduction may signify the self-replacement of a quantitatively and qualitatively fixed system of relations. Alternatively, reproduction may entail self-development considered either as the purely quantitative expansion of a qualitatively fixed structure ('steady state growth'), or as the uneven development by which the structure determines itself both quantitatively and qualitatively. The specific form of growth relevant to the science of wealth is not arbitrary. On the contrary, the characteristic mode of development of wealth is implied in its inner nature, so that the articulation of the most general relations of wealth also makes explicit the determinateness of its reproductive cycle. In order to establish that development, and especially uneven development, is not an historically contingent form, but an intrinsic law, it is necessary to isolate the dynamic force latent within the most general characterization of economic interaction. Thus, the necessity of a specific form of movement derives from the analytic specification of the elementary structural relations within which wealth is given its most general determination.

The starting point for the investigation of economic relations is not, then, the totality and its self-development,[8] but the abstract investigation of the relations in their most general form. It is this abstract investigation which is also the most difficult. Indeed, it is at this level that the methodological issues make themselves most sharply felt, and it is here that the argument deviates most obviously from the prevailing methodology of the sciences.

By its nature the argument regarding the most elementary relations is concerned exclusively with their immanent development and can make no direct appeal to evidence. The intelligibility of the evidence must in any case presuppose the clear articulation of a structure of ideas. Even for those sciences in which experimentation is possible, the experimental evidence must ultimately be validated by the theoretical construction which makes the experimentally achieved result no longer a striking anomaly, but only the mundane exemplification of a necessary law.

To be sure, it would be absurd, in any concrete scientific investigation, to eschew the insight provided by the empirical study of phenomena. The investigation of empirically given information can contribute essentially to the abstract formulation of an ideal relation. The statistical investigation of economic data may unearth systematic relations, including logical connections which would otherwise be difficult, if not impossible, to discover. Since the accumulation of capital is also a process of the historical development of capitalist economy, its laws are represented in the historical record. The investigation of that record, both qualitative and quantitative, may provide essential insight into the mechanisms of growth and development. Indeed, a primary object of the theoretical investigation of capital accumulation is to make intelligible the concrete history of capitalist economic expansion. None the less, it cannot be assumed that the abstract formulation of the relations in accordance with their intrinsic laws will spring immediately out of the empirically irreducible facts, no matter how numerous or varied. The initial enquiry into the subject-matter is simultaneously logical and empirical, requiring that all available information be appropriated in detail and that the essential be distinguished from the inessential by a process of abstraction. The ultimate result of the theoretical treatment of economic relations is not, however, the derivation of empirically contingent correlations, but of the necessary laws which govern economic life. It is precisely to the extent that such laws are taken to be the object of the science that the empirical investigation, taken by itself, remains inadequate. The objective of the theoretical work is neither to ignore nor to present the evidence, but to transcend it (in part upon the basis of the evidence itself) in order that the concrete history, represented abstractly by the 'data,' can be grasped as a living reality. At this stage the force of abstraction is the only means by which a truly theoretical treatment of the subject-matter can be achieved.

The object of the present volume is the exposition of the intrinsic logic of economic interaction considered in its most elementary aspect. This object cannot be achieved by the presentation of a compendium of empirical observations and arbitrary definitions. The various distinct subjects dealt with theoretically do not emerge within the argument as results of empirical generalization. Instead the logic which connects theoretically the seemingly disparate economic relations (e.g. prices, profits, wages, etc.) constitutes those relations not as phenomena immediately present in their full determination, which need only to be described, but as different modes of determination of the most elementary relation. In the case of economic theory this elementary relation is that of wealth taken in general (the commodity and its determinate features). The empirical description of phenomena, however necessary to the emergence of a scientific conception, must give way, in the theoretical argument, to the explication of the intrinsic logic of the system of relations. The theory concerns itself with the inner determination of the subject-matter. This inner determination entails the constitution of the particular relations as logically implied in the most general and elementary conception.

Exchange is the relation of wealth by which its elementary unit expresses and realizes its intrinsic determination (especially its value). Labor is the process out of which wealth emerges as a product. Competition is the system of interactions through which wealth realizes its drive for unlimited expansion. The particular relations of wealth, which together compose the subject-matter of economic theory, are all relations into which wealth enters in order to fully realize its intrinsic nature. The intelligibility of the complex structure of wealth taken as a totality derives from the demonstration that the concrete relations which make up that structure are relations into which the substance of economic interaction – wealth – enters in its self-constitution and self-development.

The present volume considers the elementary relations of wealth. The starting point is wealth in the abstract, considered without reference to any of the concrete relations by which it constitutes its self-determination. For the treatment of wealth in general, the subject-matter presents itself in its most elementary form. The elementary relations of wealth are immediate or indeterminate to the extent that abstraction is made from the concrete interactions which, taken as a whole, represent the process of wealth's self-determination. The object of the theory is to show how these concrete interactions are implied in the general conception of wealth. This demonstration establishes the concrete structure of wealth (the system of economic relations as a whole) as the mode of existence necessary to the subsistence of wealth.

The particular relations within which the concrete determination of wealth is effected determine wealth only by existing as relations of wealth. They establish wealth within a living process which is determinate only by *being* the living process of wealth's determination. Exchange is not an extrinsic event which 'happens to' wealth, but to which wealth remains intrinsically indifferent. Exchange is only made intelligible as that self-relation of wealth which expresses, in the interrelation of its elements, their intrinsic determination as wealth. Here, wealth is concretely determined as means of exchange, and means of exchange is made intelligible as a relation of wealth. This holds also for laboring, which constitutes wealth as the result of a process, thereby establishing the determination of wealth as, for example, means of production. The determination of wealth as means of production is necessary if wealth is to be situated within a process of self-generation. The constitution of wealth as a self-renewing system requires the conception of a productive activity made specific to economic life. This specification is the object of the theoretical investigation of commodity production. The theoretical investigation of production establishes its specificity as the self-generative process of wealth, and in this sense makes production a determination of wealth.

In order for this result to be achieved, wealth must be intrinsically determined in accordance with the requirements of its own productive consumption. This determination is also the division of wealth into the productive requisites of laboring. The determination of wealth within its productive activity establishes a specific economic subject, e.g. means of production, upon the basis of its contribution to the development of wealth as a total structure. Determination entails the inner differentiation of the elemental relations – value distinguished into its different forms: commodities and money; capital differentiated into its component parts: fixed and circulating capital; etc. When these differences, and the inner relations which they imply, are established as implications of the general conception, they are established substantively as determinations of wealth. It is the general conception, out of which the concrete relations have yet to emerge, which is the starting point; and it is the emergence of the concrete relations out of this abstract and as yet undetermined relation, which constitutes the theoretical argument.

Wealth, as Marx asserts at the outset of his investigations, is 'an immense accumulation of commodities.' The elemental unit of wealth, considered upon the basis of its defining qualities taken in the abstract, is the commodity, the unity of value and use-value. The theoretical treatment of wealth begins with the investigation of useful property. The value of the commodity is here considered to measure the extent to which the commodity participates in the system of property relations; it is the quantitative measure of the unit of wealth considered as so much property.

The confusion of this abstract, and therefore indeterminate, starting point with the full determination of wealth provides the methodological foundation for the primary confusions of the classical theory of value. The immediate equation of value with labor time makes the value relation fully determinate prior to the determination of wealth as a total structure. This equation violates the indeterminateness of the elementary relations, and undermines essentially the theoretical force of the conception of the totality as that system within which the complex structure of relations discovers its own full determination in its inner process. When value is determined in labor time prior to its self-determination within a system of commodity relations (including market relations), the determination of value within that concrete system of relations must inevitably come into conflict with the original constitution of value as so much labor time. This is especially the case where the equation of value with labor time is not established by any systematic logic which could connect that equation to the theoretical determination of wealth. The starting point for the analysis of economic relations is not the determination of value in labor time, but the abstract conception of value and use-value considered as defining qualities of wealth.

First, the general nature of the needy individual and his property are considered. This analysis of the most general determination of wealth as useful property resolves itself into an analysis of exchange-value as the means by which the intrinsic qualities of wealth are expressed in the external relations sustained among its composing units (the commodities). The expression of the intrinsic qualities (value and use-value) in an external relation is necessary to the subsistence of those qualities. Without the interrelations of commodities, the defining qualities of the commodity would be effectively suppressed. It is also necessary, however, that the mode of interrelation of commodities fully express their intrinsic determination as useful property. In particular, commodity relations must adopt a form which is adequate to the full expression of the commodity's value. This form is the exchange-value of the commodity for money, or the commodity's price. Money is also a determination of wealth in that the differentiation of wealth into commodities on one side, and money on the other, is necessary in order that the mode of expression of value be adequate to its inner nature.

The opposition of commodities to money makes possible the conception of the purchase and sale, or exchange, of commodities. Within the system of exchanges, wealth is not simply expressed in the interrelation of its elements, the qualities of wealth are also realized in a movement. The circulation of commodities and money establishes the mode of existence of wealth as a commodity flux. Wealth is here constituted as the inner force revealing itself through a form of motion.

The total movement within the circuit has as its objective the realization of wealth as an intrinsic force existing as a system of commodity exchanges. The logic of the system of exchanges is that of their own continuation, since that continuation is synonymous with the subsistence of wealth. Commodity circulation made subordinate to the laws of its own self-subsistence and self-development is capital: the self-ordering movement of wealth. Capital is not a 'type' of wealth, nor even a particular 'use' of wealth. Capital is the ongoing process of the self-subsistence of wealth. The position of the concept of capital in the theoretical treatment of economic life is therefore paramount. Without the concept of capital there can be no conception of the system of economic relations renewing itself within its specific determination. Wealth existing as capital is wealth existing within a process of self-determination and self-development. Capital is this self-development, and therefore represents the further determination of wealth as a self-generative process.

It is now possible to consider wealth (capital) as situated within an ongoing process, and therefore as the result of a process. Wealth is produced in its own process of movement, so that the objective basis for the production of wealth is also wealth. Laboring is the self-generative process of wealth. When wealth results from its own consumption, it sustains itself by positing its existence as the result of its own activity. The determinate qualities of wealth are now formed in an original process. Those qualities are determined in accordance with the exigencies of the production process, while the process of production is made determinate in accordance with the peculiar qualities of its products as the components of wealth.

Production, then, is neither an added factor in the conception of wealth, nor an alternative use for wealth (alternative to its direct consumption). Commodity production is the generative moment in wealth's characteristic life-cycle. The necessity of the productive consumption of wealth is implied in the constitution of wealth as a self-sustaining process. Production is a mode of determination of wealth which is essential to its full development, and therefore also to its scientific conception.

The analysis of commodity production completes the investigation of the most elementary relations of wealth: the relations of price, exchange, and production. The cycle within which these relations are united as a continuous moving process is the circulation of capital. The circulation of capital constitutes wealth as the process of the realization of a produced substance. The analysis of the circuit provides the basis for the inner differentiation of capital in accordance with its characteristic forms of circular motion. The concrete determination of capital in accordance with the totality of its circuit is the differentiation of capital into its component parts: fixed and circulating capital. The analysis of the circuit of capital, which completes the present volume, begins with the investigation of the general qualities of the circuit, shared in common by all concrete forms of movement of capital; and proceeds to consider the concrete determination of the circuit into its constitutive circuits. This decomposition of the circuit establishes the circuit as a whole as the unity of a system of circuits, therefore as a circuit of circuits. This unity of the system of interdependent movements is the unit of capital.

In sum, the determinations involved in the constitution of wealth as a totality within a process of self-development are:

1 The investigation of the elementary unit of wealth (the commodity), its intrinsic or defining qualities (value and use-values), and the interrelations by which these qualities are expressed (exchange-value, especially in money).

2 Wealth considered as the system of actively interrelating elements of which it is composed; wealth considered as a sequence of commodity movements ordered in accordance with its self-subsistence: capital.

3 Wealth considered in its process of self-generation: labor or commodity production.

4 Wealth considered as the connected process of its own production and realization: the circulation of capital.

Volume II, now in preparation, considers wealth as a totality within its process of self-determination. It is here that the concrete investigation of economic relations must be pursued, and that the links which bind the abstract analysis of the elementary relations to the concrete process of capitalist development are made manifest. The starting point for this construction of a conception of the concrete structure of economic relations taken as a whole is the investigation of the system of particular producers and of the market relations by which they are sustained. This entails the analysis of the concrete determinants of the price system as the basis for a derivation of the general laws of capitalist development. The investigation of these general laws requires the analysis of the market, its inner structure, and its mode of development. The interaction between the system as a whole, especially the market, and its particular elements, especially firms, provides the basis for the analysis of the expansion of capital into a world system, and of the laws of its development. The characteristic process of the self-development of wealth is the accumulation of capital. The laws of accumulation constitute the primary object of this analysis, particularly as regards the uneven character of capitalist development, and the modes of concentration implied in its growth cycle.

In sum, the two volumes together consider the determinate, or defining, qualities of wealth, the life-cycle within which these qualities are revealed, and the intrinsic laws by which the development of wealth is governed.

The effort to treat the system of economic relations without immediate reference to the state will, no doubt, strike a discordant note. The abstract constitution of wealth as the object of a scientific investigation was the first great achievement of classical political economy. In the present state of the science this abstract standpoint has been all but lost. The theoretical investigation of economic life invites criticism on the grounds of being too great an abstraction not because of any demonstrably greater *presence* of the state during the current historical period, but because of the preoccupation of modern social science with the economic activities of the state (a preoccupation which is by no means original). This preoccupation derives from the specific historical conditions within which the social sciences find themselves, and from the congenital propensity of social science to allow nothing which is not immediate to enter its line of vision, thereby repudiating all abstraction from the immediately given situation. It is all the more important, in this intellectual context, to forcibly assert those abstractions which, by leaving aside the historically specific conditions, thereby provide the conceptual basis for making those conditions intelligible. That such an abstraction does not imply any relegation of the state to the status of an epiphenomenon would be obvious were it not the case that social science has come to mistakenly identify abstract thinking with formal analysis.

Economic theory, while it must be pursued abstractly, is not a self-contained and independent body of knowledge. Indeed, the concrete subsistence of the system of economic relations can only be made fully intelligible when it is considered in the context of a political structure. On one side, the specification of the state requires a fully abstract conception of economic life; and on the other side, the theory of economic interaction cannot make that interaction comprehensible independently of the transcendence of the relations of civil society and the constitution of the state. The systematic analysis of the state is essential to any full constitution of the economy as a sphere of social interaction. It is within the state that the intrinsic sociality of the economic relations is fully realized, and that the inner contradictions of the self-development of capital adopt their definitive forms.

Finally, it needs to be stated without qualification that the object of this work is solely that of laying bare the intrinsic logic of bourgeois economy. By so doing, it is to be expected that the limits of the bourgeois epoch will be made manifest, but only as inner contradictions of the process of its self-development. The arena within which these limits must ultimately work themselves out is not economic but political, so that the abstract investigation of economic relations could provide a full account of the limits of capitalist development only by falsely depicting its fundamental contradictions. It is here also that the analysis of the state is primary. The treatment of the state, both theoretical and historical, is essential to the full consummation of the project to which these volumes seek to contribute.

PART ONE

Introduction

CHAPTER ONE

The object of economic science

I Self-subsistence

1 The social determination of individuality

Historically, the conception of the individual within a social order first situates that individual immediately within a complex system of divisions and particularizations. This constitution of his particularity as an *a priori* condition makes impossible any full development of individuality as a social condition. Thus, for Plato, the differences which underlie the social division of labor are differences of natural aptitude and endowment. As such, they are fixed without regard to the inner determination of the system of social relations. This starting point contrasts sharply with that of Adam Smith, for whom the differences among men are considered to be the result of the growth of the market system and, as such, a product of economic life rather than an externally fixed condition. The notion of equality as the primordial condition of man, which develops in the seventeenth century, constitutes the differences among men as originating in their social condition. The emergence of this conception is the essential logical basis for the development of economic science. The work of Smith, Ricardo and Marx represents the culminating point in the development of the idea of the social determination of individuality.

Prior to the emergence of political economy as a science, individuality is not grasped as it exists within society, so that the social order is not considered to be composed of 'individuals.' The differences which separate and oppose men make of them different members of the species but cannot establish their real individuation. These differences are seen as fixed conditions rather than as particularizations accounted for by the inner determination of a social principle. Society takes responsibility for the adjudication of differences, never for their origin. Where concrete differences connected, for example, to the family or to the division of labor taken as a fixed condition are adopted as the *a priori* basis for a conception of social life, the common quality which sustains itself in and through these differences, and which ultimately accounts for them, is obliterated.

For the inner determination of the concrete conditions of social life it is essential that those conditions be grasped as particularizations of a social principle whose general conception is prior to the treatment of the particular qualities through which it sustains itself. The abstraction from the system of differences finally establishes this social principle as the logical foundation for the differences which concretely establish social life as an internally determined and self-developing system. Barring the attainment of this abstraction, the theory is constrained to take its departure on the basis of already given conditions which divide and oppose the members of society. So far as these conditions are taken to be irreducible, not only is the fully abstract and general conception of the social relation impossible, but it is equally impossible to develop the theoretical conception of the socially determined differences which constitute the social order taken concretely. Without the initial abstraction by which the most elementary and general conception is isolated, it becomes impossible to conceive the concrete differences in a systematic manner as social conditions. To consider such divisions to be premises of analysis is to consider them premises of social life itself; and to consider these differences premises of social life is equivalent to their treatment as fixed outside of society, for example in nature.

The immediate fixing of the person according to his situation within a social order makes that situation something distinct from a real social determination. The origin of the determination of the person as a member of a social order is given to him prior to the constitution of that order, so that the content of his personality is made up of extra and even anti-social elements. The whole of the striving of the individual within society is determined as the expression of fixed conditions, ultimately of natural instincts. There is, in this case, no emancipation of the member of the species from those instinctual ends the pursuit of which exhausts his life-process. Individual freedom is the social form; the natural determination of the species is the substance. The freedom of the individual existing within a social condition is no longer a real emancipation from the life of the species within nature, but only the form which that natural striving adopts for the species as a whole. The content of personality is not freedom but naturally given attributes and instincts, capacities and desires. Where this real content is an instinctual one, the form – subjective freedom – can be at best a passive receptacle for a substance foreign to it. At worst the form becomes a real antithesis to its substance and the conception of a distinctively social determination cannot be sustained.

For the development of the conception of social life, it is necessary to move beyond the immediately given system of concrete relations which make up the life of the species. The abstraction involved in this movement is the basis for distinguishing between those relations which constitute the social life of the species and those relations still bound up in its natural determination. This abstraction constitutes the object of the analysis as a social order established upon the basis of a distinctively social determination.

In order to consummate this conception, however, it is necessary to consider social life not as an immediately given complex of institutions and relations, but as a logically ordered totality the reality of which is not immediate, as in its empirical conception, but mediated by the full development of its inner logic. Since the conception of the system of social relations as a whole is the idea of a social order, and since the theory consists solely in the presentation and development of that idea, the system of relations implied in the idea of society must form not the beginning but the endpoint of the theory. In order to arrive at the true starting point it is necessary not only to leave aside the natural determination of the species, but also to abstract from its complex determination within a social order. Through this abstraction it is possible to extract from the complex of social relations that common element which marks the point of origin of a real social determination. This origin is the conception of that common element which concretizes itself within the system of social relations as a whole, and whose life within that system establishes it as substantively a social condition. In this sense only the most general conception of the social being is able to account for the development of a conception of the social order within which that being pursues his concrete social determination.

2 Property rights

The attempt on the part of social theory to move beyond the immediate natural determination of the social being and to constitute his concrete condition as a social reality entails first the opposition of the social being to the mode of existence of the species within the 'state of nature.' In society, according to Rousseau, 'man becomes other than he is.' The sociable man adopts a 'false face' when he constitutes himself as a personage within a system of persons. This emergence is the development of the public man who lives not 'within himself,' as is the case for the man in the primordial condition, but instead within his external relations, with others. The sociable man draws from others 'the sentiment of his own existence.'[1] The bifurcation of man into an existence which is 'within himself,' and an existence which is exclusively in his relations with others, first establishes the independence of the social being from any determination within a fixed external condition. But, having first grasped this independence which is characteristic of the social life of man, social theory displaces it to the 'state of nature' outside of the social order.

Social theory locates outside of society the abstract person determined only by his own self-subsistence.* Social theory locates within society the reality of the person in his relations of depend-

---

* Since Hobbes, the raw material out of which the system of social interaction develops is made up of individuals whose self-subsistence is synonymous with their absolute autonomy and independence of any determination either natural or social. The full determination of social interaction is given immediately in the self-determination of the 'individual' who generates his own 'preferences,' 'intentions,' or 'ends.' The idea of self-subsistence is not in this case the abstract starting point for a real social determination of individuality, but the basis for a determination of social interaction in accordance with a system of individuals wholly determined outside of the social order. For a critique of this idea as it appears in classical and modern economics see D. Levine, *Economic Studies: Contributions to the Critique of Economic Theory* (London: Routledge & Kegan Paul, 1977).

ence upon the members of the social order. It is for this reason that social theory fails, at first, to grasp the social determination of the abstract person, placing him instead outside of society, in the 'state of nature.' Society is the world not of the self-subsistent person, but of greater or lesser personages subsisting in their relations of difference and opposition.

The origin of these differences is outside of society, in the natural aptitudes and inclinations of men. However, these natural differences only express themselves in relations of inequality and dependence in society. It is the differential respect among persons, accorded upon the basis of their different natural endowments, which makes the social order an arena for the development of inequality. Since personality is endowed from the outset with fixed natural attributes, society is constituted immediately as a system of greater and lesser personages. The quantitative differentiation is taken to be directly primary, and the latent equation of men *as persons* is suppressed. This inequality and dependence of men is not natural since nature-given differences do not become, in the state of nature, the basis for differential recognition and therefore inequality.

The personage is only established as such in his recognition by other personages, and it is upon the basis of their respect that the individual is raised to the status of a true person. Even where the original basis for his elevation is presumed to be in his natural aptitude, he only really becomes a person in society. This striving to be a person marks the achievement of personality not as a natural attribute, but as the development of man's social condition. The development of personality is considered, especially by Hobbes and Rousseau, to be immediately a striving for respect and ultimately for domination. The member of the species can only exist as a person within society. The specific differences which distinguish among persons (those of differential respect) are created in society and are, therefore, substantively social differences. Thus, even while differences in society appear originally as the simple transposition of differences in natural endowment, this transposition is made into the substantive constitution of differences among men which are wholly socially determined.

To the extent that these differences must be a violation of the 'natural' equality and freedom of men, their social determination is severed from and opposed to the most elementary existence of the individual who, in the natural state, is not even considered a person. Yet, once having excluded inequality from the natural state of man, it is no longer possible to attribute equality of men to their natural condition which encompasses a system of interaction wholly indifferent to the conditions of equality and inequality. Equality as much as inequality of men is the result of mutual respect and recognition; it is necessarily equality of persons. Thus, relations among persons cannot be excluded in the constitution of freedom and equality, so that, especially for Hobbes, the natural right attached to the freedom and equality of the natural condition must lead inevitably, and of its own inner force, towards a social determination of right. This also makes social dependence and inequality the mode of existence of equality and freedom.

The opposition between the state of nature and civil society is the mode of expression of a contradiction deeply embedded within the implied conception of nature. This contradiction forms the methodological basis for the whole of the subsequent analysis. To the extent that within the state of nature man lives 'within himself,' his sole recourse in the determination of his existence must be to the fixed drives and instincts with which his natural being is originally endowed. In this respect, the liberation of man within the state of nature is a false liberation since it liberates the individual from the bonds of society only to subordinate him to the bonds of nature. This is true so far as the state of nature is taken to be a true arena of natural interaction. The identification of the state of nature with the natural life of the species, however, obliterates the true specificity of the conception of a state of nature within social theory. The natural instincts which rule in the state of nature are those instincts which mark the distinctively human nature of man. This human nature is anything but a truly natural attribute, and, while explicitly denying man's innate sociality, implicitly constitutes his social determination as intrinsic.

To the extent that the state of nature is grasped as that condition within which the real inner nature of man is realized in its purity, therefore in its fully abstract and general form, man in his natural state is not determined by natural instincts and drives, but by his intrinsic independence and freedom. Freedom and equality define the state of nature not because they derive from man's instinctual determination, but because they are the inner nature of man. Since these conditions are in man's nature they do not bring about his reduction to a real natural condition, but instead establish the distinctiveness of the human condition from the animal life of the species. This natural condition is one of liberation from the natural life of the species, of man's elevation above any determination in accordance with naturally fixed drives. In this respect, the nature of man which is violated in civil society is not his real natural determination, but the original basis for the liberation of man from the life of the species within nature. This reality exists in its pure form not in the system of social relations, but in their absence, only because that system of relations is seen to violate man's inner nature and not his instinctual determination.

The difficulty entailed in this construction is apparent. The nature of man is unable to realize itself within the natural state to the extent that, within the latter, man is reduced to the level of animal existence. At the same time, the nature of man is unable to realize itself within civil society since its conditions are in direct conflict with man's intrinsic character, his inborn freedom and independence.

The concept of natural right is the result of the purification of the idea of right and its constitution in a form which is fully elementary. This purification brings with it a confrontation with the question of the manner in which that which is in the nature of right relates to the full development of right within a concrete totality (society). For seventeenth- and eighteenth-century social theory this relation is one of irreconcilable opposition. This opposition is already implied in the methodology which considers the elementary conception of right to be given naturally, and to be therefore fixed independently of any full realization as a system of reciprocal and mutually dependent rights.

The relation of the concept of natural right to the system of social relations is that of inward reality to its outward expression. The latter is made up of contingent and accidental circumstances which violate the purity within which right exists in the state of nature. This concretization, since it is considered to be intrinsically unnecessary to the constitution of right, is grasped as its negation. Rather than the concrete determination of freedom, the social condition represents the subordination of freedom to external restraints which violate its real subsistence within the state of nature.

This result reveals the profound methodological link between

35

classical political economy* and the social theory which forms its historical point of departure. For classical political economy the treatment of the value concept follows the same methodology employed in the treatment of freedom in the political philosophy of the seventeenth and eighteenth centuries. The natural price is determined independently of the system of price relations taken as a whole and, indeed, conflicts essentially with that price which emerges within the totality of economic relations. The original problem of the relation which is sustained between that which is in the nature of right and the full development of right within a total system of property relations appears, within economic theory, as the problem of the relation of that which is in the nature of exchange (value) to the fully developed exchange system. In both cases the connection of the elementary relation to the system within which it exists concretely is not one of its realization but one of its obliteration. The method employed in constituting the elementary relation as a natural determination inevitably sets up a contradiction between the substance, or inner nature, and the form, or outward expression. This contradiction makes impossible any consistent conception of social and economic relations. Such an opposition can only be overcome when the system of social relations is constituted as the system within which right sustains itself by subsisting within the process of its concrete self-determination.

Social theory first discovers that human quality, which provides the basis for the development of a condition which leaves aside the natural determination of the species, in the ideas of freedom and equality. It is in man's nature to be free, free to determine himself by an act of will. It is this inner nature which distinguishes the nature of man from the natural condition of the species in its instinctual determination. This notion of freedom sets up an opposition, within the state of nature, between those components of that state which are substantively natural and exist for man simply as objects or things, and that component, man, whose

---

* The term 'classical political economy' is employed throughout to refer to the main representatives of the first systematization of economics as a science, especially the British school of Adam Smith and David Ricardo. The line of development of classical thinking also extends through the work of Karl Marx who is, in certain respects, the last representative of the school, while at the same time breaking fundamentally with certain of its presuppositions. For a comprehensive characterization and critique of the classical conception of economic life see D. Levine, *Economic Studies*, part I.

innate freedom renders the objects existing before him nothing more than an external sphere for the realization of his will. The germ of the development of a distinctively human sphere into a social order exists originally in a condition of freedom determined only in its opposition to a world of objects, since this opposition implicitly necessitates the development of a sphere of human life outside of any natural determination. The starting point is the right of man to exert his will in a sphere which lacks any self-will of its own. This is the right of 'every man to all things' (Hobbes). Such a right (1) distinguishes the natural condition of man from all naturally determined relations, and (2) constitutes this difference, which provides the basis for the development of man's social condition, in abstraction from its own full determination within a social order. Abstract right is, then, a natural right in that its conception is developed in abstraction from the idea of a social order taken as a whole, in particular of a state. Right is at the same time not a natural condition since it opposes man to the natural sphere, giving him the right over that sphere and, further, leading him into the development of a social order in the form of a state.

The appropriation of objects is the means to the constitution of the object as property and of its owner as substantively a property owner. Appropriation is the act by which the embodiment of freedom is effected as 'itself a substantive end.'[2] Indeed, the right of every man to all things expresses that infinity of desire which denies all determinacy of need as the basis of appropriation. Where the illimitability of desire is taken as the basis of appropriation, possession has as its object not the fulfilment of desire, but the appropriation of the external world as a substantive end in itself. Such appropriation is not limited in any way by need and, therefore, cannot be traced back to need as its ground. To be sure, appropriation must ultimately be seen also to eventuate in the fulfilment of needs. None the less, where the object of appropriation is the satisfaction of desire, the relation of will becomes no more than the means to the fulfilment of desire and stands opposed to the freedom of the individual within society. For the fulfilment of need to realize the freedom bound up in the right of the abstract person, that need must be itself determined in terms of an abstraction characteristic of a distinctively social condition. Otherwise appropriation as the means to the satisfaction of need becomes once again the social form within which the natural life of the individual is developed as its substantive content. The content of willing becomes the complex of natural desires in that those desires, once established as independent of the system of property rights, cannot be conceived in terms of their social determination. The abstraction of right cannot, then, be immediately limited in need. This is expressed in the link between appropriation and the universality of external objects, appropriation which is in principle without limit, that is, of all things.

The right of every man to all things is equivalent, however, to the absence of right. The latter disappears, as Hobbes points out, in the clash of right. Where proprietorship does not entail exclusivity, the right of each is always immediately the violation of the right of others, so that the assertion of right is directly its negation. The real constitution of rights always entails the renunciation of right. The abstract act of 'taking possession' cannot, in and of itself, effect either the recognition of property or the valuation of property. Without the recognition of proprietorship by others the possession remains substantively only an external object which is possessed.

The determination of rights and of the freedom of the abstract person requires a sphere within which right is recognized and limited. This is not, however, an external limitation of right on the part of a principle which opposes and excludes the free development of will. Instead, right is limited within a system of opposing rights, particularly by the necessity that right be recognized if its reality is to be fully established. Within society there is a limitation of right. But in this case right is limited by and within a system of reciprocal and opposing rights. Here right is determined, and therefore limited, by the necessity of its own subsistence and development. This determination and limitation of right is the object of social theory and especially of economic science. Yet to begin with the fully developed system of rights which makes up civil society is to begin with the limitation of right and to that extent with its negation. Where this limitation is taken to be present from the outset, and not developed out of the realization of rights within a system of property relations, the opposition of society to freedom as the sphere of its limitation and negation excludes any realization of freedom within society. This makes the suppression of freedom the starting point of social life. But, for society to be grasped as a system of rights, it is impossible to consider its starting point to be in the limitation of rights with which the member of the species is already endowed outside of society. The limitation of right within society must be shown to be necessitated by the conception of right, and must be shown to be the sole sphere within which the subsistence of property rights can develop. In so far as the social being is a locus of rights, and is thereby distinguished within his social condition, that social condition must bring with it a limitation of right which is capable of realizing rather than suppressing individual freedom.

The recognition of right within the system of rights and of possessions brings with it the explicit constitution of the property owner within a system of property owners and of objects as property within a system of property. For property to 'really exist' it must be recognized as such, and this recognition is tantamount to the relinquishment of right in that it is a relation of will to will in which each recognizes its intrinsic limitation. What limits my right is first the necessity that it be recognized as mine by others so that this limitation has the form of a relation of rights, therefore a self-limitation of right. This recognition of right which comes with the renouncing of right situates the object within a reciprocal relation of will. Within this relation, the contract, the object ceases to be a mere 'object' in that it 'contains the moment of will.'[3]

The contract does not simply recognize an already fully developed condition, proprietorship, but substantively brings the property and its owner into existence. In this sense the object ceases to remain a mere thing, and becomes instead a social substance – property. The quality which the possession adopts as a piece of property is not external to society but exists only in society, so that the substance – property – is brought into existence by a social act. Once proprietorship is recognized, the existence of the object as a possession ceases to be a quality which is external to it. The social substance, property, is not an object which precedes the emergence of rights and is subsequently appropriated. The social object is created within that same relation which recognizes and thereby constitutes the act of appropriation itself. The relation of will to will does not appropriate property as the means to the constitution of rights within society; it creates property as the embodiment of the act of recognition of will.

Seventeenth- and eighteenth-century political theory hardly goes beyond the standpoint within which the opposing parties to the relation remain nothing more than 'immediate self-subsistent persons.'[4] Relations among persons are not seen to entail a system of particularization and mutual dependence. To the extent that civil society and the state develop such relations of mutual dependence, the existence of the person within 'society' obliterates his freedom and self-subsistence. The relation of right to society becomes essentially the contradictory one of the negation of right within society. This negation is at the same time essential to the subsistence of right, since it is only within society that the recognition of right can be assured. The absorption of the idea of the person into that of independent self-subsistence makes the member of civil society and the state ultimately an immediate self-subsistent person who, as such, is incapable of developing any real social existence. Among such persons any mutual dependence must remain purely external to the independent self-sufficiency which is their defining condition. The interrelation of will is only necessary abstractly, in order to constitute each party as bearing the capacity for entering freely into contractual relations. The freely contracting person is bound to other property owners solely by the unifying force of the contract, and by the reciprocal recognition of their property and of their property-owning status. The mutual relations of persons in no way overcome their independent self-subsistence, so that any real development of mutuality is excluded. Mutual dependence remains arbitrary and extrinsic to the social condition of the property owner. The relations which transpire among property owners need not involve the development of a sphere within which the parties to the contract and the property which it brings into existence are given a full determination connected to the development of concrete social relations.

At this level there exists the property taken qualitatively as the substance brought into existence through the reciprocal relation, and the property taken quantitatively as so much property or value measured in the relation of properties effected in the contract. The property and its value exist only within the system of property rights. In this respect the relation of contract brings the property and its value into existence. At the same time, only that which has value can be substantively appropriated, and only property can be the object of a contract. In this respect the contract takes the property and its value as its presupposition. The object of the contract must be already implicitly of value so that the contract achieves the explicit social recognition of that social quality already implicit within its object. This necessity leads social theory subsequent to Hobbes to the conclusion that property and value are *first* produced, by 'labor,' and only subsequently appropriated because of having been made worthy of appropriation. This marks an advance in conception in so far as it makes explicit the necessity that property be produced as such in order that its appropriation be more than purely formal.

The development of the theory of value along the lines first intimated by Locke and Rousseau, seeks to constitute value as a substance intrinsic to property, and therefore to constitute the object's full determination as a social substance. What is lost in this development, however, is the realization that the origin of all relations of property including that of its production must be in the reciprocal recognition of right. The latter constitutes the object of social life as a social substance and can alone constitute the activity by which that object is produced for society as an activity which transpires within society. Property is a social substance brought into being within society. Where property is an exclusively social reality, not appropriated into society but having its substantive origin within society, the production of that property must be its creation as property. Such production brings into being a social object. This production must be itself socially determined, so that its conception must develop not outside of the idea of right but within the full development of that idea.

To this extent the idea of right precedes, logically, that of the production of property, and provides the logical basis for the social determination of the productive activity. At the same time, the idea that the property and its value exist prior to and independently of the particular contract, and in this sense *precede* that relation, establishes clearly the objective force of property and value.

The contract creates the property in so far as the property is nothing more than the relation of immediate self-subsistent persons finding their determination exclusively within their mutual contractual agreement. The constitution of property hinges upon the thus far arbitrary expression of will. The person enters into the contract only in order to exist abstractly as a self-subsistent person, and not in accordance with his concrete social determination as a particular personality. The existence of the property appears to be the accidental result of the self-determination of the abstract person whose abstraction eliminates his social determination in accordance with the intrinsic necessities of a system of property and of property owners. The object of the person is nothing more than his constitution as a person, which constitution entails no specific content with regard to his needs, capacities, and resources. Thus, the property and its value exist at the will of the abstract person whose abstraction is equivalent to his lack of determination. In this relation, the necessity of property and of its emergence within the relation are clear, but the concrete determination of the property and its value are still absent. The immediate self-subsistent person seeks out, for example through the exchange of property, his constitution as a person. In this respect the object of the contract is precisely the same on both sides. Each person appears as a property owner, and as nothing more than a property owner, whose sole end is his constitution as such through the constitution of his property. While this makes the relation of property necessary, it does not make its real development possible since the moment of difference, in which the parties are opposed in their concrete determination, is suppressed.

For the contract, the opposition of property owners, while necessary, is insufficient, since the identity of the poles as property owners does not in itself account for that difference which entails the concrete development of their relation (i.e. the concrete possibility and necessity of the contract). Indeed, the abstract constitution of the person as a property owner within the contract is impossible where there is no concrete differentiation of property owners. To be sure, the constitution of the parties to the relation as distinct, or opposed, wills renders them *ipso facto* (or, formally) different. It is precisely this difference and opposition which the relation of contract, taken in the abstract, sustains. None the less, such an opposition must remain purely formal unless the real content of the concrete differentiation of persons in accordance with the system of property rights is developed. The abstract difference of persons is not sufficient to establish the reality of their relation. For the latter an abstract necessity must be connected to a concrete necessity of interrelation built out of a system of intrinsically determined differences. It is within this concrete development of differences that the abstract opposition of persons sustains itself.

II Self-seeking

1 The content of self-seeking

The freedom of the property owner is only limited by the necessity that his property be recognized as such. This recognition of the right of the property owner is effected in the contract into which he freely enters. This contract brings the property into existence and is, therefore, the only means by which the freely contracting person can establish himself as a property owner. Such a contract, freely entered, is a relation within which the freedom of the parties subsists within their reciprocal constitution. But for this constitution to be realized, it is necessary to consider the determinacy of the relation as a matter also of the concrete differences which oppose the parties to the relation. It is necessary, then, to consider the manner in which the freely contracting person establishes his individuality. The concrete determination of the abstract person must (1) be a self-determination which will not violate his freedom, and must be equally (2) a self-determination which sustains itself only within the self-differentiation of a system of individuals. The activity by which the individual discovers himself within a system of now concretely determined persons is his self-seeking.

Prior to the emergence of classical political economy, self-seeking refers essentially to an abstract condition in that the object achieved through self-seeking – the 'self' – is an accidental amalgam of motives, desires, instincts, compulsions, etc. Whether these are considered to be 'natural' drives and capacities, or simply to be the arbitrary content of the self-determination of the actor, their real determination is not part of the subject-matter of social theory. The content of self-seeking is here determinate only in its abstract opposition to other selves, so that its content is neither more nor less than the 'self.' Since the determination of the individual, in so far as his individuality is concerned, is given without regard to his social condition, that determination contributes nothing to the conception of the full realization of the concrete person as such.

Where the desires and motives which determine the individual are given by nature, they stand in opposition to the freedom of the individual as its antithesis. In this case, the content and result of self-seeking conflicts essentially with the objective of that self-seeking which is the full development of individuality and freedom within a system of the free interrelation of persons. The form remains that of the activity of the independent property owner or even the immediate self-subsistent person, while the content is that of a more concretely determined individual fixed, however, only by naturally given drives and capacities which exclude any free self-constitutive activity.

Similarly, where the content of self-seeking is considered to be not the complex of natural drives but the free act of the self-subsistent person, taken by himself, his self-constitution defies any real determination. The moment of difference which establishes the opposition of individuals is a matter of individual whim, or of exclusively 'subjective' preference. The differences which account for individuality, and therefore for the emergence of the person substantively as an individual within and among a class of individuals, have nothing to do with the intrinsic constitution of the social order. This determination of difference is not a social determination and, indeed, it defies fundamentally any possibility of a social determination, since the development of the individual takes place wholly outside of his relations with other individuals.

The self-determination of the individual on the basis of preferences in no way connected to his social condition is his constitution by desires which have no force capable of driving the individual into relations with the system of individuals. Such desires lack the quality of need which is a substantial requirement for a system of relations and is the basis for the social constitution of individuality. The mutual relation of persons is conceived exclusively at the abstract level of the contract, either as the means to the realization of the full independence of persons, or, at best, as the accidental self-constitution of the person as a moral and social being. For such a conception the content of self-seeking is only consistent with freedom in so far as that content remains socially indeterminate and arbitrary.

The consistency of this standpoint with subjective freedom is, however, illusory. While it asserts the untrammelled freedom of the moral actor with one hand, with the other it deprives the self-subsistent person of any legitimate sphere of self-determination. For self-seeking to realize, within a concrete sphere, that self-constitution which is identified with freedom, the individual taken by himself is wholly insufficient. The self-seeking person must look outside of himself into an external sphere within which he can establish the subsistence of his own concrete determination as an individual. And this external sphere, if it is not to erase the freedom of the individual, must be nothing more than the particularization of the system of property and property rights, so that the development of the particularization of persons is the development of their reciprocal constitution as property owners, or concrete persons.

2 *The needy individual*

This concrete social determination is first accomplished by classical political economy. And, indeed, the object of the science of economics is precisely the conception of this sphere within which the free self-seeking of the individual becomes the process of his self-constitution as a social act.

In self-seeking, the individual pursues the concrete determination of the whole of his existence in needs which are particular and individual. The need, as means to this determination, must be itself intrinsically determined in accordance with its purely social end. In this respect the determination of the intrinsic character of those needs typical of the social life of the individual is essential to the scientific treatment of social interaction. The constitution of particular need as the basis for the self-determination of the social being makes his determination in accordance with particular need the basis for his emancipation from all determination in naturally fixed needs.

Need is not a quality attributable to the otherwise abstract property owner. It is instead the content of his self-determination, and the objective of his self-seeking. The determination of need is equivalent to the determination of the needy individual. Need, then, is bound up with the freedom of the individual in that it provides a specific and determinate content for that freedom. The concept of need summarizes the relation of the individual to the system of individuals within which he subsists. The life of the member of the species within nature relates the individual member to the biological system as a whole on the basis of a fixed complex of needs which together define the whole of the life of this naturally existing being. The biological relations between species, between the members of a given species, and between the individual species and its total environment can be grasped for the individual as a complex of needs which he has in order to sustain himself within the natural system and therefore as a component element of that system. Needs within society have this same logical status in so far as they summarize the relation of the individual to the complex system of individuals within which he subsists. His needs are the requirements which he must fulfil in order to exist within such a system as a constituent element. Individual needs represent equally the concrete determination of the need to be individual. The totality of the fulfilment of natural needs is the animal life of the member of the species, and can never bring its members to a higher level of existence outside of the system of natural inter-action. The fulfilment of needs within economic life is equivalent to the existence of the person as a needy individual within a system of needy individuals. The social determination of need is also, then, the determination of the need of the person for a social life. The fulfilment of such a need is no matter of individual whim but is incumbent upon the individual if he is to exist as such. Upon the satisfaction of these needs rests the very constitution of the individuality essential to the member of a social order. These are the needs which the individual has, not in order to be a member of a natural species, but the needs which he has in order to be a person within a system of persons. The articulation and fulfilment of need is what makes the individual one among a system of individuals determined in his individuality only by merit of his membership within the system as a whole.

Natural needs summarize the life of the species existing con-cretely in its interrelation within a biological system. Within society, need also designates the subsistence of the individual within a system, and the relations by which the individual and the system of individuals subsist as such, not as biological factors but as substantively social beings. To consider those needs which summarize the life of the self-seeking individual to be natural is tantamount to considering the social being as a natural entity, and social life as nothing essentially different from the life of the species within nature. The social determination of need is not, however, achieved on the basis of the interposition of a 'social' determination which is extrinsic to the real life of the individual seen as an element of a biologically determined species, and imposed upon him. Since social determination is always bound up with the development of personality, the needs by which the individual is determined within society are needs by which he determines himself. The fulfilment of need is the activity by which the individual constitutes his freedom as a determinate condition subsisting within a social order. This fulfilment is also the activity by which the social order constitutes itself as the sphere of the subsistence of a system of needs.

The freedom in accordance with which needs are developed and fulfilled within society leads social science to the notion of the indeterminacy of need. Indeed, historically the social sciences all seek to constitute the needs existing within society as different from natural needs by merit of this indeterminacy. Corresponding to the needs by which the species renews itself within a determinate system of natural relations are the 'desires' or even 'preferences' by which the individual expresses the absence of any concrete determination of his life within society. Need comes to be relegated to the life of the individual outside of society, since the concept of need entails the element of constraint and determination which is connected to a requirement of life but not to an individual whim. Within society the individual can at best articulate a set of preferences, which as such cannot be considered to constitute any real determination. Ultimately the idea that there are needs articulated exclusively within society stands as a reproach to the whole of the history of social theory.

While classical political economy is unable to make any explicit break with this conception of need, the logical content of classical theory argues forcefully in favor of the necessity of a conception of a sphere of need not determined by any natural interaction. This requires the idea of a distinctive sphere for the development and subsistence of needs, a sphere of economic life. Classical political economy asserts the equivalence of the concrete determination of the person with his articulation of needs which are requirements for his subsistence and therefore necessary, while also constituting the basis for the realization of his freedom. In this way, subjective freedom develops within a system of needs which are particular, which are necessary to the subsistence of freedom, and which provide a sphere for the development and realization of freedom.

The first subject-matter of economic science is the type of need characteristic of 'civilized society' and the means to its fulfilment.[5] Within civilized society self-seeking is the activity of the needy individual who is determined not simply in the abstract, as a

47

property owner, but also concretely by his particular needs and by his property as the means to the satisfaction of need. The relation between opposing property owners as abstract, self-subsistent persons brings into existence the social substance, property, which then becomes the basis for their constitution as property owners. For the needy individual who seeks to constitute himself concretely as a person, the ownership of property is inadequate. Property, as such, is not the means to the fulfilment of need but the embodiment of will and nothing more. Its value, and its value to its owner, is exclusively in its recognition as the embodiment of will, and the implied recognition of its owner as substantively a property owner. To the needy individual the value of his property lies in its constitution of its owner as a personality not only abstractly, but also concretely. Here property is also determined as the means to the fulfilment of need. Property is not only valuable, it is also useful. Indeed, it is valuable, as Smith and Ricardo affirm from the outset, only in so far as it is useful. Within economic life property is wealth and it is within economic life that property is constituted as wealth.

In economic life self-seeking is the pursuit of (1) the self-determination of the individual on the basis of his needs and of their particularization within a complex of particular needs, and (2) the development of individual need in and through the system of needs and of needy individuals. This system of needs, of needy individuals, and of the relations through which the pursuit and development of need is accomplished is the starting point for the conception of civil society. Civil society is society within which this system of needs develops in a multiplicity of directions made possible by its social determination. The means by which society satisfies needs which expand and multiply without limit is the wealth of society.

To the extent that wealth is property it is valuable, and its value is the result of a social relation. Value is first brought into existence as the objectification of will within the reciprocal relation of right embodied in the contract which establishes the reality of the property of the property-owning person. This reciprocal constitution of right, at the level of economic life, also entails the concrete determination of the individual and of relations among individuals on the basis of needs and of property as the means to the satisfaction of needs. The social substance which emerges within the system of needy individuals is useful property, or wealth, and owes its existence as wealth, both in the fulfilment of need and in the recognition of right, exclusively to its generation within the reciprocal relations of needy individuals.

III Mutual dependence

1 The system of needy persons

For the existence of wealth it is not sufficient that the needy person own property which is useful to him. It is further required that this usefulness becomes an intrinsic quality of his property. The individual can no more constitute the object of his desire as useful than he can constitute that object as property. Wealth comes into existence only where need is connected not to the whim of the individual but to his striving for a self-constitution within the differentiation of a system of needy persons. Since it is that difference which emerges within such a system that the individual grasps as the inner content of his freedom, his needs are tied to his differentiation from and among the system of owners of wealth. This difference must, then, be acknowledged by the system of needy individuals as its own product. That original abstract difference of property owners, as property owners, which establishes their right within the reciprocal constitution of rights and properties, is now determined concretely as an opposition of persons whose differences are also contained within their mutual constitution within the relations of a system of concretely determined individuals. Concrete differences of need and of property establish that opposition of needy individuals which is sustained within their mutual relations. Just as the constitution of the property owner requires a reciprocal acknowledgment of right, his constitution as the owner of wealth springs out of a mutual provision of the means to the fulfilment of need. The difference which establishes the individuality of the property owner makes him the owner of wealth. And this difference exists only within a system of needy persons which sustains each individual. Property becomes wealth when its determination is within a system of wealth and the abstract person becomes the needy individual when he is determined concretely by his situation within a system of needs, therefore by his particular needs and by the means which he possesses for the fulfilment of some part of the system of needs.

In civil society the fulfilment of need is not the subsistence of the individual as a member of a species determined within a natural system. Instead, the pursuit of the means to the satisfaction of needs is the pursuit, on the part of the individual, of his social condition. This social condition is, however, nothing more than the dependence of the individual upon a system of needy individuals as the sphere within which the fulfilment of his own needs must occur.

The system of needs is, therefore, a system of mutual dependence in the fulfilment of need. Each individual has as the means to the satisfaction of his needs two conditions: (1) the wealth of other individuals as the means to the fulfilment of his own needs, and (2) his own wealth as the means by which he acquires the substances which satisfy his needs. To the extent that the satisfaction of the needs of the individual requires his relating to other needy individuals, the relations among needy individuals together provide the means to the constitution of each as a person determined concretely on the basis of needs. The provision of needs becomes the concrete substance of the reciprocal relations among persons.

The system of mutual dependence of needy individuals is a system in which the ownership of wealth is not the means to the immediate satisfaction of need, but the means to the acquisition of the substances capable of satisfaction of need. Each needy individual, in order to subsist as such, must acquire the property of other needy individuals, while the sole means available for such an acquisition, which is consistent with the recognition of the independence of each, is through the provision to the other of the property possessed by the needy person. The system of mutual dependence of needy individuals is, then, a system of the exchange of property. The needy individual is the property owner determined concretely in terms of the needs by which he constitutes his social existence. Wealth is his property in so far as it fulfils his need only by first satisfying the needs of others. The exchange of wealth is the contract by which recognition of personality is bound to the mutual provision of the means to the satisfaction of need. Within civil society, differences between properties are essential so that the constitution of property as such is its constitution as the means to the fulfilment of a particular need. Property is now valuable not only as property, but also concretely as useful property. It has a use-value particularized within a system of use-values.

The private fulfilment of personal desires cannot constitute the person as a social being. It excludes his recognition in and among a system of needy individuals, excluding both the recognition of his abstract individuality and the recognition of the concrete content of that individuality – its determination in terms of needs. For the isolated consumer, the satisfaction of wants is a deprivation of all recognition and excludes his constitution as an independent person. Thus, the freedom of the isolated consumer is purely negative in that it has no possibility of recognition. For the isolated consumer there exists no order within which his individuality can be established in a positive way through a system of relations. Neither is it possible for the isolated consumer to objectify his will and relate to an external substance which is anything more than an inert object incapable of sustaining his constitution concretely as an individual.

The constitution of the abstract person as a property owner requires the recognition of his property as such on the part of another property owner equally constituted as such within the same relation. This recognition originates, then, in the bilateral or reciprocal constitution of property and right in the contract. For this reciprocity to be sustained the contract, as the sole means to the constitution of the freedom of the individual as a real, positive quality, must become the active element rather than simply the passive expression of abstract right. This develops within civil society where the relations among persons are necessary not only to their abstract determination as persons, but equally to their concrete determination as needy individuals.

2 Civil society

If free interaction is to eventuate in a positive, determinate result, that freedom must itself be determinate. Such a determination does not oppose freedom by fixing it within a system of needs inconsistent with the self-determination of the needy individual. The system of needs is, instead, the arena within which freedom is sustained and developed. The circumstance under which freedom can be realized is that freedom contain within itself the compulsion to reciprocal dependence as the only real basis for its own development. Within the exchange system, external coercion is unnecessary precisely to the extent that the self-seeking of the needy individual provides the driving force in his participation within a system of mutual dependence. In order that the individual pursue his own needs, and therefore seek out his *self*-determination as a needy person, he must immerse himself within a system of mutual dependence in the provision of need. Self-seeking is the driving force in that seeking after others which develops into a system of mutuality. This result establishes explicitly the inner determination of self-seeking not in the autonomy of the isolated being, but in the social life of the property owner. Such self-seeking has, implicit within it, a real social determination.

Pursuit of individual need becomes the inner force in the development of a system of relations termed 'civilized society' by classical political economy. Each individual pursues his own ends, and pursues therefore himself as end. But, in the course of this pursuit of the individual as end, that individual must, in order to realize his own ends, contribute to the realization of the ends of other individuals, and therefore also to their realization as ends in themselves.[6] Self-seeking develops of its own inner necessity into a seeking after others, so that eventually the individual finds himself, but he does so only in his relation to other individuals. This reversal is not the denial of self-seeking but is already latent within its conception as a social condition. It is not the external determination of the pursuit of private interest but the expression of its intrinsic nature. These relations entail his articulation of needs consistent with the totality of the system of needs. Therefore, when the individual finds himself, he finds himself in his relation to others so that the self which he discovers as the outcome of his self-seeking is nothing more than his relations of mutuality with other self-seeking individuals. Within these relations of mutual dependence individuality becomes substantively a social condition which is sustained only within the system of needy persons. Self-determination exists substantively as such for the individual only where it develops simultaneously outside of that individual in his relations with others, so that his most private determination is not only the basis of his social relations, but the inward reflection of his relations with the system of individuals. The needs by which the concrete person determines himself in opposition to other needy individuals, as different from them, are all determined in his relations with the system of property owners. It is this system of differences which sustains the relations within which property can alone subsist. The need of the individual is substantively his own, it is the content of his self-seeking; at the same time need is nothing more than the relation of the individual within a system of mutual dependence of needy persons.

Classical political economy grasps this notion of the mutual dependence of independent self-seeking in its conception of the market system. The latter is composed of commodity owners interrelating exclusively through commodity exchange. Since the provision of need takes place through exchange, the force by which that provision is pursued is no external instrument but the already implicit interdependence of needs. Mutual dependence is a quality intrinsic to the determination of need. Freedom, in economic life, is a quality of the market and of the particular commodity owners who together compose that market. The free market is a self-ordering system in which the unfettered activity of the needy individual, constrained exclusively by his own needs and consumed by the pursuit of his own ends, leads to the sustenance and development of a system of interdependence. This principle of the self-organization of the system of freely self-determining subjects is the 'invisible hand' of Adam Smith.

That free self-seeking eventuates in an integrated system of economic relations reveals the social determination of that free self-seeking. In economic life, the development of the free market is the development of a sphere within which the mutual relations among commodity owners are an expression of, and realization of, their freedom. Such freedom can only exist where it is itself the driving force in the self-constitution of the needy individual in strict accordance with the needs of others. Particularization and differentiation of needs relate the particular individual to a distinct set of needs connected to his subsistence as this particular person. Since each man can provide for his own needs only by providing for the needs of others, the provision of his needs becomes equally the means to the provision of the needs of other individuals. Thus, according to Smith, the development of the system of needs is synonymous with the development of that specialization in the provision of the needs of others which makes every man 'in some measure a merchant.' This development, traced by Smith to the division of labor, entails a specialization of the individual. And

53

this specialization of the individual in the provision of the needs of others turns back upon the individual, determining the content of his own needs. Thus, within the division of labor individual need is defined by specialization and therefore by the division of labor, or system of needs, taken as a whole.

In civilized society, free self-seeking is the substantial origin of mutual dependence, and the system of mutual dependence is the realization of the inner nature of self-seeking. The development of the independence of the individual, and the development of his dependence within a system of individuals, are the two aspects of the development of the market. This dialectical relation is grasped by Smith as a relation between the division of labor and the extent of the market. First, the division of labor is limited by the extent of the market. Mutual dependence, then, can only emerge and develop within a system of freely self-seeking individuals. The division of labor, and the system of interdependence in the provision of needs, grows with the liberation of the individual. The individual is set free to express and develop that inner nature to 'truck, barter and exchange,' to enter into relations of reciprocity in his constitution as the embodiment of subjective freedom. At the same time, the specialization implied in the division of labor, and in the system of mutual dependence, is the cause which makes every man in some measure a merchant. Where, originally, the development of freedom in the form of the unfettered market system is the basis for the growth of mutual dependence in the form of the division of labor, the reverse is also established and the growth of mutual dependence, of the division of labor, is the force which sustains the expansion of the market by making every individual necessarily a member of that market. The system of mutual dependence is the ground of subjective freedom. The more the individual frees himself the more he becomes dependent, and the greater his dependence upon other individuals the more extensive the arena for the development of his freedom.

These two aspects of the growth of the system of mutual dependence among free self-seeking persons are united by Smith in his conception of wealth. The development of wealth entails precisely that expansion of mutual dependence which is also the sole foundation upon which the liberation of man from his natural state is built. The wealth of nations sets man free. But it only sets him free within the system of wealth. This is the market system grounded in a social division of labor. The market system is the sphere within which the division of labor effects its full development, and that full development is the origin of the wealth of nations which is synonymous with civilization.

IV Economic science

In the history of social theory, freedom always stands in opposition to that mutual dependence out of which the concrete life of the social being is developed. Need and its mode of provision stand outside of, and opposed to, the system of rights which constitute the social order. The development of the notion of freedom brings with it the abstraction of the person from all concrete determination in needs. Freedom and equality are conditions of man outside of civil society, while dependence and inequality (differentiation) are his condition within civil society. This is the standpoint of seventeenth- and eighteenth-century social theory, and especially of Hobbes and Rousseau. Even here, however, there always lurks the beginnings of the realization that the freedom which is suppressed within civil society is also incapable of subsisting outside of civil society. Still, it is only with the emergence of classical political economy that these implications can be developed in a positive way. Up until the emergence of economic science there existed no conception of a concrete determination of the person which is in accordance with his freedom.* On one side the social life of the individual required abstraction from all concrete determination of that individual, especially on the basis of needs. On the other side, this exclusion of the determination of the social being in needs excluded any inner determination of his social existence, and obliterated any sphere within which his freedom and rights, sustained within society, could develop concretely as the inner substance of his particularization. Civil society is that sphere within which individual freedom provides itself with a determinate content and therefore comes to be the element of a system of relations of reciprocity and mutual dependence grounded in free individual self-seeking. The object of economic science is

---

* For political theory the sphere within which freedom is realized as a social condition is the state. The latter is, however, conceived independently of the system of economic relations and, therefore, fails to provide for the individual an arena for the social constitution of his individuality.

precisely to develop the conception of the self-seeking individual subsisting within a system of relations which are also of his own making. Economic science establishes that the unfettered self-seeking of the needy individual is subject to a determination, and that that determination is not the effect of external force but is instead the process of the self-organization and self-development of the market system.

In economic science the needy individual is determined in a manner consistent with the subsistence of individual freedom precisely in that the law which governs the preservation and constitution of freedom is the law of the self-ordering market system. It is the conception of this system and the laying bare of the intrinsic logic of its development which constitute the object of economic science.

PART TWO
Capital

CHAPTER TWO

Commodity relations

I Needs

1 The social determination of need

The needs whose fulfilment is the objective of economic life have their determination not in the natural renewal of the species, but within the system of social relations. The needs fulfilled by the species within the natural order are the needs which it has in order to exist within nature and as a natural element. The needs whose pursuit makes up the economic life of the individual are, by contrast, the needs which he has to exist as a social being. The objective of the pursuit of needs on the part of the individual is nothing less than that concrete individuation which is the process of his constitution as a social being. This constitution entails his recognition as the locus of free self-determination within the social order. Such freedom can only be recognized in the concrete determination of the person in accordance with needs which must not be the antithesis of freedom, but its particularization within a system of property ownership.

In the first instance, the social determination of need is synonymous with that abstraction by which needs are made independent of the fixed natural conditions of the reproduction of the species.[1] The satisfaction of need ceases to entail the pursuit of instinctually fixed ends and entails instead that the individual order his life in accordance with an idea whose content is freedom and self-determination. The need for food ceases to be synonymous with a fixed natural substance pursued instinctively, and comes to involve the pursuit of a substance which is not provided by nature, and which cannot be grasped instinctively. This substance is ideal and emerges only within the social order.

The abstraction of need which is implied in its ideal determination entails a particularization and multiplication of needs and of the means to their satisfaction. The severing of the determination of need from the relation to the fixed natural substance is also the multiplication of substances and of needs. The multiplication and particularization of needs realizes and also expresses their determination independently of any natural condition. This particularization of needs, which marks their separation from the natural sphere, connects the needs to the particularization of persons within civil society. In nature need provides no basis for the differentiation of the members of the species and is, in this respect, uniform and undifferentiated. In society the pursuit of needs is the process of individuation of personality, so that the system of needs is inherently a system of the multiplication and expansion of needs. To the extent that the individuation of personality implies the distinguishing of persons in accordance with their needs and with the means which they possess for the fulfilment of needs, the multiplication and expansion of needs is directly implied in their social determination. For the member of the species existing within nature, particular needs serve only to identify and equate the different members of the species in their concrete existence as such. The concrete life of the species, defined in terms of its mode of subsistence within a natural system (i.e. by the concrete relations sustained with the other elements of nature, which the species consumes in its own maintenance or is consumed by for the preservation and development of the natural system), is composed of particular pursuits and relations held in common by all members of a given species. On this level it is the identity of the needs of the individual members which marks their common natural origin. Equally, it is the opposition and multiplication of needs which marks out the individuation of the members of the social order, and therefore their common social origin. The investigation of the needs whose articulation and satisfaction transpires within the system of economic relations considers first the general nature of social needs, and then the laws by which their development is governed.

Within economic life, the provision of need is a form of mutuality and of reciprocal dependence. This interdependence of needs
and of needy individuals becomes the sole basis for their independence as property owners. It is the arena within which their
individuality develops a concrete content defined by particular
needs. Such needs do not provide for the individual any relation
to a natural sphere, and the fulfilment of these needs does not
sustain the individual within nature. On the contrary, the satisfaction of the type of need characteristic of economic life sustains
the individual within the system of needy individuals as one of its
elements. His pursuit of the satisfaction of need is only the pursuit
of his constitution as an individual within a system of individuals.

The mutuality involved in the satisfaction of need requires also
that the needy person provide the means to the satisfaction of the
needs of others. The relation which effects the reciprocal satisfaction of need must constitute the satisfaction of need as the
development of individuality and freedom simultaneously. In
economic life the reciprocal recognition of freedom and autonomy
finds a concrete determination within a system of needs. The social
determination of the person as a property owner is equivalent to
the social determination of his needs and of the means to their
satisfaction. What is entailed in this social determination is the
recognition of the needs and of the activity aimed towards their
fulfilment as the self-constitution of the person as an individual
within a system of individuals.

The social determination of need has two aspects. First, social
determination is synonymous with individuation and social needs
are always individual. Needs oppose individuals as concretely
different, and they do so by the acts of those individuals themselves. In this respect needs are subjective and effect the expression
of individual personality in all its particularity. It is possible for the
satisfaction of need to achieve this purely subjective and personal
end, however, only through its recognition within the system of
individuals. Particularity is that of the particular personality only
in and through the recognition of particular subjective need as the
content of individuation. Need has its real goal in the relentless
striving for recognition, and it is in the intrinsic necessity that
subjective need be recognized as such that it displays its objective
side. For subjective need to be recognized it must exist not only in
the immediate relation of the object of need to particular person-

ality, but equally as the objective social basis for the constitution of individuality. Thus the relation of need which constitutes the subjective particularity of the person also mediates the inter-relation of persons, and is in this respect objective. Need is subjective in that it exists directly for the particular individual, providing the content of his individuation, and it is simultaneously objective in that it provides for the individuation of personality only by existing for the system of individuals. The objectivity of need does not stand in opposition to its subjective determination, in relation particularly to psychological factors, but instead finds itself existing within the whim of the individual personality. That the consumption of food or clothing is the means neither to nutrition nor protection but to the satisfaction of a psychic need is not a violation of the real inner nature of need, but the realization of the very objectivity of individual personality. The need characteristic of economic life derives its determinacy from its exclusive subsistence within the system of needy individuals, and in the recognition of individual need as such by other needy individuals. It is not the subjectivity of need which, in economic life, violates its real natural character, but, rather, the retention of any natural determination which violates the real economic determination of need. The recognition of need is the only way in which its satisfaction can sustain the individuation of the person as a social condition and it is, therefore, the determination of that need within the act of recognition which stamps it irrevocably as a social condition. Since the objective existence of need is only realized in its recognition, that need is itself a purely social condition and wholly determined within the system of social relations. The mutual provision of need is, then, the mutual recognition of need and the reciprocal provision of the means to the satisfaction of needs.

The social substance which embodies the reciprocal recognition of will is property. The object, then, which fulfils needs is also property, since it is the objective basis for the recognition of the person as a needy individual. Property existing concretely as the means to the satisfaction of need is useful property, property determined by its utility or use-value.*

---

* The term most appropriate to signify the usefulness or use-value of the commodity, or the commodity as a use-value, is utility. The notion of utility has, however, taken on the connotation of the relation to the indeterminate whim of the isolated self-subsistent person. To this extent the concept of utility has lost

2 *Useful property*

The substance which fulfils the need of the individual is not
determined in its relation to that individual taken in isolation, but
only within his individuation within the system of needy persons.
The substance is brought into existence with the mutual constitution and provision of needs. As such this substance is no natural
material employed for social ends. Its very materiality or objectivity
with respect to the individual is a social quality developed within
the system of needy persons. Since the need is not determinate
within a natural condition, the means to the satisfaction of that
need, the use-value, cannot be defined as a natural substance or
material. Within nature the satisfaction of need is irrevocably
connected to a particular substance itself also provided by nature.
The subsistence of the biological organism requires that that
organism related itself to other biological elements and subsist upon
them as the means to its existence and renewal. Here the substance
which satisfies need is also fixed biologically. Within social life the
substance which satisfies needs is not connected to any given
biological function and material. Food and clothing, so far as they
constitute the individual not as a biological organism but as a
social being, are not connected to any given natural substance but
may be formed out of a wide range of substances. In primitive
society food may be connected to a single set of nature-given
materials, plants and animals. Here, the prevailing natural determination of life expresses itself as a determination of the means to
the satisfaction of need within nature. By contrast, in economic life
the food which satisfies the needs of the individual can take on a
multiplicity of forms and be formed out of an unending variety of
natural materials. In this respect the determinacy of the need and
of the means to its satisfaction, the use-value, is not connected to
a natural substance but to a social constitution of need.

So far as the economic life of the commodity is concerned, the
specificity of its physical substance is now contingent. Since the
physical material within which the use-value presents itself does
not account for its utility (which may be present indifferently in a
variety of physical forms, and even, for certain use-values, in no

its social determination. For purposes of the present analysis, the terms use-value
and utility will be used interchangeably to signify the relation to a socially
determined need.

physical form whatever), that physical form does not contribute to the economic determination of need and of the means to its fulfil-ment. It is not implied by this that the particular use-value cease to require a material form, but only that, for the use-value, its materiality as such become a matter of indifference. Indeed, it is now the social life of the material substance which gives its existence a new dimension. A paper cup is by no means of the same utility as one made from silver. And yet, it is not the brute physical materiality of the silver which directly provides its useful form with its exalted utility. On the contrary, by becoming an element of the determination of utility, the silver acts not as a chemical substance, restricted to a series of naturally fixed chemical interactions; instead the chemical substance is here endowed with a social recognition and determination. Indeed, it is the value of the silver, and its physical properties as they exist for the social being, which alone provide the silver cup with its unique utility when opposed to cups made of more 'mundane' substances.

Since useful property is determined independently of any natural condition, its measure must also be independent of any relation to a natural substance. The quantum of use-value is defined not in relation to natural material, but to social need, for example the need fulfilled by the shirt in clothing the body. Where the use-value is the shirt, it is measured in the number of particular shirts and not in the quantity of any natural material (e.g. cotton) out of which it may have been formed.

The measurement of use-value is, then, in accordance with its social constitution and in units relevant to its original social deter-mination. In this respect, the measurement of utility has a sub-jective dimension. It by no means follows from this, however, that the measurement of use-value proceeds upon the basis of the purely subjective and personal desires of that individual who happens, by chance, to possess or consume it. The subjective relation of need develops only within relations involving the mutual constitution and recognition of need. Since the emergence of need entails its social recognition, social need requires an objective measure independent of the accidental whims ('preferences') of the individual.

That the quantum of shirts is the single shirt, and not the unit intensity of desire on the part of its owner, makes the use-value independent of the particular individual and his personal whims precisely by making that use-value dependent upon the system of needs and of needy individuals. The need which the shirt fulfils is purely objective, even where the consumption of the shirt is individual, so long as that individuality is a social condition. Indeed, the social constitution of the individual becomes synonymous with the individual determination of need once individuality is grasped as a social condition. One shirt can clothe one individual. To be sure, it can, under normal circumstances, clothe only one individual and therefore be consumed individually. But the use of the shirt remains objective when it is the means to the objectification of the individual personality. It can be neither determined nor measured in any purely contingent qualities of the particular personality which are not accountable to its universal social determination. In this respect, the use-value has an objective measure which, while by no means independent of individual personality, is indifferent to that personality so far as it is considered outside of its social determination. The quantum of useful property is, therefore, indifferent to the purely personal 'intensity of desire' of the particular consumer.

Property, within civil society, is embedded within a system of individuals interrelating through the mutual provision of needs. Property exists concretely as the means to the satisfaction of need. The social objects which mediate the relations between persons determined concretely in terms of need are use-values which are also owned by particular needy persons. The use-value is the means by which the needy person acquires the means to the satisfaction of his needs when it is the means by which he acquires other use-values from other needy individuals. Through this reciprocal provision of need the individual is determined, on the basis of his particular needs, as this concrete person. The content of his individuality is a specific complex of needs. At the same time the individual, as the owner of property capable of satisfying the needs of others, owns the capacity for the acquisition of the use-values specific to the satisfaction of his own needs. The property which the needy individual owns is both the means to the satisfaction of a particular need, a use-value, and the means by which the needy individual acquires from another needy person that use-value which satisfies his particular need. The property is both specific to this particular need and independent of any particular need. By merit of the ownership of property the individual is not constrained to the satisfaction of the need to which that property is specific since, as property, it is capable of replacing itself with other particular use-values. Property, within civil society, is the means to the satisfaction of need, and is at the same time the means to the emancipation of its owner from determination in relation to any particular need. Property is the access to need in general, to a determinate part of the system of use-values which compose the wealth of society.

To the extent that the use-value is necessarily also property capable of being replaced through exchange with other use-values, the use-value is measurable independently of its relation to particular need. This measure is the worth or value of the property. Just as the property, in order to realize itself as such, must be useful, so also the use-value, in order to realize its social determination, must be property. The recognition of need existing within a system of needy individuals is the recognition of the means to the satisfaction of need as the means to the constitution of the needy individual as a person, therefore as a property owner. Such a means is itself property.[2]

The quantitative measure of property, taken in the abstract as the embodiment of will, is its value. When abstraction is made from the object as the means to the fulfilment of need and from its owner as a needy individual, what remains is, on one side, the abstract social object – property – and on the other side the abstract person – the immediate self-subsistent person or property owner. Within economic life, however, the notion of value is not reducible to a relation between immediate self-subsistent persons. Property, existing within economic life, is wealth and contains within it the potential for abstraction from particular need only in and through its relation with the system of needs and of use-values. Whereas for the immediate self-subsistent person the property is the determination of his immediate relation with another person, and is brought into being in their reciprocal constitution, for the needy individual determined concretely the property is already determined as a value and a use-value by the system of individuals and by the system of wealth. For economic life the value and the use-value, which together constitute property as wealth, are intrinsic to the wealth, so that it is as much the concrete determination of the property as wealth which determines the interrelations of property owners as it is their interrelation which determines the object as the social substance – property. Within economic life, then, value is the measure of property taken as such. At the same time, value is intrinsic to the property not by merit of the immediate relation of self-subsistent persons, but by merit of the prevailing relations among concretely determined needy individuals. The constitution of the property as valuable requires that it be capable of the satisfaction of need, and the abstraction by which the property becomes the means to the satisfaction of need in general is the abstraction by which its owner is emancipated from determination in fixed needs. This abstraction is here constrained to exist concretely as a relation in and among the system of particular needs and needy persons. The value of the commodity, within economic life, is its indifference to need and is by that fact a relation to need. The property determined in its relation to needs both negatively and positively is the commodity – the unity of value and use-value.

In order to be realized as values, commodities must interact one with the other in such a way as to allow their universality to express itself. On one side, the use-value, as a relation to particular need, can only exist fully as such where it is the component of wealth and therefore also, implicitly, a value; while on the other side, the value, as freedom from determination in any particular need, can only exist as such where it expresses itself in a use-value which provides for it a determinate form. The form which the value adopts is therefore the commodity and the expression of the value is in the particular use-value.

II The commodity

1 Exchange-value

While the commodity as a value implies an indifference to particularity of need, to the degree that the commodity exists alone in its relation to its owner, it exists inseparably from particularity of need. The single commodity is also the single use-value, so that as such it is incapable of expressing any indifference to particularity of need. It is restricted to its immediate identification with the means to the satisfaction of one particular need.

The commodity is such only to the degree that its use-value is the basis for the expression of its indifference to relation to particular need, and in so far as its value provides the basis for the constitution of the objective social determination of its utility. It is the interchangeability of commodities which constitutes both their value and their utility as explicitly social conditions. The use-value existing simply as so much property – value – is the equivalent of other use-values existing also as quantitatively equivalent amounts of property. But, for the existence of property it is necessary that its value be tied to the satisfaction of particular need. Within economic life property is always connected to the fulfilment of need, so that the object can only be worthy of appropriation, be valuable, to the degree that it is useful. Equally the use-value exists only within the system of needy individuals and the realization of use-value develops in and through the system of property relations.

Value reveals itself only in the relation of commodity to commodity, therefore of use-value to use-value and of value to value. This relation, taken in its most primitive form, is the exchange-value of the commodity. Since the commodity exists as such only where it stands in a relation of interchangeability with other particular commodities, the commodity is such to its owner only to the extent that it has no use for him. Since he sees in it no use-value, its use-value being temporarily suppressed in the exchange, it becomes pure exchange-value. In its use the commodity finds its commodity character, its exchange-value, suppressed, while in that expression of its commodity character through the interchange of commodities the useful character of the commodity disappears. The use-value as a commodity properly considered ceases to be a relation to particular need and becomes instead the means to the acquisition of other commodities: it is the command over other commodities. The commodity as so much command over other commodities, over the world of use-values, is a value, a relation not to particular need (it is, rather, wholly indifferent to particularity of need) but to the entire system of needs taken as a whole.

The exchange-value of the commodity is, then, a relation of different commodities and not a property of the commodity taken in abstraction from the system of commodities. The exchange-value of the commodity is its command over another particular commodity, equating the two different commodities in a fixed proportion:

$$x \text{ commodity } a = y \text{ commodity } b$$

This equation of commodities is simultaneously the most elementary and the most difficult formula of economic theory. It presents itself as the abstract formulation of the most commonplace of economic relations. And yet, to grasp theoretically the properties expressed in this equation and the laws by which the relation is governed remains among the most difficult tasks of economic science; and it remains a task yet to be fully consummated in all its necessary detail and complexity. Even Marx, who understood most profoundly the abstract relations of commodities, failed in his effort to fully account for the system of commodity relations considered in its full theoretical determination.*

Since the exchange-value of the commodity is its relation to another particular commodity, and since the commodity always presupposes a system of commodities, exchange-value can never be singular but must always be multiple. The commodity has many different exchange-values, as many as there are different commodities with which it can express its interchangeability. The commodity is not, then, an exchange-value, but is, rather, capable of entering into a series of exchange relations and thereby taking on a sequence of exchange-values corresponding to the series of commodities with which it is capable of being equated.

Exchange-value is the external form of expression of the intrinsic commodity character of the object, of its value. It is precisely through the sequence of exchange relations that the presence within the commodity of a substance – value – which transcends its particular use-form and, by equating indifferently the commodity to all particular use-values establishes a commonality, is revealed. Underlying the entire series of exchange relations (of particular exchange-values of the commodity) is a substance which relates the commodity not to another particular commodity but simultaneously to all particular commodities.

Exchange-value is, first, an equation:

$$1 \text{ shirt} = 2 \text{ books}$$

---

* Marx attempts to make concrete his abstract conception of commodity relations in the third volume of *Capital*, and particularly in the 'transformation of values into prices,' together with the conception of the market system implied in that transformation. The weaknesses of the method employed by Marx will be considered in the following discussions of value and exchange-value, and especially in the second volume of the present work which will reconsider the full theoretical determination of commodity relations.

Here the commodity character of the use-value is expressed in its indifference to particular use-form, its capacity to be equally the property of one shirt and of two books. The shirt, taken as a use-value, cannot be equated with the book also taken as use-value. It is precisely as use-values that one shirt and two books are distinguished. The shirt is the use-value shirt only to the extent that it excludes the book, is differentiated from and opposed to it. This exclusion hinges upon the correct comprehension of the concept of use-value. As we have seen, the quantum of use-value is specific to the particular use-value so that its measure is connected to its particular, and therefore distinct, relation to need. For shirts it is the single shirt, for trucks the single truck, for oranges the single orange, etc. As use-values, shirts, oranges, and trucks can no more be equated than they can be summed. It is no more sensible to write the equation:

$$1 \text{ shirt} = 2 \text{ bushels of wheat},$$

if we are speaking of use-value, than it is to write:

$$3 \text{ apples} + 2 \text{ oranges} = x \text{ apples}.$$

The equation which expresses the exchange-value of the commodity can be meaningfully viewed not as an equation of use-value, but only as an equation of a substance indifferent to the particular use-value. This is, of course, immediately implied in the notion of an equation of apparently disparate objects. The problem is to discover in what respect the two objects are to be equated and therefore what substance they possess in common whose existence is revealed in their equivalence. So far as the equation of exchange-value is concerned, since exchange-value is itself no more than the mode of expression of the value substance, it is evident that the substance shared in common by the distinct commodities is nothing other than their commodity character, their value; therefore the fact that, as commodities, shirts and books each contain value in a quantitatively fixed proportion. In the exchange relation it is not the book as such which is equated with the shirt (any more than in the equation of masses the oranges as oranges are equated with apples), but the value substance as it presents itself in particular quantities within the different commodities. Thus, if the equation $5 \text{ apples} = 3 \text{ oranges}$ equates their weights it does not equate the apples and oranges. The apples and oranges as weight are wholly indifferent to the fact that the weight is the weight of the apples or the weight of the oranges. In either case it is simply so much weight and it is the latter which is, in fact, found to be present in equal quantities on both sides. As so much mass, oranges and apples are the same, but, as so much mass, oranges and apples cease to be oranges and apples. Equally, where we consider the equation of exchange it is not the use-values which are equated, although the manner of expression seems to imply this, but the values, the shirts and the books not as use-values, therefore not as shirts and books.

The distinction between value and exchange-value is predicated upon the conception of value as a substance indifferent to the particularity of the commodity owner and his desires. This universality of the value relation constitutes it as intrinsic to the commodity so far as its owner is concerned.* The use-value is incapable of effecting the equation of commodities in a quantitative sense so far as that equation involves the mutual dependence of individuals in the provision of needs. Since the equation brings about a reciprocal provision of need, it presupposes an opposition of use-values so that the equation of commodities within the exchange is not an equation of use-values, but an equation brought about in the abstraction of the property from determination in relation to use. Exchange opposes different commodities as particular use-values while equating different commodities as equally valuable.

2 Equality of commodities and of commodity owners

The expression of value in exchange-value takes the form of an equation of use-values and, therefore, implicitly an equation of disparate particular needs. This equation effects the identification of all distinct commodities as equally the repositories of value. This equivalence of commodities as values stems originally from their indifference to the particular personality of their owners and from the particular need which each fulfils. As values, the particu-

---

* The notion that the value of commodities is 'intrinsic' to them is common in the classical period. This notion is expressed in R. Cantillon's *Essai sur la nature du commerce en général* as well as by Ricardo in his early writing on money; see *The Works and Correspondence of David Ricardo*, ed. P. Sraffa (Cambridge: Cambridge University Press, 1951) Vol. III, p. 52.

lar commodities relate to their owners as the bearers of the capacity to enter into contractual relations. Since the value character of the object stamps it as indifferent to particularity, either of the use-value of the commodity or of the personality of the owner, the owner appears in relation to the commodity only in its abstraction from his particular personality. This abstraction affects equally all commodity owners, establishing each as bearing indifferently the abstract capacity for ownership. As we shall see, implicit in the relation of exchange-value is a real interchange of commodities, an actual exchange in which the indifference of the commodity to its owner is matched by an indifference of its owner to the particular features of the commodity.

The equation of exchange, therefore, establishes an equivalence of commodities which is at the same time an equality of commodity owners. Equality, within economic life, is not the abstract equation of mutually indifferent principles, but the equality of individuals concretely determined as different. These concrete differences relate to the determination of the individual on the basis of needs; it is only in so far as the individual is determined by the particularization of need within society that that difference forms the basis for an equality of individuals. In the relation of exchange-value, the equation of commodities expresses the necessity that they interrelate both in the fulfilment of particular needs and in the acquisition of the means to the fulfilment of particular needs. The relation of the commodity to need is a two-fold relation, on one side positive and on the other negative. The negative aspect of the relation, in so far as it entails an abstraction from determination in need, develops within the system of needs as the command over wealth without limit. Property in economic life is command over commodities, therefore over particular use-values. It is the means to the fulfilment of need, but it is the means to the fulfilment of need not limited in a given particular use-value. Property becomes wealth when it is the means to the fulfilment of need without limit. Existing in this way, property is valuable, and the commodity as so much property is so much value. The force of the relation of equivalence is precisely in that, through the interchange of commodities, each commodity owner retains without diminution or abrogation his status as a property owner. He must, in the exchange of commodities, retain his property if he is to sustain himself within the relation of exchange as a property owner. The retention of property on both sides develops with the exchange of equivalents. The equivalence of the exchange is an equivalence of the values of the commodities exchanged, so that on each pole of the exchange there exists property in the same measure. This relation sustains the status of the property owners as such, so that in the relation of commodity exchange the equality of commodity owners as commodity owners is sustained in the interchange of particular properties.

The recognition of rights existing equally on both sides of the exchange is revealed and preserved in the relation of commodities and of commodity owners. The commodity owner is established as free from determination in particular needs, as the owner of wealth, only in so far as he is the owner of commodities specified to the fulfilment of particular needs. In economic life, freedom from determination in fixed needs is also the determination of the commodity owner in needs, and the emancipation from fixity of need always takes place in the interrelation of particular needs. Thus, the content of freedom is the equality of individuals as commodity owners. And this equality, far from the determination of the whim of the individual, is always determined in relations of reciprocal recognition of rights and mutual provision of needs. Here we confront not the abstract freedom which dissolves into the maze of particular whims and passions, which always remove the individual as the complex of passions from any social context, forcing him to commune always with himself, but that freedom whose content is a social determination and which therefore has as its other side the strict determination of the individual as a commodity owner. This determination presupposes freedom from specification in need, and at the same time involves the determination of the individual within a complex of social relations. Individual freedom as self-determination is located by the individual in other individuals, and in the system of individuals whom he recognizes as equally the embodiment of this same freedom and in whose recognition the substance of his own freedom is alone to be found.

The equation of commodities, within which their value is expressed, is therefore also an equation of commodity owners which indicates, on the most general level, the determination of the commodity owner by a social condition. Equality is, therefore, a substantive social condition which provides for the freely self-determined individual a content and determination. The real content of this freedom comes to light once its social determination is established. In this case the needs of the individual are also an expression of his social determination, and therefore of his participation within a concretely determined system of social relations.

The social determination of the exchange relation can only be grasped where two conditions have been definitely established. The first entails the idea of equality and universality of the social being as the foundation for the conception of social life. The second is the determination of the differences between persons as a self-determination in accordance with their social reality. Thus, the absence of a true conception of exchange in Aristotle's *Ethics* is already implied in his starting point, which is that of fixed and irreducible differences among men. While he grasps correctly that in exchange 'people who are different and unequal . . . must be equated,' he refuses to see this as a real equality, instead always considering it 'impossible that things differing so much should become commensurate.'[3] Since the differences between men and things are fixed prior conditions, their equalization in the exchange must violate their intrinsic character. Where it is impossible to abstract from these fixed conditions it is impossible to constitute the social being in his full universality. Without such an abstraction there can be no logical basis for the conception of the equality of commodities and of commodity owners. In the absence of the conception of the full universality of the members of the social order it is equally necessary that any conception of a universal social substance which mediates their relation be excluded. The irreducible differences of men are reflected in the irreducible differences of the objects which mediate their relations. The idea of value is excluded. Where the object is not considered to be a value, its exchange cannot be the use which is implied in its inner constitution. While exchange is the proper 'use' of a value it is necessarily the 'improper use' of an object which is not a value.[4] This is no simple moral judgment but a judgment concerning the intrinsic character of the object necessarily implied by the absence of a concept of value.

The conception of equality is fully achieved with the development of moral and political philosophy in the seventeenth and eighteenth centuries. This development provides the necessary stepping stones for the emergence of a scientific conception of exchange. The latter requires in addition only the notion, first established by classical political economy, of equality as grounded in socially determined differences. With the rise of political economy the investigation of the 'anatomy of civil society' can for the first time be fully consummated.

3 *Value and use-value*

In the first instance exchange-value appears as a relation of two particular commodities which, taken as individual and independent commodities, appear only as use-values. Since exchange-value relates these individual commodities, it appears not as a relation of value to value but of use-value to use-value. It is the equation of use-values which reveals the equality of values within the inequality of use-values. Since the equation of commodities as useful objects contradicts their useful character it must, in reality, be an equation of use-values as embodiments of value. Value can only be expressed in the relation of use-value to use-value since it cannot exist independently of the commodity form, therefore of the embodiment within a particular useful form. This useful form hides the value substance, requiring that it express itself in a relation. Value is expressed as exchange-value – the command over another commodity, therefore over another use-value. Therefore, value is only expressible in use-value. Yet, this is also a contradiction since the mode of expression of value contradicts the nature of value by tying it down to a particular useful form, denying thereby its intrinsic independence of particular useful form. Within the single commodity as unity of value and use-value the form adopted by value – the individual commodity or use-value – contradicts the nature of value. The relation of exchange-value reproduces this contradiction within the commodity in the form of the activity of one commodity upon another. Exchange-value appears as an external manifestation of the contradiction which originates within the commodity; indeed, within the concepts of value and use-value.

In this unity of opposites a relation of the universe of commodities (value) is only expressible as a limited relation to particular commodities. The disaffection of value with its limited mode of expression drives the value relation to adopt more and more concrete forms in an effort to effect its emancipation from the contradictions intrinsic to it. The opposition of value and use-value is the driving force which underlies the development of the entire system of economic relations. Such an opposition cannot, therefore, be grasped as a simple inconsistency of the differing poles of the commodity relation. The latter cannot be understood to move apart into a dead opposition – on one side value, on the other use-value – since that opposition does not exist except as a contradiction within the commodity which unites the poles as determining aspects of a single relation. Since this is a contradiction not to the value substance, but within the concept of value, the relation of value to use-value is as much a necessity as is the independence of value from use-value intrinsic to the notion of value. The constitution of social needs can no more be grasped independently of value than the value relation can subsist independently of the system of needs. It is in the relation of exchange-value that this unity forcibly asserts itself as an interrelation of commodities and of commodity owners.

III The forms of exchange-value

1 The elementary form

The most elementary form in which value is expressed is that of exchange-value, and particularly that of the expression of the value of one commodity in its relation with another particular commodity. This is the expression of value in the equation of two particular use-values which Marx terms the 'elementary' or 'accidental' form of exchange-value:

$$\text{10 bushels of wheat} = \text{1 ton of iron.}$$

Viewed as a simple mathematical equation this says no more than that there exists, within each commodity, a common substance in equal amounts – value. Taken as an equation, and therefore as symmetrical, the expression of value as such remains implicit. It is clearly present as the rule according to which the commodities are equated, but it remains lacking in a positive expression. We as yet do not know what the value is, or precisely how the value of the iron, as of the wheat, is expressed in the equation.

On the other hand, considered not simply as an equation but as a dynamic expression of value, the symmetry gives way to a distinction between the poles – the wheat and the iron. This distinction within the equation of value was grasped by Adam Smith, who equated it with the concept of value itself. Smith considers the subject of the analysis of the value concept to be the relation of the commodity – its value or worth – to the person who possesses it but does not wish himself to use or consume it.[5] The existence of the commodity as a possession but not as an object of need is revealed in the alienation of the commodity. When the commodity is alienated by its owner it retains the characteristic of a possession while denying its immediate determination in need. To its owner the commodity ceases to be a use-value and, at that instant, becomes for the first time, in fact, a commodity, a value. This relation of the commodity to its owner who has no use for it is, according to Smith, its value. And this relation of property, which is the value of the commodity, is the useful object which it purchases in the market. For Smith value is the labor which the commodity is able to command.

The comprehension of the equation of exchange depends, therefore, upon the angle from which it is viewed. For the owner of the wheat the wheat has no use-value and exists only as so much value which is to be determined in its relation with another use-value. Thus, viewed from the standpoint of the commodity owner, the two sides of the expression are not, in fact, symmetrical. On one side there is use-value and on the other there is value. Thus the equation of use-values viewed as the expression of value expresses that value by distinguishing the relation of the poles of the exchange, specifying one pole as the value and the other as the use-value. As the command on the part of wheat over iron (implicitly the amount of iron purchased by wheat in the market) the equation is:

10 bushels of wheat is 'worth' 1 ton of iron

or

the 'value' of 10 bushels of wheat is 1 ton of iron.

It is clear that the equation of exchange-value, while symmetrical when viewed as the simple manner of revelation of the presence of the common substance of value on each side, is asymmetrical when viewed as the particular form of expression of the value of the particular commodities from the standpoint of each pole. Accord-

ing to this form of expression of value, the use-value on one side
is equated with the value of the commodity on the other so that the
value of the commodity on the left of the expression – in the
'relative form' – has a real expression in the use-value of the commodity on the right, while the commodity on the right-hand side
of the expression – in the 'equivalent form' – since it is value (the
value of the commodity in the relative form) has itself no expression. The 'value' of ten bushels of wheat is the use-value one ton
of iron so that we know from the expression what is the value of
the wheat. But this value is the use-value of the iron so that the
real intrinsic value of the iron has no expression. When we write
that the wheat 'is worth' so much iron we say nothing (except by
implication) as to what the iron is worth.

Since the value of the commodity in the relative form is the use-
value of the commodity in the equivalent form (the value of the
wheat is so many tons of iron and not so many of the units of value
of iron), the former has a real expression. That is, from the side of
the relative form the value of the commodity is different from its
use-value. The commodity in this form goes outside of its particular useful embodiment, and directly denies its particular useful
form. Its value, indifference to useful form, is given expression
when it is revealed to be an altogether different useful form (iron),
and when it is equated with and implicitly replaced by that other
form. For the commodity in the relative form, the value is not the
use-value since it is another use-value. The value of the wheat
cannot be the use-value of the wheat since it is the use-value iron;
by implication, so far as the owner of the wheat is concerned, its
value stands always opposed to its use-value. Here the value of the
commodity is that other commodity which it commands, so that
the value of the commodity is not its use-value at the same time
that it is asserted to be another use-value. It is for precisely this
reason that the commodity requires a relation to another use-value
if its value is to be expressed. If we were to write the equation of
value as

10 bushels of wheat = 10 bushels of wheat

there would be no revelation of value but only the statement that
the use-value wheat is the use-value wheat. The expression of value
requires an interaction of use-values and, in the first instance, the
expression of value is nothing more than a relation of use-values.

By contrast, on the side of the equivalent form the use-value of the commodity is directly equated with value, it is the 'worth' or the 'value' of the commodity in the relative form. Value, in so far as it is given concrete expression in the equation of use-values, is identified with one of the use-values. Here, value is not the abstract social substance of the commodity which relates it to its owner simply as so much property, but the relation to particular need, in this case to another particular need. And, indeed, here value appears as the interaction of need, as the mediating stage in the reciprocal provision of needs among the system of needy persons who, as commodity owners, fulfil each other's needs through the exchange of commodities. Viewed in terms of the elementary form it is still the difference of need which determines the value relation. In the elementary form the inability of value to divorce itself from a relation to particular use-value implies the equation of value not only with use-value but with this particular use-value. Value is iron.

In the equivalent form, just as in the case of money, the use-value – × amount of gold – is value. The social substance of the commodity which makes the latter implicitly indifferent to its useful form now appears to be (1) identified with use-value, as when we state that the value of the wheat is so much iron or that the price of the commodity is so many ounces of gold, and (2) identified with a purely material, natural substance. Here it is not even the use-value in its relation to a socially determined need but, apparently, the use-value in relation to so much of a physical substance. As a result, the value of the commodity in the equivalent form has no expression since it is directly equated with its use-value.

This absence of expression appears most vividly if we anticipate the more advanced form of the expression of value – money. Here the asymmetry between the two sides of the value expression is evident. The exchange-value of the commodity is the expression of its value in the particular use-value – money, or the money commodity. To say that the exchange-value of bread is $3 (so many units of the money commodity) is not the same as to say that the exchange-value of $3 is so many pounds of bread. To be sure, such a statement may be reversed and the equivalent form given over to the commodity which originated in the relative form so that the value of the latter may now be expressed in the former, but now the asymmetry is not eliminated but affects the two commodities in reverse. Since money is characteristically and intrinsically re-stricted to the equivalent side the peculiarity felt in the switch of forms in the case of the expression 'three dollars is worth five pounds of bread' is accounted for by the opposition of forms and therefore attests to the intrinsic asymmetry of the expression of value. To switch the objects in this way is not to eliminate this asymmetry but to apply it differently to the commodity pair. The impossibility of eliminating the difference of form appears clear in the case of money, which has no price, and which, because of its peculiar useful character, cannot be switched from one form to the other.

The idea that exchange-value is the command over another particular commodity, which we have noted for example in Adam Smith, eliminates the presence of value as a principle which exists within and yet stands opposed to the system of particular needs. Here, value exists only as exchange-value, and this fact not only indicates the mode of expression of value, but leads to a substantive reduction of value to exchange-value, so that the value of the commodity is its command over another particular commodity and therefore no intrinsic property of the commodity itself. This equation of value and exchange-value implies the elimination of the value substance and thus marks the elimination of the explicit social principle from the system of needs. The social character of needs is then directly identified with their multiplication and not with anything intrinsic either to the particular needs as such or the individual commodities taken as related to the system of com-modity owners. The real universality of the value relation is suppressed.

Once value is equated with exchange-value, value becomes exclusively a relation of need and can find no independent sub-sistence. As a result, it becomes equally the case that exchange-value, and with it price, can find no intrinsic law according to which it is determined. The reciprocal interaction of commodities is immediately their value so that the interaction does not express the activity of a social principle which might give for it an account. As a result it becomes impossible to ground the exchange system in the life process of a determinate social reality. In the absence of the value principle, the system of exchange can only appear as an expression of the system of need; thus the reduction of value to need characteristic of modern economic analysis becomes inevitable. To begin with exchange-value is to posit an interaction with no reason outside of the irreducible particularity of a reciprocal provision of arbitrarily fixed needs.

2 *The expanded form*

While all exchange of commodities places those commodities in the elementary form, it by no means follows that the elementary form is adequate to the expression of value. On the contrary, the weakness of the elementary form is apparent in the identification of value with the command over one particular commodity, one particular use-value. In this form value has no expression independent of particular use-value and, indeed, is directly equated with the particular use-value. Value, or the indifference of the commodity to particular need, appears as a relation of the commodity to one particular need; command over the world of commodities, over the totality of wealth, has the form of command over a single commodity, a limited expression of wealth.

The elementary form of value makes explicit the independence of value of any relation to a given particular need. Yet this independence is achieved here only in the relation of the commodity to another particular commodity which is posited arbitrarily as the means to the expression of the value of the original commodity. When the elementary form establishes the independence of commodity-value it thereby also establishes the necessity that the expression of value pass beyond the limitations implied in the abstraction of the elementary form.

Where this abstraction is not overcome, the exchange-value ceases to be the expression of value, and becomes instead a direct relation of need. As a result, the systematic nature of exchange is replaced by the accidental interaction of particular need. Here the exchange seems to express the relation of two irreducibly autonomous commodity owners whose interaction adopts the form of an interchange of use-values according to conditions wholly bound up with the immediate exchange itself. The fact of the interchange, and its quantitative dimension, appear both to be fixed in the needs of the individual and not in the system of need and of interaction among commodity owners. Primacy is given to the immediate interrelation of two commodities in the elementary form, so that were this expression to be taken by itself exchange of the commodity would appear to be accidental.

In order for value to be expressed in the relation of commodities, that relation must go beyond the interaction of a single commodity pair. In particular, if we consider the expression of value from the standpoint of the commodity whose value is to be revealed in a relation of exchange-value, that relation must, if it is to express the value of the commodity, go beyond the equation of the commodity with another particular commodity. The particular commodity, in order that its commodity character may be allowed to surface, must come into a relation with the system of commodities, therefore simultaneously into relation with the world of commodities taken together. This is accomplished first in what Marx calls the 'expanded form of exchange-value.'

In the expanded form the simultaneous interaction of the system of commodities as a whole is effected, so that the equivalence of use-values, which reveals their equivalence as values, is now the equivalence of all commodities as equally embodiments of the value substance. The original equation of exchange-value now is extended to take in an unending chain of commodity relations:

10 bushels of wheat = 1 ton of iron = 30 yards of cloth
= 4 chairs = ...

Taken from the standpoint of the expression of the value of the particular commodity, the expanded form reveals that the accidental equation of commodities is, in reality, only a determinate element in a series of equations. This result is implicit in the conditions that (1) the commodity is a repository of value, and (2) as a repository of value the commodity exists from the outset in an implicit relation with a world of commodities. This relation is implied in the elementary form and first made explicit in the expanded form, which expresses the universality of the value of the individual commodity:

$$10 \text{ bushels of wheat} = \begin{cases} 1 \text{ ton of iron} \\ 30 \text{ yards of cloth} \\ 4 \text{ chairs} \\ 1 \text{ ounce of gold} \\ \cdot \\ \cdot \\ \cdot \end{cases}$$

Now the relative form is faced with an unending string of equivalents each equally able to express its value. The commodity in the relative form (the wheat) is now simultaneously, and indifferently, the equivalent of any and all other particular commodities. Its relation of equivalence can no longer be taken as an accident of its interaction with another particular commodity. Equally, the interaction of the commodity in the relative form must be assumed to go beyond that of two independent commodity owners to constitute each as a single element of a total system of commodities and commodity owners. In the expanded form the manifold nature of value is made explicit in its mode of expression.

In the expanded form of value the value is, then, no longer tied to any particular commodity or useful form and is, as a result, constituted for the first time as really independent of expression in any particular use-value. Now the value of the wheat appears indifferently as so much iron, so much cloth, so many chairs, etc. Since the value of the wheat is all of, or any of, these particular use-values, it is not tied to any one of them and, in its mode of expression, denies identification with any particular useful form. The mode of expression of value in the expanded form, therefore, denies identification with use-value and begins to appear as really distinct from use-value. The opposition of value and use-value develops towards the necessity of the independence of the value substance. In the elementary form the value is identified with a particular use-value. In the expanded form the value is no particular use-value. In the elementary form value is so many tons of iron. In the expanded form value is so much iron, so much cloth, so many chairs, etc. The value in this form is by that very fact *not* so much iron, so much cloth, and so many chairs. Since value is indifferently iron, cloth, chairs, it is therefore none of them. Value appears here for the first time as a relation to the world of commodities. Value sees the world of commodities as it really is, as so many forms of its own existence. Value is now the participation of the particular commodity in the whole of the wealth of society.

Yet, at the same time that value takes on a universality in the expanded form it also loses all real expression by adopting that form. In the elementary form the value of the wheat is expressed as so much iron. Value is iron. Value is given a determinate expression as the commodity iron. Here, in the expanded form, however, the value of the wheat is unknown except as an unending series of relations. As a result of the multiplicity of equivalents it becomes impossible to express the value of the wheat, to uncover the substance of value itself. There is no way of extracting from the infinite series of equivalents the real value, the common substance, and of grasping that substance itself in an expression; no way, that is, of concentrating out the substance of value. In this respect the two opposing forms of the expression of value (the elementary and the expanded) each suffers from a complementary inadequacy:

1 Elementary form – value is expressed, but is restricted to a single commodity, a relation to particular use-value. Value exists and is known but only in the inadequate form of particular use-value. We know that the wheat has a value independent of its useful properties and we know what that value is: so much iron. Yet this knowledge is intrinsically unsatisfactory since as knowledge of value it contradicts the nature of value.

2 Expanded form – now value is no longer tied to an inadequate form of expression so far as its universality and indifference to particular use-value is concerned. To this extent the expanded form overcomes the contradictions of the elementary form. But at the same time, the expanded form denies to value any real expression and existence which it has, however inadequately, in the elementary form.

3 The general form

In order to overcome these limitations the two forms must be united on a higher level. In the elementary form the expression of value possesses unity but lacks universality. In the expanded form that expression possesses universality but lacks unity. In order to adequately express the value of commodities it is necessary to develop that form of expression which possesses simultaneously the universality of the expanded form, which relates the commodity to the world of commodities, and the unity of the elementary form, which relates the commodity to its value in a single substance. The equivalent which expresses the value of the commodity must now be a single substance which is, as well, penetrated with the universality of the commodity relation. This substance is the commodity in the equivalent form in what Marx calls the 'general form of value':

$$\left.\begin{array}{l} \text{10 bushels of wheat} \\ \text{1 ton of iron} \\ \text{4 chairs} \\ \text{1 ounce of gold} \\ \cdot \\ \cdot \\ \cdot \end{array}\right\} = \text{30 yards of cloth}$$

The general form allows the value an independent mode of expression, as in the elementary form, without denying that relation to the world of commodities sustained in the expanded form.

The general form expresses the value of each commodity in a particular use-value, but now that use-value appears in a different relation to the commodities whose value it expresses than did the single commodity acting as the equivalent in the elementary form. The commodity in the equivalent form (cloth) now expresses value for the world of commodities as a whole and therefore simultaneously expresses the value of all diverse use-values. The general form appears as the transposition of the expanded form in which the series of commodities exists now on the relative side. The result of this transposition is to alter essentially the expression of value. Now the equivalent has immediately impressed upon it a universal character as simultaneously the equivalent of all commodities, the universal mode of the expression of value. Since the expression of value is concentrated in a single commodity, particularly in its use-value, the substance of that commodity, as regards the expression of value, has undergone an alteration. Its existence in the equivalent aspect of the general form brings about a change in its inner character and in the nature of its use-value.

Knowledge of the value of the commodity in its command over a particular commodity (the equivalent in the general form) is knowledge simultaneously of its command over all commodities since the equivalent is the expression of the value of all commodities. The single commodity within which all commodities express their value is also the concentrate of value for the universe of commodities. Thus the general form retains that property of the elementary form of expressing value in a unified manner and also that property of the expanded form of relating the commodity in the expression of its value to a world of commodities.

But, while the general form limits the expression of value to a single use-value, as in the elementary form, that use-value is no longer simply a particular use-value. It is a use-value marked out by the system of commodities as universal. As such it is the socially recognized embodiment of value. The expression of value in this commodity is its expression in a use-value whose use-value is the expression of value. In this respect the universality of the expanded form is united with the unity of the elementary form. Even while value is expressed in particular use-value, it is expressed independently of particular use-value, thereby adopting its own mode of expression. The commodity which expresses the value of all commodities in its own use-value is the commodity whose use-value is universal: the universal equivalent, money.

IV Money

1 The universal equivalent

As the universal equivalent, the money commodity takes on a use-value the determination of which goes beyond the system of particular use-values existent in the more elementary forms. The one ounce of gold which exists, for example, in the relative side of the expanded form, exists as so much gold and does not possess the use-value of the universal equivalent. The latter is bestowed upon the gold only by its relation within the general form and therefore does not exist prior to or independently of the development of the general form and of the universal equivalent. The expression of value requires a commodity defined in its relation to the world of particular commodities. Money is the socially recognized existence of value which is outside of the bodily form of the particular commodities. Here value is a relation to a particular use-value which relates to no particular need but only to value's own need for expression. The expression of value in the money form, then, is:

10 bushels of wheat
1 ton of iron
4 chairs
30 yards of cloth = $80
.
.
.

2 The standard of value

The money form is distinguished from the general form in that for the latter the use-value which expresses the value of all commodities remains particular (so much gold). To the extent that the commodity which becomes the general equivalent is simply transferred from the relative to the equivalent form, it retains its particularity as one aspect of its economic existence in the general form. Its use-value is now duplicated, remaining on one side that of the particular commodity while adopting additionally the use-value of the general equivalent. Indeed, the particular commodity seems ultimately to derive its ability to function as the general equivalent from its prior determination as a particular commodity. This is by no means the case for money. The use-value of the money commodity is its existence as the universal representative of the value of commodities, and nothing else. The development from the general form to the money form represents, therefore, a quantum leap which entails the constitution of a commodity whose particularity lies wholly in its capacity to exist as the universal equivalent, and whose life process is determined wholly by its striving to exist as money.

The general conception of money does not involve the equivalence of the money with any single particular commodity as the source of its commoditization. On the contrary, the convertibility of the money into some particular commodity always tends towards the reduction of the money form to the general form of value. Money which is directly redeemable for some particular commodity whose value is given independently of the specific relation into which it enters with money is not immediately the representative of value, but is the derivative of the value of the commodity which it represents. This in effect places money, the universal equivalent, in the relative form of value. In this case, the money form is reduced to the general form and the universal equivalent is reduced to the relative form:

> 10 bushels of wheat
> 1 ton of iron
> 4 chairs
> 30 yards of cloth
> . $= \$80 = 1$ ounce of gold.
> .
> .

Here, again, value is the particular use-value which is also something other than value. The constitution of the particular commodity as universal (e.g. of gold as money) implies also the reduction of the universal equivalent to the status of a derivative of the particular commodity and of its value. This is the historical starting point. Conceptually, however, the general treatment of money must be fully emancipated from any immediate identification with a particular commodity.* The conception of the money form, emancipated from the particular commodity, makes possible the theoretical treatment of money and of its value. This, at the same time, makes possible the comprehension of the particular conditions under which the determination of money in its relation to one particular commodity becomes necessary.

Once money is severed from any immediate equivalence with the particular commodity, it can no longer derive its value from

---

* 'The fact that historically paper currencies arose out of metal currencies is no ground for regarding them in that manner theoretically. The value of paper money must be deduced without resort to metal money.' (R. Hilferding, *Das Finanzkapital* [Frankfurt am Main: Europaische Verlagsanstalt, 1968] p. 67.) It needs to be emphasized that what is really implied by 'paper money' in this connection is money in general, taken without regard to the concrete conditions by which its value and its specific circuit are determined. Marx, while grasping the specificity of the money form for the first time, still clings to the precious metals as the irreducible basis for the valuation of money. Thus, even when at certain points he recognizes the monetization of the metals as the origin of their value, he always returns to their intrinsic valuation in their direct production as the ultimate foundation of their value. Hilferding attacks this aspect of the Marxist conception directly and insists, above all, upon the theoretical priority of money taken without regard to a specific relation to a particular commodity (i.e. paper money). None the less, after once making explicit the theoretically necessary standpoint, and particularly the determination of the value of money not in terms of the labor-value of the precious metals, but in terms of a 'socially necessary circulation value,' he proceeds to vacillate on the issue and eventually to return to a non-monetary standard for the value of money.

the value of that particular commodity. The first effect of this is that money appears to lose its value. And, indeed, as the universal equivalent money has no value of its own since, in particular, there can be no means by which the money could express its value without giving up the universal form. For the money to be the universal equivalent, it must be excluded from all existence in the relative form. Any failure in this respect is a failure of the money to constitute itself as such. Since the money cannot express its value, it in effect has no value. This absence of value is equivalent to the lack on the part of money of a value which is distinctive to it as one particular commodity determined in a manner equivalent to that of all particular commodities. In this sense it is substantively correct to conclude that money lacks any intrinsic value, deriving its value exclusively from the valuation of other commodities and from its relations with those commodities.

To the degree that money is the universal expression of value its own value is its amount, so that rather than having a value, money is value. The money is value not because of any contingent material property (e.g. durability) but because of the relations into which it enters with the system of commodities.* The value of money is, in this sense, completely derivative of the valuation of the totality of particular commodities. Money, then, extracts its own value from other commodities and is able to be itself valuable only by existing as the value of other commodities. The absence of the process of its own valuation is also the condition which makes it possible for the money to find its own value exclusively in its relations with other commodities and therefore to exist as the external manifestation of *their* values. This existence of money as the value of the system of commodities finds no contradiction in any particular and contingent circumstances of its own valuation.

---

* The necessity that the material form of money (to the degree that money is required to actually adopt a material form) have the property of durability may be deduced from the functioning of money as medium of circulation (see below, chapter 3). It is in the nature of money that its consumption transpire within the system of commodity exchanges and that it retain its material form through its repeated consumption Since money is commodity value made independent of useful form, the money must be capable of sustaining itself through a sequence of relations with particular use-values. Durability of money means the ability to preserve its integrity as the unique embodiment of a given amount of value through a series of commodity relations. This also entails the ability of money to store value over an extended period of time.

The less money has its own value, the more adequate it is to exist as value (and as its standard and measure), and the more the value of the money exists exclusively in its relations with the system of commodities.

The unit of the money commodity acts as the standard of value. The unit of money-value is a unit of the commodity the use-value of which is specific to its existence as the universal equivalent. The use-value of the money commodity is not that of the material substance of which it is composed, but of the social function to which it is specified. Value is measured, then, not in ounces of gold, but in dollars, marks, shillings, etc.

It is only where money ceases to function as such (as the universal equivalent) that a particular commodity such as gold must be brought in to function as money. The latter acts as money in this case because it is also not-money. Since the activity of money has been suspended, the determination of the value of money in its life process gives way, to a greater or lesser degree, to its external determination in the value of gold. Even here, however, it must be always borne in mind that the valuation of the precious metals is not a condition given independently of their existence as money (for example by their immediate production). On the contrary, where particular commodities function as money, their own intrinsic value gives way, to a greater or lesser degree, to their valuation as money.

3 *The measure of value*

The expression of the value of the commodity in money is its price. Money is value and expresses value only by existing exclusively as the medium by which the total system of commodities establishes its unity. Money is the substantiation of this unity and expresses the value of the particular commodity in its relation to that commodity which represents the total commodity system. The value of the commodity expressed in money is, then, substantively its value since it is the relation of the commodity to the system of commodities taken *in toto* and expressed as a single magnitude.

With the emergence of the money commodity through the joint activity of the system of commodities as a whole, the opposition within the commodity between its value and its particular useful form is reproduced as a relation of money (as the universal repre-

sentative of value) to commodities (the particular embodiments of
value in useful form). The value of all commodities now has an
expression outside of those commodities in a particular commodity,
money. The exchange relation between the individual commodity
and money, its exchange-value with money or its price, now gives
independent expression to its value. Since money is the universal
expression of value, it measures the exchange-value of the commodity with the universe of commodities. Just as the exchange-
value of wheat with iron measures the ability of the wheat to
command iron in exchange, so its exchange-value with money
measures its ability to command all particular commodities – iron,
cloth, etc. – since money is the command over all wealth, the
general form of the existence of wealth. Thus the exchange-value
of the commodity with money is substantively the exchange-value
of the commodity as such. Money, which serves to measure the
command in the market of the commodity over all other commodities, measures directly the exchange-value of the commodity.

Since money measures the exchangeability of the particular
commodity it measures also the value of the commodity. The
commodity has exchange-value with particular commodities, and
therefore with money, only to the extent that it has value, so that
the degree of its exchangeability with other particular commodities
expresses the degree to which it is valuable.

The emancipation of money from its identification with the
particular commodity makes it the adequate measure of value. To
measure length in a particular substance (e.g. a metal stick) is to
make length to that degree contingent on the particular properties
of that substance. Equally, to measure value in gold is to make the
measure of value contingent upon the particular properties of the
gold, particular properties which have nothing in principle to do
either with value or with money. Empirically, all measures are
contingent in this sense. Conceptually, however, value has, in
money, a measure which is fully adequate to it since the measurement of value in money is its measurement in a substance which is,
in principle, nothing more than value itself. The price of the
commodity, grasped in its theoretical determination and not as an
empirically contingent magnitude, is the logical measure of its
value.

While the price of the commodity is the measure of its value, it
by no means follows that the concept of value can be directly

subsumed into that of price. The idea that price is the measure of the value of the particular commodity entails not only a general mode of expression of value, but also a determination of the price relation in accordance with the nature of the commodity and of value. The price is the valid measure of value; it is, therefore, the 'real' or 'natural' price, only in so far as the determination of price is bound up with value and its characteristic life process. The logical relation of value to price simultaneously allows the value a measure adequate to it and constitutes the price not as the result of contingent circumstances, but as determined by its intrinsic laws. The significance of the relation of price to value is in the conception of the exchange relation as determinate and not accidental. The conception of price without value is the conception of a commodity relation which, since it lacks any intrinsic determination, is purely contingent. The conception of value without price is the conception of an intrinsic force with no ability to express and realize itself in a relationship. As in all scientific investigation the distinction between the substance and its mode of expression is essential, as is the unity of the intrinsic substance and its extrinsic life process.

It is possible, for example, to measure extension with a meter stick. But, while it is sensible to determine with the use of a meter stick that the length of a pipe is six meters, it is not reasonable to conclude that the pipe is extended in space six meters because it is equal in length to six meter sticks. That the pipe is extended in space so many meters expresses a relation between the pipe and another object, but is not the same as the property which the pipe and the object share of being extended in space, the property which makes them commensurable in this way. An object is no more extended in space because it is so many meters long, than a commodity is valuable because it exchanges in such and such a proportion with money. Rather, an object has the property of being extended in space so many meters by merit of its mass, density and form of movement relative to a co-ordinate system. Yet, the meter stick, taken by itself, measures neither mass, density, nor motion. Thus, when we say that one meter stick equals one-sixth of the pipe we are measuring the extension of the pipe in a generally recognized unit, concluding that the pipe is six meters long. And this equation (1 pipe = 6 meters) gives us the same sort of information as the equation of value, 10 bushels of wheat = $1, namely

(1) that the two objects possess a common property – in the first case extension, in the second value, and (2) that this property is measured in a particular way, first extension in meters and second value in ounces of gold.

Similarly, it is possible to measure temperature by inches of mercury:

$$1 \text{ cup of water} = x \text{ inches of mercury} = y° \text{ F}.$$

This is possible because both water and mercury share the common property of containing energy. Without this common property it would not be sensible to attempt to relate the two in terms of their temperature. In this context it would be senseless to attempt to measure the temperature of the dollar (at least to attempt to measure it in degrees Fahrenheit), or the distance between today and yesterday (in meters), or the velocity of stupidity, the price of the moon, etc. The equation of temperature is possible because both water and mercury are made up of molecules in motion which can, in their movement, contain differing amounts of energy expressed in the differing temperatures. But, while these energy levels are expressed in temperature, to say that they are equivalent to temperature would be to collapse energy into its particular form of expression as heat, and thereby to deny any distinction between temperature and energy and any substantive theoretical significance to that distinction. Even while knowledge of energy and its properties allows for a direct transformation of information concerning temperature to information regarding energy, the property which underlies temperature goes beyond the simple notion of temperature by accounting for it, and without the difference between the property or substance and its mode of expression there could be no such theoretical account.

It is for this reason that it is possible to measure length (extension) prior to the development of any rational theory of space, and to measure temperature prior to the development of a satisfactory theory of the molecular structure of matter. Equally, the measurement of value in price takes place with no knowledge whatever (of a theoretical nature) regarding the laws by which that value is determined. Indeed, prior to the publication of the *Wealth of Nations*, it was the typical procedure of economic thinking to take the measurement of commodities as a purely practical problem having nothing to do with economic theory. This is the other side of the absence, prior to Smith, of a theory of value. In the absence of any concept of value, the measurement of commodities proceeds directly in terms of their market price, taken as an *a priori* condition and not as the specific subject-matter of a theory. Even for Smith, who constitutes value as the object of a theory for the first time, the measurement of value in price brings with it intractable difficulties. These are the difficulties connected with the labor-commanded conception of value within which the value of commodities is measured in their exchange-value with the particular commodity labor-power. Here Smith sees, if only for an instant, the deeper problems connected to the conception of the relation of value, exchange-value, and price. It is only with Ricardo that the difficulties in the measurement of value begin to expose the really problematic character of the categories of value and price. For Ricardo these deeper problems, while never satisfactorily resolved, take on their true proportions, challenging the whole of economic theory, and indeed, the very possibility of an economic science.[6]

The difficulty which is evidenced in Ricardo's inability to find a measure adequate to the concept of value is that brought about by the notion, characteristic of Ricardian economics, that value is the substance and determinant of exchange only in so far as it is intrinsically independent of exchange. This conception is the logical starting point for the classical and Marxian theories of value and of money. Value is, or is determined by, a substance – labor – which is externally fixed. Since this substance is given outside of the system of exchange relations, it can act as their independent determinant and cause. Such externality is essential to the methodology of the classical theory for which determination ultimately implies recourse to an irreducible condition – labor and its distribution. Exchange is a social form for a substance which must originally be constituted as a fixed natural condition. The identification of labor with value makes possible a theoretical determination of exchange in the form of a reduction of the exchange relation to its prior determination in an act of 'labor.' The social determination of the latter, once posited outside of the system of commodity relations, must be either explicitly denied, or reduced to an empty empirical assertion. This independent determination of the value substance, while it appears to make possible a theoretical account for the system of exchange relations, in actuality establishes an intractable barrier between the substance of exchange – value –

and the real relation as it subsists within its own process of self-determination. The system of price determination leaves untouched the determinant of price – value. The determination of price within the system of commodity relations as a whole now opposes the determination of price in value.*

In order to overcome this contradiction it is necessary to give up the idea that the value substance is fully determined independently of the system of commodity exchange, to reunite the substance with its mode of expression, and to constitute the price system as also the real determination of the value relation. This makes price the logical measure of value since the determination of price and the determination of value are now united. The distinction between value and price now expresses not their opposition, but the real determinacy of the price relation. In particular, the relation of price to value makes the price relation a lawful one subject to a necessity in its movement, and for which a theoretical account is possible. Thus the idea that price is the result of contingent circumstances is overcome, and price becomes instead an element in an objectively determined social process. Since the price relation has this determinacy, it can no longer be considered as an external relation of objects which are intrinsically indifferent to exchange. No more could the conception of the relative motion of massive bodies be grasped as a relation indifferent to their intrinsic determination and constitution as substances – mass. While relative motion and intrinsic mass are not independently determined, neither can they be immediately identified. So also in the case of the commodity. The notion of value is the notion of an *intrinsic* determination of the commodity as a social substance, which intrinsic determination is only possible in the context of its rela-

---

* In Ricardo this opposition expresses itself most sharply in the search for an 'invariable measure of value.' Invariability in this case is synonymous with indifference of value to the processes which are specific to the system of exchange relations by which the self-development of capital as a whole is effected. Invariance means, therefore, indifference of value to the concrete system within which its own self-determination is accomplished. For Marx this same contradiction manifests itself in the problem of the so-called 'transformation of values into prices' whose function it is to establish that the system of price relations is nothing more than a phenomenal form for a condition – value and surplus value – already fully developed and determined within the immediate production process and without any reference to conditions bound up with the self-realization of the total capital. It is, therefore, not surprising that, for both Marx and Ricardo, there develops a contradiction between value and the system of price relations.

tions and its movement, therefore, within the system of price relations.

Value, then, is not a natural substance, but the inner determination of the commodity in accordance with its life process. Value is the inner reflection, within the commodity, of the system of economic relations as a whole. It is this intrinsic determination which makes value a substance, not its reducibility to an external material condition. Value is as much a substance as is mass, and it is as little reducible to an external condition given independently of its relations and movement.

The identification of the measure of temperature with knowledge of the property of the material which gives to it a temperature, or the length of the pipe with the property of the pipe that gives it extension in space, is comparable to the assumption that the exchange-value of the shirt is also the property of the shirt which allows it to command commodities in the market. Even though the value of the shirt, which is that property which makes it exchangeable, is only expressed in the opposition between particular commodities, therefore in exchange, and is there expressed in a determinate manner so that knowledge of value is knowledge of exchange-value and knowledge of the latter together with knowledge of the laws of its emergence is knowledge of value, none the less the distinction between value and exchange-value is essential. What is involved in this distinction is the account for the relationship of exchange (as of extension or of temperature) rather than its mere practical description and the measurement of its effects. Without the distinction between value and exchange-value there is the abstract statement of exchange but no explanation of the force whose activity gives rise to exchange. Value is precisely this force within the particular commodity which ties it into a system of exchanges and of particular exchange relations but which cannot be identified with any particular exchange relation. And, while a strict relation can be expected to subsist between this force and its expression, it does not follow that it is reasonable to identify the two. To do so is to lose altogether the conception of the value substance and with it the possibility of a theory of exchange and of exchange-value.

4 *The representative of wealth*

With the development of the value relation and of its forms of expression, especially the money form, the wealth of society ceases to appear simply as the sum total of commodities, the multiplicity of use-values. Wealth exists now substantively as the command over all use-values. Wealth is in direct proportion not to the command over a particular commodity, or over any limited set of particular commodities, but in direct proportion to the command over commodities in general, over money. In the first instance, then, wealth exists independently, as wealth, when it exists as money – money is wealth and wealth is money. Just as in the history of the conception, so also in the conception itself the starting point is the identification of wealth with money. It is precisely the weakness of economic thinking prior to the emergence of classical political economy that this identification forms not the starting point, but the whole of the conception of wealth, the fixed point to which the whole of the notion of wealth is restricted. It is for this reason that, prior to physiocracy, the real origins of wealth are never uncovered, so that the conception of wealth, and as well the conception of money, is never raised to a truly theoretical level.

Money as such, while expressing the wealth of society, does not exhaust the life process of wealth and does not account fully for the oppositions implicit within the commodity form. This is grasped implicitly by classical political economy. Money expresses the wealth of nations but it only *expresses* it, and even that only under special circumstances. Wealth, on the other hand, is a relationship which goes beyond any fixed expression in money, a relationship which actually determines the movement of money and the development of the money form. In order for money to express the value of commodities, and therefore to represent the wealth of society, it is insufficient that it merely relate to commodities as the expression of their commodity character. It is further necessary that money realize itself in relation to the world of commodities, and that within this relation there be posited the production and reproduction of the opposition of commodities and money as well as of the value substance which accounts for the relation of commodities and money. The simple opposition of commodities and money already presupposes the presence of commodities as the repositories of value and the money commodity as the universal equivalent. The full determination of this opposition requires that the analysis go beyond the mere expression of value to consider the process by which and within which the value relation is determined.

CHAPTER THREE

The circulation of commodities and money

I Exchange

1 Purchase and sale

In the relation of exchange-value the commodity comes to be situated within the system of commodities in a quantitatively and qualitatively determinate manner. Exchange-value, and especially exchange-value in money, expresses the value of the commodity through the interrelation of commodities. This simultaneously emancipates the value of the commodity from any connection to an isolated need, and situates that value within a system of commodities and therefore of needs. Thus the relation to the whole which is implicit in the commodity is made explicit. The constitution of wealth as a system of commodities linked via a series of exchange-values establishes the indifference of commodities to the particular need to which their use-value is inextricably connected. In this way the concept of wealth refuses to remain fixed in the form of an aggregate of use-values and comes instead to entail a system of determinate relations which integrates the aggregate of commodities. This integration involves the constitution of value as an active force which connects the commodity to the world of commodities, constituting thereby the full social determination of the commodity as an object of need and as the embodiment of value.

The exchange-value of the commodity relates the commodity to other commodities and especially to money. The expression of value in the relation of exchange-value involves, however, nothing more than the possibility or potential for the emancipation of the value locked up within the commodity from its particular, restricted, embodiment. For the full emancipation of the value from its fixity to a particular use-value and need it is necessary that this potential be not only revealed, or expressed, but that it also be actualized. This requires that the commodity not only be equated with other commodities in the relation of exchange-value, but that it be replaced by other commodities and especially by money. Involved here is not only the passive expression of value as a potential, latent within the commodity, but an active existence of value as a movement. Value is not a latent force, hidden within the commodity form and restricted to its given embodiment, but constitutes itself as an active force in the determination of the life of the commodity and of the system of commodities.

The realization of value through the interchange of commodities requires the replacement of the commodity with money. Since money is the commodity embodiment of the value relation, the acquisition of money is also the acquisition of value. The commodity is both the means to the acquisition of value, and is itself value due to its equivalence with the money commodity. The commodity is realized as a value when it becomes value in the form of money. The commodity becomes money when it is replaced, through exchange, with the money commodity.

Exchange-value in money expresses the value of the commodity in that commodity which is the general form of exchange-value and in which all expression of value is concentrated. Money is able to purchase all commodities because it is in that purchase, and only in that purchase, that the commodity is able to establish its commodity character. Thus, in the sale of the commodity for money, the commodity realizes its own value and simultaneously enters into its characteristic process of movement. In this case, while the value remains constant in quantity, its form is subject to continuous alteration. This result, that of the fixity in amount of value, rests, however, on the continual movement of value as regards its embodiment and as regards the particular commodities within which the value resides.

The purchase of money by the commodity is at the same time the purchase of the commodity with money. On one side commodities purchase money (in the sale of commodities). On the other side the money purchases the commodity. In its sale the commodity has as its objective the realization of its value, while in the purchase of the commodity the money has as its objective its realization as value. The rationale for this movement in the realization of value is evident in the case of the purchase of money, which is more precisely the sale of the commodity. In this way the particular commodity realizes the value within it as the equivalent of money, which is the generally accepted form of value. The particular use-value must establish that it is in fact the embodiment of value since the latter is intrinsically opposed to fixity within any given commodity form. On the side of money, however, the realization of the value of commodities leaves no room for the realization of any value intrinsic to money since it is impossible for the money to be equated with, and exchanged for, the universal equivalent. Instead of realizing its intrinsic value, the circuit is the arena within which money establishes itself as the universal representative of value. In order to do so the money must not only express the value of commodities, it must realize that value in the interchange of commodities and money.

In the case of exchange-value, money serves only notionally as the substance in relation to which value is estimated. As a result, no legally recognized relation to the money commodity is implied, and the money may exist only ideally. Indeed, the association of the exchange-value of the commodity with so much money as means of expressing its value may or may not imply that the commodity is, in fact, able to purchase that amount of money. The valuation of a commodity, for example a shirt, is not completed when its owner labels it with a specific relation to a fixed quantity of money (marks the shirt as having a price of $10). It is also essential that the purchase of the shirt transfer to its original owner the title over ten units of money. This entails the constitution of the price not only ideally, but also in a socially (economically and juridically) recognized transaction. With this transaction the expression of exchange-value is made an objective property of the commodity which is worth so much money only in so far as it can be exchanged for that quantity of the commodity money. By contrast to the mere expression of value, the elementary exchange entails both the expression of value, in a relation of the commodity notionally to a sum of money, and the actual confrontation of the commodity with its monetary equivalent. While this may take the form either of an immediate physical counterposition, or of the recording of the transaction strictly 'on paper' (in the accounts of the respective parties), there remains the reality of the transfer of proprietorship over the commodity and over money. The reciprocal transfer of proprietorship which marks an exchange distinguishes the exchange of commodities from the simple expression of their values. In exchange the commodity and money 'change hands,' and must, to that extent, be present for the relation to ensue. They must be present in that the parties to the contract are presumed to rightfully claim proprietorship over the commodities involved. This is not immediately implied in the expression of value for which no direct counterposition of commodity owners is entailed in the association of the commodity with a fixed sum of money.

As a reciprocal transfer of property rights the exchange is the unity of two distinct, if mutually implied, movements: the acquisition of the commodity and the acquisition of the money. While each movement must be accomplished for the consummation of the exchange, it is not implied that the two poles of the relation be contemporaneous. Just as the legal claim to ownership may precede in time the actual taking of possession, so the exchange may take the form of a claim on the commodity or money prior to the actual transfer of commodities.

Where the payment of the money equivalent of the commodity deviates temporally from the transfer of the commodity, the money is said to act as 'means of payment.'[1] While in the separation of money payment from commodity acquisition the two poles may confront one another in any order, the payment of the money subsequent to the transfer of the merchandise plays a distinctive role.

The claim which the commodity has over money is by no means equivalent to the claim which the money has over the commodity. When the receipt of the commodity is temporally prior to the payment of the money equivalent of its value, the commodity has, in effect, staked out a claim to that sum of money necessary for its realization as a value. Since the valuation of the commodity requires that it be replaced by money, that valuation is always contingent upon a specific exchange – the sale of the commodity. The uncertainty of this claim of the commodity over a part of the money in circulation is built into the particularity of the com-

modity and makes the acceptance of money as future means of
payment rational for the commodity owner. By contrast, for the
money, its constitution as value is not contingent upon any
particular exchange. Indeed, money as the universal equivalent is
always directly a claim upon a proportional part of existing
commodities. While the commodity must strive to establish its
claim over money, the money as such is always directly a claim
over any particular commodity. This limits the prior transfer of
the money to exceptional cases and leads to the normal identification of money acting as means of payment with money paid
subsequent to the transfer of the commodity.

2 The realization of commodity value and the consumption of money

Exchange, then, involves a two-sided movement: on one side the
realization of the value of commodities in their sale (which is the
purchase of money); on the other side the realization of money as
the universal equivalent in the purchase of commodities (which is
the sale of money). Situated in the latter, furthermore, is the
necessity that the exchange, the purchase and sale, be united not
in isolation, but within a system of exchanges. The money must
move from exchange to exchange, realizing simultaneously and
sequentially the values of all commodities. Money really exists as
the universal equivalent when it realizes that property in its
movement from exchange to exchange; when, that is, via exchange
it actually takes on different use-forms by purchasing them.

Equally, on the side of the commodity the realization of value is
as necessary as its expression. While money can purchase all
commodities this is by no means the case for commodities other
than money. Since the commodity is a particular embodiment of
value its value remains problematic until that moment arrives at
which the commodity is turned into value. While money is value,
the commodity must become value by becoming money. Thus, so
far as the commodity is concerned, it is not sufficient simply to
express its value, it must also realize the exchangeability implied
in that value. Expression of value must give way to the realization
of value, to exchange of commodities for money.

Just as the commodity realizes itself as a value by becoming
value to its owner in its replacement with money, the money
establishes itself as value by acting as the agent through which the

commodity reveals the independence of its value from its given useful form. By exchanging with money the commodity is not only revealed to be of value to its owner, but it actually becomes the means to the acquisition of all commodities, in effect becoming value for its owner. The commodity is, then, of use to its owner not by merit of its particular use-value, but, so long as the commodity enters into exchange, by the means which it provides for the acquisition of money. In this respect the exchange of the commodity for money is not its real consumption but only a mediating act which forestalls and thereby makes possible that consumption. This is by no means the case for money. Money can only be consumed in the purchase of commodities, and the purchase of commodities is the consumption of money. The use-value of money is, in this case, that of realizing the values of commodities through exchange. The use which money has for its owner is not simply that of expressing value. This latter is, rather, the use-value of money to the commodity owner who has himself only commodities and no money. The use of the money to its owner resides instead in its ability to purchase commodities and, indeed, to purchase all commodities. In this respect, the consumption of money, since it is synonymous with the exchange of commodities, is nothing more than a prelude to the repetition of its consumption.

Since the money commodity is consumed in exchange, and since the exchange simply serves to alter the location of the money, the latter can only be consumed in a continuous process of movement. The state of being of money is always a state of motion. 'When money does not circulate, it is the same thing as if it did not exist. . . .'[2] To its owner, its use must ultimately involve its alienation in exchange. Thus, the exchange of commodities, viewed as the replacement of commodities with money, can only exist as an element of a series of exchanges through which money can alone realize its universality.

Exchange effects the reciprocal movement of commodities and money. What remains constant or fixed within the exchange of commodities is their value, the equality of which is the underlying principle of the exchange. Value exists only within the movement of commodities and of money and yet, within that movement, the value always represents a fixed point. The movement of commodities and of money is also the active life process of value. Just as gravity is a principle of the movement of bodies in space, and is therefore not conceived itself to be in motion, so value is a principle of the movement of commodities which cannot itself be conceived to move. The analysis of commodities and of value must consider, then, the totality of movement as the mode of existence of value and analyse value as the movement of commodities.

II The circulation of commodities and money

1 *The commodity flux*

The fluctuation of value from the commodity form to the money form and back is a process through which the continuous inter-change of commodities and money brings about the independence of money from relation to particular, fixed, useful form. Money, by purchasing particular commodities, realizes itself as the universal representative of value. This process, which incorporates the purchase and sale of commodities and the realization of the value of commodities in money, is the circulation of commodities and money.

The system of commodities and money adopts the form of an interwoven sequence of exchanges. Any conception of the isolated exchange is wholly expelled, and the involvement of each exchange in the series of exchanges is made explicit. The prerequisite for the exchange is exchange itself, which leads inevitably into continued exchanging.

The circulation of commodities and money integrates the system of particular commodities into a single unified process, and makes the system of needs an organic whole rather than an externally aggregated sum. In the circular movement of com-modities the universality of the use-value becomes explicit. Here, the commodity as a use-value relates to a need defined within a system of needs and of needy individuals. The need to which the use-value of the commodity is specified is, however, no longer immediately that of its owner. In this respect the commodity exists as such for its owner precisely because it is of no use to him. The use of the commodity is no longer in its use-value but in its ability to acquire for its owner the world of commodities in the sale of the commodity for money. In the circuit, the value of the commodity is the relation which it bears 'to the person who possesses it, and who means not to use or consume it himself, but to exchange it for other commodities.'[3] Within the circuit, the relation of the use-value to the need which it fulfils has also this negative quality that the commodity cannot find that need in its owner and must leave its point of origin in order to realize itself as a use-value, as well as in order to realize itself as a value.

The system of circulation of commodities and money is, then, no less the means by which the needs of society are fulfilled than it is the means to the realization of value. Indeed, within the circuit the realization of value implies as well that the realization of use-value take place through the interchange of commodities. Money, as the embodiment of value, is the mediating term in the interchange of use-values, while use-values are mediating terms in the movement of money. The circulation of commodities and money is the mode of existence of the wealth of society. It is the total movement implied in the circuit which constitutes the wealth of the whole and of each commodity owner. In this case wealth is clearly distinguished from any dead aggregate of objects. Just as wealth cannot be conceived without the systematic interconnection and interchange of commodities, so also the particular use-value comes to presuppose not only a system of needs and of commodities but the circulation of use-values. The separation of the need fulfilled by the commodity from its owner establishes the social determination of that need in the form of its complete dependence upon a system of needs and a system of exchanges. To the extent that the fulfilment of need presupposes exchange as much as the exchange of commodities requires the system of needs and needy individuals, the need so fulfilled cannot be that of the isolated individual but must be that of the individual already determined as a commodity owner. The fulfilment of need through exchange involves the abstract determination of need on the part of the exchange system as a whole so that the use-value of the commodity, far from being defined by and for the particular individual, is determined only by and within the system of individuals. The latter is alone capable of setting in motion the machinery requisite to the fulfilment of need and the realization of use-value. In economic life, the satisfaction of need is a social act undertaken by the system of individuals and by the individual so that the need satisfied in this way has an existence only within the system of needs and of needy individuals.

Classical political economy grasps this result explicitly in its conception of the division of labor. Within the latter the interdependence of needs is the determining factor in the constitution of each particular need. This interdependence has as its corollary the mutual dependence of needy persons in the satisfaction of their needs. The division of labor not only establishes a system of mutual dependence in the provision of needs, it also establishes an interdependence in the constitution of the needs themselves. Each particular need derives from the division of a total system of needs where the whole is not only made up of the separate parts, but equally accounts for the particularity of the distinct elements of which it is composed. It is this determination of needs within a totality itself made up of needs and of the means to their fulfilment which classical political economy designates as the division of labor. This idea involves the forcible assertion of the social determination of need, therefore of the determination of need within and only within the system of needs.

2 The realization of commodities and money

The circulation of commodities and money is a unity of two opposed and yet mutually presupposing movements: on one side the realization of the use-value of the commodity in the consumption which is made possible only through the exchanges which compose the circuit; on the other side the realization of the money commodity as the universal equivalent in the continuous purchase and sale of commodities within the circuit. The circuit, taken as a whole, simultaneously constitutes the money as a mediating term in the interchange of particular commodities – implicitly therefore in the fulfilment of particular needs – and the particular commodities as mediating terms in the movement of money. Viewed on one side the circuit is that of the interchange of particular commodities facilitated, indeed made possible, by the intervention of money. Here it is the commodities which are made to appear explicitly in motion while the money appears to be fixed. Viewed on the other side, however, the roles are reversed and it is the movement of the money which has primacy.

The circuit, grasped in terms of the movement of commodities, achieves first the realization of the value of the commodity in its interchange with money. In this way the owner of the first commodity alienates its use-value in order to acquire its value equivalent in the form of money. This act, the sale of the commodity, makes possible the acquisition of the second commodity. At this stage the subsequent life of the commodity is of no consequence. So far as the circuit is concerned, it is the active life of the commodity within the movement which is alone of interest. Where the commodity is consumed it falls out of that movement; where it is exchanged once again it continues to participate. But, whereas for the money the return to the circuit is directly implied in each particular exchange, this is by no means the case as regards the particular commodities. This fact reveals already the asymmetry embedded in the exchange of commodities.

The acquisition of the second commodity makes of the money, which is also exchanged, a mere means to the transposition of use-values. It is in this respect that the necessities bound up in the money relation are suspended. From the point of view of the needy individual the total exchange appears as the replacement of use-value by use-value, and the many-sided system of commodity exchanges is simply the mode of existence of the system of needs in its relation to the system of commodity owners. The sequence of exchanges which compose the circuit form together a movement of money, for which the system of needs acts as a fixed point. First, the sale of Commodity 1 is the means to placing Commodity 2 into the hands of the original owner of Commodity 1. Second, the sale of Commodity 2 is the means to placing Commodity 3 into the hands of the original owner of Commodity 2, and so on.

The movement of commodities is, however, simultaneously the movement of money: in one direction commodities in motion, in the other direction money in motion. In this way the circuit makes possible the realization of the use-value of commodities only by effecting the realization of the money commodity as purchasing power in the abstract. The money, within the circuit, moves through its own cycle, which cycle is identical to that of commodities except that the latter appears as the former reversed. In this respect the circuit is the movement of commodities in one direction and the movement of money in the other so that the movement of commodities is always simultaneously the movement of money. By realizing the values of commodities, money serves to establish a quantitative relation of exchangeability between particular commodities and the system of commodities as a whole. Money acts, here, as the 'medium of circulation,' as the means to the interchange of commodities. The capacity of money to circulate commodities is measured in its own rate of movement, the 'velocity of money.' This measure grasps directly the fact that money can exist only so long as it remains in motion. In a given period of time a given quantity of money is capable of realizing the value of a given number of commodities of given value, therefore of realizing a fixed total sum of value. The rapidity with which money circulates, realizing *seriatim* the value of one commodity after another, is its velocity. And this, together with the amount of money, determines the quantity of value realized per unit of time. The total value realized in a given period of time (V) is equal to the product of the quantity of money (m) and the number of circuits through which it passes (R) within that given period of time. Thus, if the total value circulating is equal to $100, and if the money circulates twice per period, then the quantity of money required for circulation is $50. Given the value of commodities, the quantity of money needed for circulation is given by the reciprocal of its velocity:

$$m = V\left(\frac{1}{R}\right).$$

It is with the idea of the velocity of money that the state of money as a state of motion and never of rest is recognized and that the quantity of money is tied directly into the movement of commodities and of money.

This incessant movement of the money commodity through an unending series of exchanges establishes that commodity as the universal equivalent, realizing its ability to represent the value of all commodities. It is by establishing itself in motion through its circuit that money is enabled to act also as a 'store of value,' and in this capacity to fall, at least momentarily, outside of the flow of commodities. In this case the sale of commodities does not provide an immediate prelude to the purchase of commodities and the money remains fixed at a given point. There is a break in the circuit which may even constitute money as a hoard, preventing the continuing circulation of both commodities and money. It must always be borne in mind, however, that in order for money to act as a store of value it is essential that money establish itself as the embodiment of value. The endless motion of money, by establishing money as concentrated purchasing power, makes possible the immobilization of money. Thus, for money to store value it must also circulate as value.

This result may be deduced directly from the constitution of money as value within the system of exchanges. Money exists as the objectification of commodity value exclusively in the totality of the relations into which it enters with commodities. Money is capable of storing value precisely to the degree that money is the substantiation of value, and money is the incarnation of value precisely to the extent that it is constituted as such within the sequence of exchanges. Indeed, ultimately the valuation of money is distinguished in that it transpires wholly within, and therefore is determined wholly within, its circulation. Money is exempted from the necessity of grounding its own valuation within a process of commodity production in order that its valuation be made the expression and realization of commodity value. The money relation concentrates the relation of the commodity to the system of commodities into a single sum. The proportional relation of the commodity to the totality of commodities is its value. Money, by constituting itself as the crystallization of the system of exchange relations, becomes the substantiation of that value.

For money to assert its special function as universal purchasing power it is by no means sufficient to refer to the subjective predilections of the commodity owners present within the circuit. It is, rather, the active life of money within the circuit which enforces upon the consciousness of the individual commodity owners the fact that money is the embodiment of value and that, therefore, to acquire money is to acquire value. When this idea fully imposes itself upon the commodity system, it is then, and only then, possible for money to act as a store of value. Similarly, were money to fail in its efforts to realize the value of commodities, it would thereby fail to exist as money. It would cease to be the embodiment of value and could not act as a store of value. In this respect it is always the objective mode of existence of money which makes it the subjectively acceptable medium of circulation and store of value.

3 Barter

The idea that the acceptability of money in exchange is purely subjective, depending upon the whims of the parties to the exchange, derives from the constitution of the exchange act as the result of individual preference. Once exchange ceases to be considered a function which is qualitatively and quantitatively imposed upon the individual by his very existence as a commodity owner, neither can money as the means of exchange be considered to function as a coercive reality imposed upon the individual exchange by its determination within an exchange system. Where the objectivity of money is built into the objectivity of the exchange, and therefore into its social determination, the idea of the subjective determination of the money relation is built into the exclusively subjective conception of exchange as the product of caprice. Here, money is not only unnecessary for the exchange, but its particular functions become wholly accidental, dependent upon the psychological predispositions of the exchangers. Within the scientific conception of economic life, however, this condition cannot be sustained. The requirements of the money relation are embedded within the nature of exchange and within the system of exchanges. It is, then, the objective life process of money which is alone able to make intelligible the specific attributes of the money commodity.

The attempt to consider exchange without money, as a barter relation, is equivalent to draining the exchange of any intrinsic necessity emergent within a system of exchanges. Money represents the crystallization of commodity value existing as a substance outside of the commodity. The commodity is driven to enter into the exchange with money precisely because of (1) the objectivity of its own value and, therefore, (2) the necessity that that value be realized in objective form – money. Exchange in the absence of money establishes particular commodities in direct relation one to another, and excludes any expression of value as a substance whose universality establishes its intrinsic independence of any particular commodity form. In barter, the commodity exchange is established upon the exclusive basis of the elementary or accidental form of the expression of value. This condition transpires where the full development of the commodity relation and the market system, as of the various forms of the commodity and of exchange, are impeded. Value is blocked from any constitution as an objective social condition, and dissipates into a determination based upon the purely contingent circumstances surrounding specific exchanges. In particular, where commodity exchange is not fully integrated into the life process of society, exchange is not subject to determination by an intrinsic force and comes to depend instead wholly upon accidents of climate, geography, history, etc. Here, exchange is unable to establish itself within the ongoing process of the self-renewal of society as a relation determined by the exigencies of the ongoing social process. Exchange takes place on the periphery of society to the degree that exchange is peripheral to the activity by which the system of social relations is reproduced. Under such circumstances, any idea of the determination of commodity exchange in value and its realization in the exchange for money can develop at best only to a limited degree.

The ideas that the intermediation of money within the exchange is a matter of 'convenience' and that money is purely 'conventional' (ideas which typify the history of economic theory) rest essentially upon the presupposition that commodity exchange is indeterminate and not the expression of the commodity's intrinsic determination as a value. Where the exchange is necessitated as the mode of realization of commodity-value, it is necessary that the exchange system generate a commodity which represents the objectification of value and in whose acquisition the realization of value can alone be fully accomplished. This commodity is money, and its objective necessity is directly implied in the objective necessity of the exchange relation itself. To deny the objectivity of money (therefore its necessity) is equivalently to deny the objectivity of commodity exchange.

4 *The reciprocal provision of need*

The use-value of the commodity can only be realized in its consumption to the extent that the commodity both has value and is able to realize that value in its sale. If money makes possible the use of the commodity, it is only because it is the value of the commodity which is the prior condition for its consumption. Classical political economy always recognizes explicitly the necessity that a commodity have a use-value in order that it have a value, and always implicitly that it must also have a value if it is to be capable of realizing its use-value. In this respect, it is no less true that for a commodity to have a use-value it must also have a value. The purchase of money on the part of the commodity establishes precisely this property of the commodity, of having value in a fixed proportion, which value is the *sine qua non* of its consumption. Within the circuit the existence of money as the medium of circulation establishes this essential condition together with the mechanism by which it is fulfilled.

The social determination of the individual commodity owner, as of his needs, is only implicit for that commodity owner taken in his immediate relation to the commodity. Yet, even here, in this apparently immediate confrontation, the complex social constitution of the relation is always present. This social determination becomes explicit for both the commodity and its owner when the fulfilment of need is seen to require the intervention of the system of exchanges, and when the apparently immediate relation of commodity owner to commodity is recognized as no more than a limited aspect of that system of exchanges.

The circulation of commodities effects a reciprocal provision of need through the exchange of commodities, thereby revealing the social determination of the system of needs. Indeed, it is with the development of the exchange system that there proceeds, *pari passu*, a development of the system of needs and the immersion of the individual within a system of reciprocity in the provision of needs. In this way, each individual is fully developed into a commodity owner or, as Adam Smith observes, every man 'becomes in some measure a merchant.'[4] The independence of the commodity owner is directly a function of the wealth which he possesses, and within the system of commodity owners independence comes with, and only with, the ownership of commodities. Since the latter bestows upon the individual his freedom, it is the value of his commodities which sets him free. And since that value, joined to the use-value, constitutes his property as wealth by merit of its existence within an exchange system, it is the latter which stamps the individual as wealthy by stamping his property as valuable and as useful. For this end the individual is wholly powerless. He does not make his property valuable nor does he make it useful. It is the system of needs, of which he is nothing more than a dependent element, which determines the character of his property as wealth, therefore as really property, worthy of being appropriated. It is the *society* of independent merchants which makes the merchants independent, indeed which makes them merchants by making them proprietors of merchandise.

The circulation of commodities differs from the simple exchange of commodities in that the circuit is sustained beyond the changing of hands of the particular use-values involved in each exchange act taken by itself. In this respect the circuit is more than the sum total of the exchanges of which it is composed. It connects those exchanges together, absorbing them into a process of exchanging which is implicitly without limit or end.

The starting point for the treatment of the commodity relation is the mode of expression of value in the relation of exchange-value, and particularly of exchange-value in money. This expression of value presupposes no actual interchange of commodities but only their equation, as equally the embodiments of a common substance in given proportions. With the expression of value in money the actual interchange of commodities for money and the purchase of commodities with money can be considered. The sale of the commodity is the means by which the value latent within it can be realized in the replacement of the commodity with the universal equivalent, therefore with value. With the circulation of commodities and money the value relation is no longer restricted either to a purely formal expression or to a limited movement, but comes to exist as a continuing process.

Within the circuit money is freed from specification to any particular exchange by its movement through an endless series of exchanges. To this degree, value is itself emancipated from its determination in relation to any given use-value since it subsists now within the manifold relations which constitute the circuit. Commodity circulation is a value process within which, once viewed as a whole, value is emancipated from restriction to any given exchange. Thus, the emergence of money makes possible the realization of the universality of the value relation; and the emergence of the commodity circuit makes possible the full development of the money relation.

III Capital

1 The self-ordering of the commodity circuit

The movement of commodities is the precondition for the realization of those commodities as use-values and, in this respect, commodity circulation has as its moving force the system of needs taken in relation to a system of use-values. For the circuit to exist it is necessary that the movement within it be continuous, that each particular exchange lead itself into a connected series of exchanges. This necessity resides in the medium of circulation which can sustain itself only within the circuit and, therefore, only so long as its movement provides the force which sustains that circuit. In this respect the money sustains the system of exchanges for the sole purpose of sustaining itself as money. In order to establish the circuit on a sound foundation, the system of needs must not only be *integrated* as a sequence of exchanges, it must also be *sustained* in and through those exchanges. For this end, exchange and the mere interlocking of the system of exchanges within the circuit, taken in the abstract, are insufficient. It is further required that there exist, within the circulation of commodities and money, an inner force by which the flux, in its entirety, is governed. It is this force which orders the circuit in such a way as to sustain the system in its entirety and thereby make possible the continuous movement which is its sole mode of existence.

This inner force is also a principle of self-organization. The commodity circuit, taken by itself, appears to move without object or direction, to constitute as a whole nothing more than a chaos of commodity exchanges the effect of which is altogether indeterminate. The comprehension of the inner law of the total movement requires that each exchange be subordinated to a principle and that the circuit as a whole be, in this way, subject to an ordering. This principle of order exists as an inner force which is made explicit in the analysis of the movement of money and of commodities. Formulated externally, this principle is the 'object' or 'goal' of the circuit. Formulated in terms of the requisites of the circuit itself, the principle is that of the self-organization of the commodity circuit, the object of which is nothing more or less than its own maintenance and continuation. The determination of the circuit according to the law of its continuation is the only basis on which the system of exchanges can be constituted as viable. Any other basis for the determination of the circuit must necessarily make the latter contingent upon extrinsic relations over which it exerts no force. This would necessarily make the circuit itself the accidental result of capricious conditions and would exclude any systematic conception. The ordering of the circuit according to the law of continuous movement is the constitution of the circuit as a process of self-movement.

In the first instance it is not a matter of deciding whether the object of the circuit is the fulfilment of need or the acquisition of value. Clearly the circuit, by definition, subsumes simultaneously a movement whose object is the fulfilment of need and a movement whose object is the acquisition of value. What is essential is not to graft on to the movement a goal which is extraneous to it, but to find within the continuous flux of commodities a determinate form within which alone it becomes possible for the circuit of commodities and money to move according to its intrinsic laws. The form which is adequate in this sense to commodity exchange and circulation is that which has as its sole objective continuous movement. This objective can never be fulfilled where the acquisition of particular use-values is isolated as the end of the commodity cycle. In this case the consumption of the commodity made possible by its purchase marks simultaneously the end of the use-value, which disappears in that consumption, and the end of the value, which disappears along with the use-value. Since such movement always leads outside of the circuit, disappearing into a consumption act which curtails rather than sustains the movement of commodities, the acquisition of use-values to meet particular needs cannot, in itself, constitute the objective of the circuit. Neither, however, can the acquisition of money in itself sustain the movement. This acquisition is only the acquisition of a hoard of value in the form of money. Such an act is, taken by itself, irrational, since it absorbs the medium of circulation in order to use it as a store of value and in so doing deprives it of that quality of incessant movement which enables it to function as the store of value. Value in the form of a money hoard is value confined to exist only as a potential, incapable of realizing its power over and within the system of commodities. Such a potential, which fails to realize itself as an active force, ceases to sustain even the possibility of movement. Money which fails to circulate ceases to be money.

The objective of the movement of commodities, then, can be neither the acquisition of money nor the acquisition of use-values. And, yet, the circulation of commodities and money is composed, *in toto*, of nothing more than the interlocking of purchase and sale. It is nothing more than the acquisition of commodities on one side and the acquisition of money on the other. It is, therefore, not in the elements of the circuit, the acquisition of money and of use-value, that it is possible to discover its law, but only in the merging of the two movements into a single connected process. Within this process the acquisition of use-values, of particular commodities, is the means to the acquisition of money, which is the means to the acquisition of more commodities. The circulation of commodities and money is constituted as a single connected process:

$$\ldots C_1 - M - C_2 - M - C_3 - M \ldots$$

The sale of commodity one (C_1) is the means to the acquisition of money (M) which is the means to the acquisition of commodity two (C_2). This act constitutes, however, no terminus for the movement but is itself nothing more than the means to the acquisition of money as the means to the acquisition of another commodity (C_3), and so on without end. Here it is equally arbitrary whether the starting point is said to be the commodity (C) or the money (M). The movement of commodities and money is not simply the mutual interchange of commodities and money; it is the subsistence of value in and through its various forms. The common element in the circuit is the interchange of commodities and money and the preservation of value through and in that interchange. Where the object of the circuit is its own self-movement the circuit must be constituted as the mode of existence of value.

The necessity that value take on a form of existence which is adequate to its conception is the necessity that it subsist within a process whose moving principle is value itself. At the same time the movement always requires that value adopt both the form of particular use-value and the money form. In this respect the circuit requires the interrelation of particular need. The conditions for the self-determination of value within the circulation of commodities and money include the necessity that value emancipate itself from specification to particular need – fixity in a given use-value – only in and through its relation to particular needs, so that it is through the interrelation of particularity that the universality of the value relation can alone be realized. The movement through needs, by which value emancipates itself from determination in all fixed need and fixed systems of need, is the commodity circuit. In order to be adequate to the conception of value the circuit must subordinate the system of commodities and money to the subsistence of value. The mode of circulation which realizes this quality of the value relation is capital. Only as capital can the value substance provide the moving force in the commodity circuit. The process of commodity circulation must emerge as that process whose starting point and ending point are equally value; for which value, therefore, is end in itself. Capital is 'exchange-value which preserves and perpetuates itself in and through circulation.'[5]

2 The simple circulation of commodities

In the course of the development of economic theory the organization of the circuit has been conceived to follow two radically opposed principles. Originally, in Marx and to a lesser degree in classical political economy, the inner law which governs the movement of commodities and money is that of capital, and the self-movement of the circuit is made primary. From this standpoint the circuit is constituted as the process of the self-liberation and self-determination of value, therefore of value constituted as capital.

At the same time, however, as this conception is beginning to emerge (especially in Quesnay and Smith), the conception of the circuit is pursued in an entirely different direction, a direction in which the inner logic of the circuit is thrown outside, and the movement of commodities and money is considered to establish the provision of fixed needs. This is the origin of the present-day conception of commodity exchange as the means to the allocation of resources among fixed and given ends. In this case the question of the inner law by which the interchange of commodities is governed becomes instead the question of the 'object,' 'end,' or 'goal,' of the circuit. The unifying principle according to which all exchange is determined and by which each particular exchange is determined both quantitatively and qualitatively is that of the 'provisioning' of the members of the economy in accordance with their given requirements. According to this conception, the exchange system does not order itself in accordance with the necessity of its self-preservation through continuous movement. Instead, the exchange of commodities is determined according to a fixed principle which stands outside and determines, externally, the existence and magnitude of the particular system of exchanges.

This is the conception of the 'simple circulation of commodities,' the formula for which is based on exchange of commodities for the sole end of the reconciliation of the use-value of the commodity with the need of its owner. Within the simple circuit the purchase of money in the sale of the commodity has as its only purpose the purchase of another commodity which is more closely connected to the given needs of the owner of the original commodity. The simple circulation of commodities is made up, then, of a sale in order to purchase, whose sole end is consumption:

$$C_1-M-C_2.$$

Within this circuit, the movement of money is subordinated to the circulation of commodities, as the means to the end of the movement of commodities. From this standpoint there can be no self-movement since the principle of movement latent within the money is made a principle of fixity. While for this circuit value has the form of a process rather than object and value is set loose of any fixed embodiment, that value remains none the less incapable of shaking off its encasement within a system of fixed and arbitrarily given needs.

On one side, within the simple circulation of commodities, value exists within a process of movement and thereby attains a degree of independence of the particular commodities of which that movement is composed. Still, on the other side, the simple circulation of commodities limits sharply the full constitution of the value relation. The circuit is not a self-sustaining value process but a movement restricted to the confines of externally fixed conditions – the conditions of the presence of particular use-values in fixed proportions. The movement begins not explicitly with value, but with the throwing into the circuit of particular use-values, and the circuit continues only until those use-values are thrown outside of the process to exist in their consumption as simple use-values unconnected to the commodity form.

Value within the simple circulation of commodities remains restricted to particular need. To be sure, value is tied to no particular need and to this extent expresses a degree of independence. On the other hand, this independence of particular need is achieved only through the development of a dependence upon the total system of needs which remains fixed. In this sense, value remains a determination of need. Since these needs are fixed, rather than posited within the movement as a whole, they appear to subordinate the value relation. The latter acts simply as the mediating term in the relation of need to need. This is expressed directly in the formula for the simple circulation of commodities: C_1—M—C_2. The logic which underlies this movement is independent of the money, which is nothing more than the means to an end. It is, then, possible to suppress the mediating term (M) as inessential to the conception of the process as a whole. With this suppression, the rationale for the circuit in the interchange of use-values is made explicit: C_1—C_2. Value, as expressed in this formulation, is nothing more than the relation of need to need, the quantitative equation of use-values. Within the simple circuit the logic behind the exchange of commodities is the redistribution of use-values so that value never succeeds in going beyond the conditions bound up exclusively with that redistribution. The effect of this is the determination of exchange upon the basis of a given allocation of use-values as that allocation relates to the needs of the individual commodity owners. Since exchange is determined by need, and especially by the relation of the particular needs of commodity owners to the particular commodities which they possess, the determination of exchange by value is suppressed. The determination of the movement of commodities in particular needs excludes the determination of that exchange in value.

The exclusion of any objective concept of value resolves all exchange into the accidental interrelation of arbitrarily fixed needs. Such needs lose their objective social character and are made instead into the wholly indeterminate expressions of particular and fixed conditions. The determination of value on the basis of needs fixed independently of the exchange relation is thus also the deprivation of need of any real determination. This makes impossible any conception of need within economic theory.

The effort to conceptualize exchange exclusively on the basis of the simple circulation of commodities is characteristic of the history of economic thought. The inability of economic analysis to pursue the treatment of exchange beyond the simple opposition of particular needs leads it to constitute the system of circulation founded in arbitrarily fixed needs as a comprehensive account for exchange and, therefore, as an exhaustive picture of commodity circulation. All specification of exchange is in accordance with the arbitrary specification of ends, so that the preservation of value in and through circulation appears not as that form already implied in the circuit, but as the result of an arbitrary specification of its objective. The commodity system remains fixed as a machine for the achievement of externally given ends.

3 Capital and the determinacy of economic life

The concept of capital concentrates and makes explicit the fundamental differences which distinguish that conception of exchange which provides the starting point for a real determination of the system of economic relations from that conception which predominates in the history of economic analysis. The latter is distinguished by the absence of any concept of capital as the self-subsistence of value, and the resulting constitution of capital as nothing more than a particular form of the simple circulation of commodities. Indeed, the contradictions characteristic of the conceptions of capital which dominate the history of economics are all founded in the intrinsic inadequacy of the idea of capital as a particularization of the simple circuit of commodities. The inadequacy of this conception accounts, therefore, for the inability of economic theory to move beyond the level of the interaction of fixed needs and grasp a process which is determined not by arbitrarily posited particular ends but by the self-development of capital.

Economic analysis, in the modern period, invariably takes as its object society conceived as a mechanism of adjustment of resources to individual goals or intentions. The adjustment of means (scarce resources) to ends (subjective preferences or intentions) is considered to be the inescapable foundation of all economic science. To this degree economic life is made incapable of establishing itself in the form of a connected and unified process. This inability to conceive of the system of economic relations as capable of defining a unified process of self-renewal within which the particular relations are determined because produced and reproduced, is characteristic of present-day economic thought.

The conception of the process within which society determines its own relations entails the concept of capital as value which preserves and perpetuates itself in and through its own cycle – the movement of commodities and money set loose from external determination in resource supply and fixed needs. The emergence of this concept is the endpoint of the development of the conception of the commodity and its circuit. At the same time, capital provides the starting point for the development of a theory which fully accounts for the system of economic relations in its entirety, including the determination thereby of the system of needs itself.

In the argument up to this point the conception of the commodity and its life process has passed through the following stages:

(1) First, value is a quality attached to the commodity existing as a particular use-value. The universality of the commodity, and especially the indifference of its value to its particular useful embodiment, remains submerged in the form of a particular use-value. The commodity can no more express the universality embedded in its worth than it can reveal the abstract quality of its use-value.

(2) This opposition is first given a real mode of expression as the exchange-value of the commodity with another particular commodity. It is only in the external relating of commodities that their intrinsic commodity character has any means of expressing itself. Here value adopts the form of a relation of one particular need to another. In the original expression of value the two poles of the commodity (value and use-value) emerge as concentrated into the two opposing commodities – one being the simple use-value and the other representing value. The contradiction within the commodity is thrown outward and adopts the form of a relation between commodities. None the less, this opposition remains tied down to particular use-form. In the elementary form value is expressed in a particular use-value: value is use-value.

(3) This limitation is finally overcome in the emergence of the money commodity and in the expression of value in the exchange-value of the commodity with money. The value of the commodity in money is that value expressed in the commodity whose use-value is that it is recognized by the system of commodities taken as a whole to be value.

(4) The value of the commodity is now capable, for the first time, of independent expression. This makes possible the realiza-

tion of the value of the commodity and therefore the realization of money as the universal equivalent, as the generally recognized embodiment of value. The value of the commodity is realized when it is replaced, through exchange, with money. The particular commodity becomes money when its owner alienates it for money, replacing the commodity with so much of the universal equivalent. Value is, in the act of exchange, not simply expressed but also realized.

(5) The circulation of commodities and money takes the realization of value one step farther. Rather than money realizing the value of a particular commodity it is able, within the circuit, to realize *seriatim* the value of all particular commodities. Value exists within a process or movement. The opposition between use-value and value is mediated by a process within which, taken as a whole, value is emancipated from specification to any particular use-value and need. Value is a commodity movement and in that movement value denies its designation to any particular commodity relation, to any embodiment in a given particular use-value. As a result, while value is at no single moment separate from and independent of use-value, the process as a whole constitutes value as independent of any fixed useful form. While value can never become independent of the relation to need and to the system of needs within which it is alone able to subsist, it is none the less able to establish its distinctive character as the moving force which asserts the intrinsic order and logic of the system of commodity relations.

(6) Value existing in this way is capital, value which sustains and perpetuates itself within its own circuit. The circulation of commodities and money is subject to a self-organization according to the principle of its own preservation and continuation. The law which orders the movement of commodities and money in the continuing sequence of exchanges is nothing more or less than the law of the continuation of that circuit, of the perpetual transformation of commodities into money and of money into commodities. The sole objective of this movement is its own continuation so that the transformation of money into commodities is the means to the transformation of commodities into money and vice versa. As capital, the circulation of commodities composes a never-ending cycle the totality of which is the sole objective of its particular elements.

Capital

The idea of capital grasps the inner principle of the self-organizing market system. The rule of capital is the law of the 'invisible hand' of classical political economy, and the investigation of the life cycle of capital is synonymous with the laying bare of the inner determination of bourgeois economy.

CHAPTER FOUR

The circuit of capital

I The self-expansion of value

The circuit of capital has as its object the realization of value within the process of the self-preservation of value. In this respect the sole end of the circuit is a continual movement within which value adopts sequentially the different forms which encompass its life process. Within this perpetual motion the value relation ceases to be restricted to any given useful form, not only by adopting the money form but equally by adopting within the whole of the cycle the manifold forms made available by the system of particular commodities. Thus, by existing as many particular use-values, value both remains dependent upon the system of need in all its particularity, while at the same time achieving an indifference to all specification to need. Within the circuit of commodities, the value relation is clearly established as a relation which is intrinsically indifferent to the satisfaction of any given need and which thereby effects the satisfaction of the manifold needs defined in relation to the totality of use-values interlinked within the circuit. The circuit as a whole constitutes a sphere within which the subsistence of wealth is uniquely achieved. The objective of the circuit is the acquisition of wealth not simply as a collection of use-values, nor simply as so much exchange-value in the form of money, but as a never-ending sequence of commodities and money.

But the formula of capital – ... M—C—M—C ... – realizes

125

this quality of wealth only in the form of a fixed quantity of wealth, in particular as so much value in the form of money – M. The object of the circuit is wealth – money – but only in a limited form: that of a fixed stock of money. The object of the movement as value is inherently unlimited, and yet the object as so much value in the form of so much money is inherently limited. The money within the circuit, which represents directly the existence of wealth as such, also opposes the character of capital. It is a 'limited representative of general wealth.'[1] This principle denies directly the drive of capital to realize the illimitability of value by setting it loose in a process which transcends, through continuous movement, all fixity of need. A fixed stock of money represents access to a fixed portion of the wealth of society, to a fixed part of the sum of use-values. In this sense, access to a given quantity of money is access to a limited part of the system of needs and not a real independence of all arbitrary fixing of need and of the means to its fulfilment.

The restriction with respect to the nature of value restricts in equal measure the development of the system of needs itself. The latter is limited by the given quantity of value whose circular movement defines the sphere of life of the system of needs. With a fixed quantity of money a fixed sum of use-values can be circulated. Therefore, the limited amount of value limits as well the sphere of use-value and the cycle of needs which are capable of being articulated and satisfied. The formula for capital remains restricted to the system of needs already given within the existing circuit. To the degree that capital is restricted to the given system of needs, it is impossible for need to be determined within the circulation of commodities and money as a total process. Instead, it is that process which is subject to determination on the part of the arbitrarily fixed needs. With this constitution of the circuit as the effect of the activity of externally given need, the concept of capital as the governing force of the commodity movement gives way to the notion of the simple circulation of commodities, a notion which excludes any self-determination of the commodity circuit and therefore of the exchange system. Under these conditions, the value relation becomes absorbed wholly into the relation to fixed, particular needs. Since those needs must be taken as accidental conditions which are indeterminate with respect to the system of commodity exchanges, the value relation is made into the arbitrary expression of the interrelation of needs taken in the abstract and of the given means to their fulfilment.

As capital, the movement of commodities must go beyond the limited existing forms of wealth, and it must do so repeatedly. The formula for capital cannot, therefore, be that of the self-preservation of value but must be that of the self-expansion of value where the expansion of value, considered from its other aspect, is equally the process of the multiplication and expansion of needs. The formula for capital, as self-expanding value, renewing and increasing itself through the renewal and increase of the system of use-values, is

$$\ldots M—C—M'—C'—M''—C''.\ldots$$

Capital is the process of the transformation of money into more money, of value into more value, of commodities into more commodities. In this case, the object of the movement is not simply value but surplus-value, especially in the form of an increment to the money advanced. Expansion is the means by which the restriction of wealth to a fixed sum is overcome. The increase of commodities sets the commodity system loose from any restriction to an existing world of commodities and of money. The illimitability, firmly embedded in the concept of wealth, is realized not for wealth as so many commodities or as so much money, but as the process of movement beyond all existing commodities and money, the process of wealth always moving beyond itself. Wealthiness exists, then, not in the access to wealth but in the acquisition of wealth, and of more wealth.

The value advanced, particularly as a sum of money, is value advanced to the end of its own increase. This money is now substantively capital since movement within its circuit has as its end the growth of the circuit. Capital is money which adds to itself, money which is fruitful and multiplies, therefore money which makes more money. Briefy, the formula for capital may be represented by the movement of money as the general representative of wealth:

$$M—C—M' \text{ or } M—C—M + \Delta M.$$

Where the universal mode of expression of value is money, the universal pursuit of money is capital – the process of the active self-subsistence of value.

Since the capital circuit is that of the self-subsistence of value, its realization is always contingent upon the quantitative difference between the value advanced and the value returned, or on the difference in the value advanced in this period from the value advanced in the next period. Since the value returned is always also value advanced, in the future, all value within the circuit is both an advance of money and a return. The circuit is the mutual identification and differentiation of advance and return of value. This difference provides the real rationale for the circulation of commodities and money. The value circuit in the form M—C—M—C— . . . is without any *raison d'être*. The development of the capital circuit involves the transcendence of the determination of value in its relation to a fixed system of needs and of use-values. The resulting determination of value within its own process must, however, still involve a difference. The simple identity of the poles of the circuit denies the necessity of movement. The poles of the movement must simultaneously be identified as value; and the poles must be differentiated in magnitude of value in order that the movement between them can be made reasonable. This quantitative difference (ΔM) is the surplus-value.

Where the expansion of value is denied, the circuit disappears and value takes the form of a hoard of money. In this case the money established as a hoard loses the activity by which it interacts with the system of commodities. It ceases, once established as a hoard, to exist as money, to realize the values of commodities by exchanging with them. To transform value in the money form into commodities simply in order to transform it back into money is a movement without any logical principle, an irrational cycle. Money, as we have already seen, must exchange in order for it to be and remain money. The consumption of money is only possible in the purchase and sale of commodities. The hoard can only be a hoard of money if that act of hoarding represents no more than a temporary break in the movement of money and commodities and not a permanent rupture. Were the hoard a permanent disjunction in the movement of the money, the commodity which is formed into the hoard would cease to be money. For money to exist as money it must enter into relation with other commodities, and it must do so continually. The preservation of value requires that commodities be continually in motion, while that movement can only be rational where it involves simultaneously an expansion.

The formula for capital (M—C—M') expresses the subordination of need and its fulfilment to the preservation and expansion of value. For value to realize itself as capital it must exist (1) as a value process which denies determination in any fixed complex of needs and of use-values, and (2) as a process that moves through a complex of particular commodities and which therefore requires the renewal and expansion of commodities as the basis for the renewal and expansion of value. Value ceases to be determined by given needs when it constitutes itself as the process within which the articulation and fulfilment of need is determined. Capital, as self-expanding value, is a process of movement beyond all fixed ends. It is this constitution of its own existing state as a limit, and as a limit which must be surpassed, which constitutes the circulation of commodities and money as the circuit of capital.

Capital, then, is self-expanding value. It is the value advanced which must form the basis for the increase of commodities and value. Out of the movement of the circuit there must grow an increment to that circuit, so that the circulation of commodities must provide for capital not only a process of renewal and subsistence, but equally the sphere of its expansion. The capital is first a sum of money, M. Once, however, the purchase of commodities by this money has been effected the capital takes the form of use-values, of particular commodities, C. Capital is commodities. But this acquisition of commodities is no more than the means to the expansion of value so that these commodities must also purchase more money, M'. Here, again, capital is more money; it is the return to capital existing as money to be advanced towards the expansion of capital. Thus, the return to capital is also capital since that return must now also be advanced. Money as capital is continually alienated and just as continually returned to its point of origin.

It is this return which classical political economy marks out as capital, noting in particular the identity between capital, money and commodities, each as the unique embodiment of wealth. Economics first considers wealth as the aggregate of use-values and therefore as a sum of objects capable of fulfilling needs. The characteristic of these objects which stamps them as the components of wealth is found to be nothing more than their multiplication, their many-sidedness. Yet, this multiplication gives to each of its elements a universality which it lacks taken by itself. Each object of need becomes explicitly a component of wealth, a commodity, and its owner becomes a commodity owner, wealthy in proportion to his ownership of commodities. The commodity, within the system of commodities, is equated with other commodities as a component of the wealth of society. The extent to which the commodity makes its owner wealthy is measured by the degree to which ownership of that commodity is ownership of the wealth of society. Wealth is measured, then, by the exchange-value of the commodity, its purchasing-power over the world of commodities. This power is expressly established in the exchange-value of the commodity for money. It is for this reason that, prior to classical political economy, economic analysis identifies wealth with money and wealthiness with the ownership of money. Indeed, classical thinking begins with the breakdown of this elementary conception of wealth. Wealth ceases to be money *per se* and becomes instead the peculiar use to which money is put in wealthy society. A society is wealthy not simply to the degree that it has money, but to the degree that it produces money, not by producing the money commodity but by expanding, through its own activities, its access to wealth. A man is wealthy to the extent that he is frugal, and to the extent that he puts his money to work for him in the acquisition of wealth. Here, wealth is properly identified with the process of its acquisition, which is also the process of its expansion.

For classical political economy, wealth is neither the simple aggregate of commodities, nor the simple hoard of money, but capital. A society is wealthy to the extent that its endowment of wealth is fruitful. It is wealthy in proportion to the return on its wealth, its net revenue. The analysis of exchange-value and of the circuit of commodities reveals the secret of the classical concept of wealth: wealth is capital to the extent that all economic interaction is subordinated to the self-expansion of value.

II Equivalent exchange

1 Unequal exchange

The circulation of commodities and money must constitute itself as the medium within which value preserves itself, and thereby as the medium within which value increases itself. Value can expand by circulating, and circulation must become the process of its expansion. Since the expansion of value requires the emergence of an increment to value, the process of the movement of value entails an accretion to value. And this means that within the circuit the conditions must emerge for a production of value, which is to say for the origin of a new or additional value.

Capital is made up of commodities and money and of their sequence of interrelations, interrelations having the form of exchange. The circuit of capital is, then, nothing more than so many individual exchanges. Evidently, then, there is no means, within the circular movement, of accounting for the generation of a surplus-value. Such an increment to value is excluded in principle by the conditions of commodity circulation. The circuit is a series of exchanges which effect the movement of commodities and which are founded upon the transformation of the form of value from money to commodities and back to money. Since the relations within the circuit are all commodity relations, therefore exchange relations, they are all relations in which a sum of value embodied in the commodity is preserved. As relations of exchange the relations within the circuit are relations of equality, so that the principle of movement is always that of the equality of value, and never that of an inequality of value which could provide the basis for expansion. The equality of value on each side of the exchange and, therefore, at each moment of the circuit, is the logical principle upon which the conception of the circulation of commodities and money is predicated.

The exchange of commodities is made intelligible only by the equivalence of value at each pole. Similarly, the sequence of exchanges rests upon a series of equivalences which connect each of the commodities involved in the movement as a whole, and which constitute that movement as the mode of existence of value. All of this is implicit in the concept of exchange, upon which the circuit is originally predicated, and in the analysis of the commodity relation, which originally gives rise to the necessity that value adopt the form of a commodity circuit. To abrogate these conditions and constitute the existence of value within its circuit as the origin of a difference in value, of surplus-value, requires a distortion of the conception of the commodity and of exchange. Indeed, the violation of the condition of equality of value in exchange is synonymous with the abandonment of the conception of value as an objective substance which is not given directly within the act of exchange itself.

In this case, even the notion of 'unequal exchange' is intelligible only as violation of equality which, therefore, has as its premise the condition of the exchange of commodities at their values. Indeed, were inequality of exchange to be taken to be the normal mode of interaction between commodity owners, there would be no possibility for a conception of value since the expression of value in exchange would always conflict with its conception. Since the notion of inequality of exchange is the notion of a movement of commodities in a disproportionate relation as regards the two sides of the exchange, it must have as its presupposition the constitution of exchange as intrinsically the exchange of equivalents. The measure of the inequality of exchange resides in the value substance which defines equivalence of exchange. Since this substance defines the equality or inequality of the exchange, it cannot be itself subject to determination exclusively within the particular exchange. If the value were to have its origin wholly within the particular exchange act, neither equality nor inequality of exchange would be determinable. Since the exchange always *defines* its poles as equal, the absence of any condition fixed outside of the immediate interchange of commodities would imply the direct equation of commodities as the *result* of the exchange and not as the expression of an intrinsic quality which fixes the proportions of the exchange. In this case the exchange would exclude all notions of inequality. Where the exchange of commodities is not assumed to define immediately its own conditions but to be determined by a substance which makes the poles of the exchange – the particular commodities – intrinsically equal and makes the exchange determinate, the inequality of exchange becomes a real possibility. This possibility, however, always retains as its precondition the development of the sphere of circulation of commodities and therefore the idea of exchange of commodities according to their values. The realization of value within its circuit must first be established before the law which it expresses can be violated in particular instances.

The result of unequal exchange can only be the rearrangement of value, and never its real expansion. There is no derivation from within the circuit of a systematic increment of the value advanced. Since the problem of the expansion of value is always that of the origin of a new value in the form of a surplus-value, that problem is always that of the determination of the value substance. This determination can never be restricted to the circulation of commodities to the extent that the latter takes the presence of value in fixed proportions as its presupposition. The expansion of value must always go beyond the conditions bound up in the elementary conception of the circuit since the expansion of value always involves not simply the *presence* of value but equally its full determination.

2 Direct appropriation

It is clear from the foregoing that surplus-value cannot originate within the system of commodity exchanges which constitutes the elementary conception of the circuit of capital. Since the increment to capital cannot arise within the system of exchanges, it must have its origin outside. And yet, the notion that surplus-value emerges outside of the circuit of capital also raises intractable obstacles to its conception.

The movement of wealth outside of the commodity circuit is no longer the movement of commodities based on the laws of commodity exchange. The premise of all commodity exchange is the reciprocal recognition of the freedom and equality of commodity owners and of the equality of their commodities as the repositories of value. The equality of commodities and of commodity owners brings with it the specific interaction which constitutes the form of movement of which the circuit is composed. The exchange of commodities at their values not only sustains the value of the commodities exchanged, but equally sustains the exchange system as a system of property rights. The laws of exchange are always expressive of the rights of property, rights which are realized also within the interaction of commodity owners so far as that interaction is consistent with the nature of the commodity, and particularly with the exchange of commodities at their values.

Outside of the market neither equality nor freedom constitute the basis for interaction. Such interaction is intrinsically indifferent to the law of exchange of commodities according to their values. For value to expand outside of its circuit it is necessary for capital to appropriate its increment directly and without regard to the determination of that appropriation as value. The increment is not, in this case, surplus-value since the manner in which it enters into the movement of capital explicitly excludes its determination as value.

Such immediate appropriation, by contrast to exchange, is tantamount to expansion through the direct appropriation of objects as such, which have no intrinsic commodity character and therefore possess no intrinsic value. Capital, however, is self-expanding value and never isolated appropriation. Since the appropriation of objects is not directly connected to any expansion of value, it is not the province of capital. Were such appropriation to lead, even by accident, to an expansion of value, this would still involve no *self*-expansion and therefore would violate the concept of capital. Indeed, taken by itself appropriation of objects outside of the circulation of commodities does not even involve a preservation of value, let alone its expansion. Objects which are acquired in this way are endowed with an exchange-value which is wholly accidental. This holds also for their use-value which, since defined outside of the system of commodities and of use-values, would be as arbitrary as their exchange-value. Capital requires commodities for its self-constitution, while access through forcible appropriation is never access to commodities. Forcible appropriation of objects excludes their determination as commodities, and thereby excludes in their acquisition that appropriation of value which is the essence of the expansion of capital.

To be sure, in particular instances it is possible for capital to go outside of its own circuit, indeed, outside of the market system, in its drive to expand. In this way capital, in the course of its historical development, not only generates commodities but also transforms objects into commodities by appropriating them. Such an appropriation rests upon the penetration of spheres of economic life more primitive than those already subordinated to the self-development of capital. None the less, even in such cases it is necessary that capital integrate its findings into the commodity circuit and thereby fully establish the objects appropriated as commodities. For capital to accomplish this goal it must be presupposed that capital already subsists within its circuit, so that the self-expansion of value upon the exclusive basis of the circuit without recourse outside it must be already posited. This allows the objects appropriated externally to be integrated into the circuit and thereby established as commodities. To this degree, the transformation of plunder into commodities already presupposes the self-subsistence of the commodity circuit.

It is, therefore, inconceivable that capital expand exclusively, or predominantly, upon the basis of forcible appropriation. For it to do so would be tantamount to its forsaking its capitalist character. Capital is the commodity circuit made subject to the law of its self-subsistence. Since expansion is necessary to the continuation of the circuit, the commodity circuit must involve self-subsistence through self-expansion. In this way the self-determination of the exchange system is established and a process is set loose which is capable of accounting for the sequence of commodity exchanges. It is for this reason that the expansion of value cannot be arbitrary. Were the expansion of value made the result of accident, the subsistence of the commodity circuit would equally be made indeterminate. This would necessarily reduce that circuit to an orderless chaos of movement and rest subject to no law and capable of no real subsistence. The forcible appropriation of objects places their origin outside the circuit of capital. Where this is viewed as the origin of value, especially of expanded value, that origin cannot be in the conditions established by the movement of commodities. The accumulation of wealth via plunder, even were it to expand value, could not constitute the self-expansion of value since the increment to value would have no definite connection to a value advanced.

This same condition excludes the expansion of value upon the basis of the immediate activity of the commodity owner. To the extent that the specification of this activity and of its result is independent of commodity circulation its products are just as much arbitrary accretions to the circuit of capital as are the objects acquired through plunder. Since the existence and movement of the products of such activity are determined without regard to the circulation of commodities, their existence and movement will only act to sustain (or expand) that circuit by accident. They possess no intrinsic necessity to contribute to the self-subsistence of the commodity circuit, and therefore do not constitute an intrinsic part of capital. Thus, even were the activity of the commodity owner to increase the supply of use-values thrown on to the circuit, it could not thereby contribute to the *self*-expansion of value. It could not, that is, contribute to the self-subsistence of the circuit and make that subsistence the result of a force intrinsic to the movement of commodities. Any dependence of the circulation of commodities upon the external positing of objects makes the circuit the arbitrary result of accidental cause. This excludes the existence within the circuit of an inner force which orders that movement according to the law of its self-subsistence and self-development. The movement of commodities through the system of exchanges cannot be constituted as a law-governed process and therefore cannot be considered a proper subject-matter for theoretical treatment.

The increment to capital cannot, then, be grounded in conditions given outside of the commodity circuit since all such conditions bear no innate connection to the movement of commodities and are indifferent to the operation of the inner law of that movement. The formula of capital is that of value which sustains itself through its own process. This process is necessarily that of the self-expansion of value. If its secret is to be released it can only be in terms of the creation of value by value itself. This implies that the production of surplus-value cannot be the result of an activity whose conditions are given without regard to the commodity circuit. At the same time, surplus-value cannot arise immediately within the exchange nexus since the latter consists only of relations within which the equality of value is preserved and realized.

III Labor-power

The self-expansion of value must be the result of a condition directly posited within the circulation of commodities and only upon the basis of commodity circulation. Self-expansion is always predicated, therefore, upon exchange. However, this condition, made possible only within commodity circulation, must also be a condition which goes beyond the simple system of commodity exchanges. The latter excludes any expansion of value and of commodities so that such expansion must develop outside of the system of commodity exchanges. Within the commodity circuit there is only one condition which exists outside of the sequence of exchanges and yet is made possible by that system of exchange alone. This condition does not directly involve any commodity exchange, and yet is within the circuit in that it emerges only in and through the movement of commodities in their circulation. The relation of the commodity to its owner, so far as he has purchased that commodity in the market, is the consumption not of the commodity immediately given as that of the consumer, but of a commodity explicitly purchased in the market for the purpose of consumption. This consumption is an element of the capital circuit where it has as its objective the expansion of commodities. For the self-expansion of value to take place the origin of its increment must be found in the market; must, therefore, be purchased by capital and not given immediately to it. If we take capital to be money advanced to the increase of money, then capital must purchase a commodity in whose consumption it achieves the expansion of value. That commodity, since it is purchased by capital with money, is not itself capital but is acquired by capital through exchange.

Having purchased this commodity in the market, the commodity owner proceeds to extract it from the sphere of exchange. In extracting the commodity from the exchange system the owner establishes his objective as that of the consumption of the commodity and therefore as the fulfilment of need. As a use-value, the commodity fulfils a need which, as such, involves its particularization as one among a system of needs. The use-value acquired with the objective of the expansion of value is, then, the means to the fulfilment of a need which is particular. And yet, in the case of capital, the end of consumption is never the consumption act itself, the simple fulfilment of need as such, but the sale of the commodity product which results from that consumption in order that an increment to the value advanced may be realized.

In the consumption of the particular commodity, consumption is directly the fulfilment of the need which defines the commodity as a use-value. But, even here, the act of consumption, to the extent that it involves necessarily the relation to a use-value, is not an immediate act in that the intermediation of the system of needs and of their satisfactions is already implied in the particular consumption. The fulfilment of particular need has also a universal aspect in that through such fulfilment the individual establishes as well his determination within the system of needy individuals. The mediation of exchange marks that consumption as a social act and marks the consumer as participating in his consumption within a social reality. To that extent, consumption never dissipates in the immediacy of the relation of use-value to its owner. That relation is never an isolated act, always leading instead to the further participation of the individual in the system of economic relations. Even where the consumption of the commodity directly fulfils a need, and an individual need, that direct consumption is never the final end but always a dependent moment in a continuing sequence of consumption, and therefore exchange. The fulfilment of a particular need always leads to the fulfilment of other particular needs. The satisfaction of one need cannot be achieved without the concurrent and subsequent satisfaction of other needs, and the fulfilment of a given need itself creates further needs whose satisfaction is also the objective of the consumption of the original use-value. Thus, the objective of consumption of use-values is never an immediate ending point but always a complex process which involves a continuity and multiplicity of consumptions.

Consumption on the part of capital is not, therefore, distinguished simply in that it leads beyond itself and is never dissipated in the immediate fulfilment of particular need. This condition holds for all consumption of use-values, properly considered. What distinguishes the consumption of the use-value on the part of capital is the specific manner in which that consumption constitutes an element in a sustained process of consumption and repeated consumption, the manner in which consumption creates the conditions for continued and expanded consumption.

Since the consumption relation is the putting to use of the commodity as a use-value, that relation is one in which the commodity as use-value is destroyed. The commodity as a use-value is consumed, therefore destroyed, and this is the only way in which the use-value of the commodity may be realized. This is the act by which it fulfils the need to which it is specified. But, since the value of the commodity cannot exist apart from the use-value, the consumption of the use-value, as an act which consumes the commodity, consumes at the same time the value in the sense that the latter disappears with the disappearance of the use-value. It is precisely this condition which underlies the weakness of the notion of the simple circulation of commodities. The latter represents the process in which the end of exchange is in the direct consumption of the commodity, so that the exchange of commodities leads directly into their consumption and into their consumption as an *end*, therefore into their elimination as commodities. The simple circulation of commodities always consumes, in this way, the conditions to which it owes its origin. Such a movement is never able to sustain itself through its own inner process. It is necessary, rather, that commodities be continually thrown on to the market in order that they may bring back to life the commodity circuit. The latter remains, therefore, dependent upon the external origin of the conditions which are consumed within its own process of development. Since the simple circuit leads to the consumption of commodities as its endpoint it is incapable of constituting its continuation as its own product.

In the simple circulation of commodities the endpoint is the consumption of commodities. In the circuit of capital the endpoint is the expansion of value, the increase of commodities. Consumption on the part of capital is distinguished precisely by its result – the increase of capital. It is necessary that capital find, *in the market*, that peculiar commodity whose consumption does not simply destroy commodities, but through that destruction gives birth to commodities; that commodity in whose consumption is to be found the production of commodities. Furthermore, since this principle of commodity production is to be found exclusively within the commodity circuit, it cannot be a simple natural property or object but must exist from the outset as a commodity. It must be that particular commodity in whose consumption is brought about the production of the world of commodities.

The need which is fulfilled in consumption on the part of capital, while particular in the sense that it has its specificity in the relation to capital, is universal in that its objective is to expand command over the world of particular use-values. It is the consumption of a particular use-value which, however, is no particular use-value in that it fulfils no particular need. The particular need which is fulfilled through consumption on the part of capital must always be the need for all particular use-value, for the system of commodities as a whole. Since it bears this quality of illimitability, the need stands opposed to the elementary notion of need. The particular need of capital is the need for the whole of the wealth of society, and for more wealth. The use-value which fulfils this need, then, since its particularity is in the potential embedded within it for acquisition of the totality of wealth, is the negation of particular use-value. Such a use-value stands in opposition to capital as the potential for wealth stands opposed to the existence of wealth, as its possibility opposes its reality, and as the principle of production opposes its product.

The commodity in whose consumption capital effects its expansion is the negation of specific use-value since it contains implicit within it all particular use-values. It is necessary for capital to find in the market a commodity whose use-value fulfils the particular need of capital for the universe of particular use-values and therefore for no particular use-value. This is the commodity labor-power. The need fulfilled in its consumption is that of capital to exist as the totality of particular commodities, as wealth, as the multiplicity of needs and of the means to their fulfilment. Capital can find its fulfilment in particular use-values, but never in the consumption of any particular use-value. The commodity which can satisfy the need of capital to expand to infinity its command over commodities is that commodity which shares the universality of capital – its indifference to need – but in a negative sense. Capital realizes its universality by existing in the form of a circuit of commodities and, as money, in the form of the universal use-value. Labor-power, in whose consumption capital realizes this universality, exists independently of the existing universe of particular use-values, of wealth in the form of the circuit of capital. The commodity labor-power is, then, the negation of the system of particular use-values existing in the form of a commodity, and in whose consumption capital can alone realize its command over an unlimited totality of wealth.[2]

IV The buying and selling of labor-power

1 The conditions of the exchange

As constitutive elements of the circuit of capital, the particular use-values are made subordinate to the preservation and expansion of value. The result of this subordination is the real constitution of the particular commodities as the components of wealth. Labor-power, having itself no particular use-value, stands *outside* of capital, where the latter considers all particular use-values as so many components of its own life-process. Since capital is made up of the wealth of society, of the system of commodities, it must seek out the labor-power necessary to bring it to life outside of the wealth which composes the existing circuit. Capital must confront the labor-power, through which it can alone preserve and expand itself, as a commodity existing as the property of a commodity owner standing independent of and opposed to capital. This autonomous commodity owner, who confronts capital, the existing wealth of society, as its opposite, is the laborer as the sole proprietor of his labor-power.

The autonomy of the laborer, and his sole proprietorship over his labor-power, is implied in the identification of capital with wealth existing in the process of its self-renewal. Since capital is the wealth of society, it necessarily excludes labor-power which, as the agent uniquely capable of bringing wealth to life, is also the absence of wealth. The resulting confrontation of the wealth of society with its own life-giving principle as its antithesis marks that society with the fundamental opposition of its life process. The principle of the existing universe of wealth must meet face-to-face with the principle of its vivification, and, in order to preserve itself, strike a bargain, freely accepted on all sides, which incorporates into capital the only means to its realization. This contract, through which labor-power is brought into capital and made subordinate to its process of self-expansion, is the buying and selling of labor-power. Capital, in relation to labor-power, confronts a commodity in whose consumption capital is enabled to realize its own illimitability.

The autonomy of the laborer is the logical basis for the abstraction of his laboring capacity and for its constitution as the capacity indifferently to produce the world of particular commodities. This abstraction deprives the worker of all specification to the production of particular use-value or particular commodity. Out of this deprivation springs the indifference of the laborer to the limited specification of the particular commodity products; out of this indifference springs the capacity not to produce this or that commodity product but all commodities regardless of their specification. This abstraction of the laboring capacity requires, in the first instance, that the laborer be able to abstract that capacity from himself, alienate it not only from the particularity of the commodity product but from his identity as this particular laborer. With the development of this condition there emerges, for the first time, labor-power as the abstract capacity to produce the universe of commodities, abstract because of its indifference to the production of any particular commodity; and indifferent to all such specification of production because of its abstraction from the particularity of its owner as well as from the particularity of the wealth of society.

Labor-power, since its specificity involves its opposition to the system of commodities which compose the circuit of capital, originates not as a given element of that circuit but outside of it. The exchange by which labor-power is made a part of the self-development of capital – the buying and selling of labor-power – is also that act by which capital originally makes labor-power a part of its life process. The conception of labor-power requires, then, two conditions. First, it is necessary that labor-power exist outside of the capital circuit where the latter is composed of particular commodities, of the wealth of society. Second, it is equally essential that labor-power become a part of the circuit of capital since the utility of labor-power is its capacity to bring about, through its consumption, the expansion of capital. The opposition of labor-power to capital is inextricably connected to the unification of one with the other in the purchase of labor-power on the part of capital.

This exchange has the following specific form: the labor-power exists as a commodity not already incorporated within the capital circuit. Labor-power is not, that is, posited as immediately a part of capital. In order for labor-power to become a part of capital and thereby to effect its self-expansion, capital must appear in the market, in the form of money, and purchase labor-power from the laborer. On one side there is capital in the form of a sum of money, on the other side labor-power in the form of a commodity. The conditions for commodity exchange, the opposition of money to commodity, are fulfilled. Furthermore, each pole is constrained to enter into exchange in order to fulfil a specific need connected on one side to the conception of capital, on the other to the conception of labor-power as the antithesis of capital. The resulting exchange is, then, an instance of commodity exchange whose specific conditions are given in the conception of capital as self-expanding value. For this exchange the simple notion of the confrontation of money and commodity, while presupposed, is not sufficient. It is further necessary that the needs thus fulfilled be specified and the necessity of their fulfilment through exchange be established.

The fact that it is money which confronts labor-power as the manifestation within the market of capital advanced is already implied in the elementary conception of commodity exchange which, as the transaction which effects the realization of commodity value, is never constituted as the immediate opposition of particular commodities. For capital, this necessity is also built into its characteristic cycle, which is also the life-cycle of money (value in the universal form). The idea that the purchase and sale of labor-power may as readily be conceived upon the basis of the opposition of labor-power to the means of its subsistence, suppresses the specific determination both of capital and of labor-power. Not only does such a conception fail utterly to penetrate to the inner truth of the transaction, but, by constituting the monetary aspect as purely formal, effects a retreat to the barter conception of commodity exchange. Money is thereby considered as no more than a 'veil' which masks the reality of the interaction by obscuring its material substantiation. This contention does indeed establish the essentially material determination of the capital relation, thereby obliterating any real investigation of its social determination.* The real social determination of the capital relation is inseparably connected to the specificity of that relation as an exchange sustained within a system of exchanges. This social determination requires, therefore, the intermediation of money not merely as a formal condition, but as a substantive requisite of the full constitution of the relation, and as a primary basis for the deduction of its concrete requirements.

---

* The implications of this conception of the purchase and sale of labor-power for the conception of the concrete determination of the growth process of capital are thoroughly debilitating. The suppression of the money form at the present level of analysis is the prelude to the attempt to establish the concrete determination of the wage upon the basis of the immediate counterposition of classes within the market. The elimination of money allows the transaction between capital and labor to immediately determine the value of labor-power (the purchasing power of the money wage). Since the conditions of that transaction are essentially those of the confrontation of will, the wage and along with it the net product come to be determined in a direct opposition of will. As such, the relation remains quantitatively indeterminate and the process of the self-development of capital comes to rest on a prior determination of 'struggle' which remains historically contingent. This makes the self-determination of capital also historically contingent. This conceptualization rests in its entirety upon the premise that abstraction from the monetary form, rather than obliterating the inner determination of the relation, makes possible its real comprehension. This contention cannot be sustained, however, in the light of the analysis of the real conditions of commodity exchange in general, and of the specific conditions of the buying and selling of labor-power. The concrete implications of the general conception of exchange and of the capital-labor relation for the self-development of capital will be considered in volume II of the present work.

The antithesis of capital, in whose consumption capital achieves its preservation and expansion, presents itself to capital as a commodity. Through the purchase of labor-power, capital absorbs into its circuit the active principle of its expansion. So far as the need which capital brings to the market to be fulfilled through exchange is concerned, this is a need for the *capacity* to produce commodities and nothing more. It is, furthermore, a need which capital must enter into an exchange in order to satisfy precisely in so far as the commodity labor-power remains the property of the laborer. On the side of labor-power the exchange has the reverse form. The laborer gives up the commodity which he owns in order to acquire not this or that particular use-value, but in order to acquire the exchange-value of his labor-power. The laborer, in other words, presents his labor-power in the market for sale in order to acquire a sum of money. The proprietor of labor-power is the owner of the absence of wealth. He gives up this commodity in order to acquire wealth in the form of a fixed sum of money. What he gives up is the access to wealth without limit, therefore access to real wealth. What he acquires is the access to a fixed part of wealth which is equivalently his exclusion from wealth. But this acquisition is essential to the worker since it is the sole means by which he can realize the worth of the one commodity which he owns. The exchange of labor-power for capital in the form of money is the sole means by which the laborer can acquire access even to that part of the wealth of society requisite for the fulfilment of his needs. As for any commodity owner, the exchange of commodities is the sole means to the fulfilment of need, and the starting point for this exchange is the purchase of money as the means to the acquisition of commodities. The worker, the owner of labor-power, is equally as constrained to exchange as is the owner of the capital: the worker in order to transform his property into money as the means to the fulfilment of his needs, and the owner of capital in order to acquire the labor-power without which the expansion of his capital is impossible.

The potential brought to realization in consumption on the part of capital is the potential existence of all particular commodities and is, therefore, specific to none. Capital, as the commodity circuit, is the complex of all particular use-values set in motion, and is, therefore, the capacity for the fulfilment of all particular need; it is the wealth of society. The commodity whose consumption sustains and expands capital, since drained of all capacity for the fulfilment of particular need, is nothing other than the absence of all such specification: the absence of wealth. The wealth of society existing as a potential is also the absence of wealth.

2 *The acquisition of labor-power and the realization of value in classical economics*

The development of the money form allowed originally for an expression of value in the relation of exchange-value which revealed the generality of the value relation, in particular its independence of specification to any particular commodity and to any particular use-value. Money is the commodity whose use-value is that it is the socially recognized representative of value. Money has the use-value of commanding the universe of commodities in exchange and of expressing the worth of all particular commodities. With the emergence of the money relation value is able to express itself in a particular use-value which reveals rather than obliterates the generality of the value relation. In the analysis of the circuit of capital there arises a problem similar to that resolved with the development of money. Capital can only expand itself by acquiring a particular commodity in exchange – therefore within its process of circulation – but a commodity which is, at the same time, universal in that it fulfils the need of capital for the totality of wealth. This commodity, labor-power, is that particular use-value which is no particular use-value. The analysis of the value relation gives rise, therefore, to two distinct commodities whose particularity has a universal character – money and labor-power.

The commodity which fulfils the need for the expression of value cannot, however, be the same as the commodity which fulfils the need for the production and expansion of value. It is precisely the characteristic of the commodity which expresses the value of all commodities, money, to find its consumption wholly within the system of commodity exchanges. Indeed, the circulation of commodities is the consumption of money, just as the consumption of money effects the circulation of commodities. The owner of money can only consume it by alienating it in the purchase of some particular commodity. The principle which is realized in the consumption of money is that of the equivalence of value, and therefore of its preservation through the commodity cycle. Since the consumption of money only brings about the preservation of value, it cannot effect its expansion, so that, while capital is money, the specific requirement of capital for expansion cannot be fulfilled by the consumption of money. No matter how much money may be incorporated into capital, it can only realize itself by sacrificing the money form in the purchase of labor-power. The more money capital consists of, the more labor-power it can acquire, and the more it can expand through the consumption of labor-power. Money is the means by which capital acquires labor-power, and labor-power is the means by which capital acquires more money. Capital is, therefore, never satisfied to exist as money, since for it to exist in that form is for it to give up the possibility of expansion.

Labor-power shares with money the property of being able to 'purchase' the world of commodities. As Adam Smith, in particular, recognizes, labor-power is the purchasing medium of commodities and is, in this sense, a kind of money. Through the consumption of labor-power capital brings commodities into existence; in this sense in the consumption of labor-power capital purchases commodities (for Smith it purchases them 'from nature'). This conflation of labor-power and money, founded in their shared universality, provides the logical basis for the so-called 'labor-commanded theory of value,' according to which the value of commodities is measured by the quantity of labor (i.e. labor-power) which they command in the market. What is ignored in this conception, however, is that, while labor-power is capable of purchasing all commodities by producing them, it is incapable of the real purchase of commodities, since it is not the universal equivalent. The distinction between money and labor-power is equivalent to the distinction between the realization of value and its production, a distinction never fully grasped by classical political economy. The latter tends to consider the realization of value to be immediately posited in its production, so that the distinction between money and labor-power becomes purely formal, having to do with matters of practice rather than with the intrinsic conception of value. Smith recognizes that in practice the value of commodities is measured in money and not in labor-power, but he writes this perversity off to the accidental effects of fluctuations in price rather than to the fundamental distinction of conception which is in reality at stake.

Classical political economy fails to grasp the distinction between the elementary conception of the commodity and the mode of expression of its commodity character, on one side, and the conception of commodity production on the other. The simple idea of the commodity does not contain immediately the conception of its production. For the latter to emerge it is first necessary to analyze the mediating process by which the commodity realizes its inner character. The process of commodity production must be made specific to the conception of the commodity as the *product* of a determinate process. This requires that the development of the conception of the commodity precede the conception of its production. Otherwise the notion of production would lose any quality which could account for the specificity of its product as a commodity and would appear instead as production taken in the abstract, as nothing more than the abstract logical notion of transformation taken without regard to the uniqueness and specification of its product. That is, indeed, the procedure of classical political economy, which is forced thereby to equate the production of the commodity with the most elementary conception of the commodity, taking both the notion of the commodity and the notion of its production to be already given independently of the specification of the real inner properties of the commodity relation.

With regard to the concept of labor-power, since it produces in its consumption the system of commodities, Smith considers it to be uniquely suited also to the measurement of their exchange-value. This, however, labor-power fails altogether to accomplish for the simple reason that the requirements implied in the expression of, and measurement of, value are distinct from and opposed to the requirements implied in the production of value. Labor-power, like money, is that particular commodity which is no particular commodity but potentially the world of commodities. It is access to wealth for its owner. Unlike labor-power, however, money is socially recognized as the unique embodiment of value, and its use-value is simply that it is perceived to be value. Labor-power is incapable of realizing value. Money, being just so much value, recognized as the fixed quantum of value, must possess the property of stability of value. The purchase of money with the particular commodity is the prelude to the consumption of money in the purchase of another commodity. The logic of this activity lies precisely in that the value of the money is constant in the sense that it is unaffected by its consumption. By contrast, labor-power, which is not the socially recognized embodiment of value, is not so much value but is the vivifying principle in the production of value. Money can purchase labor-power like any other commodity and realize its value, while labor-power cannot realize the value of money. At the same time, however, labor-power can produce money while money is incapable of producing labor-power. Money, by existing as a fixed quantity of value, is capable of purchasing all commodities, while labor-power can create commodities but cannot purchase them. The realization of value requires the constancy of the value of the money commodity in its consumption; the expansion of value requires the variability of the value purchased, its expansion through its consumption.

Since labor-power is not money it cannot directly purchase commodities. As a particular commodity, the only commodity which it is capable of purchasing is money, and, conversely, it is only with money that labor-power may be purchased. It is, therefore, necessary for the capital which acquires labor-power to exist in the form of money, and it is necessary that the products which eventuate from the consumption of labor-power be first transformed into money before they can once again effect the acquisition of labor-power through exchange. These requirements of the purchase and sale of labor-power are essential. They cannot be left aside without leaving aside the whole of the determinacy of capital and of the capital-labor relation.

3 *The specificity of labor-power to the circulation of wealth*

The expansion of value must be the result of a process which is simultaneously within and outside of the circuit considered simply as the system of commodity exchanges. To the extent that the circuit is conceived narrowly, as nothing more than the sequence of exchanges which effect the movement of commodities and of money, the expansion of value must occur outside. At the same time, the expansion of value, which is also the production of new value, must be based upon conditions which exist within the circuit if that expansion of value is to be itself determinate, specific to the conception of the commodity and of its value. The circulation of commodities and money, in order to establish its continuation as its own result, must extend itself beyond the elementary relations of exchange to encompass the consumption of commodities as the means to their expansion. The specificity of the circuit established on this basis lies precisely in that the expansion of value takes place as a moment within it, and that the conditions of that expansion are made available by the purchase and sale of commodities.

The necessity that the expansion of value take place simultaneously within and outside of the circulation of commodities is termed by Marx the 'contradiction in the general formula of capital.'[3] Its significance lies not in the opposition of circulation to production, but in the requirement that commodity circulation move beyond the elementary relations of exchange to itself incorporate production, and that it do so solely in order to sustain those relations of exchange through increasing them.

The opposition of labor-power to the circuit of wealth involves also the specification of labor-power to that circuit. The universality of the need fulfilled in the consumption of labor-power is specific to the circuit of commodities established as the circuit of capital. That need is the need for the expansion of wealth. It is not given immediately in the conception of the commodity and of commodity exchange, but presupposes the concrete specification of the constitution of the exchange system as the system of the generation and regeneration of capital. Thus, while labor-power has a use-value, its comprehension is not synonymous with that of the general conception of use-value, but requires the specification of the circuit of capital. For this conception it is essential that the commodity labor-power be recognized from the outset as opposing the commodity circuit and having no immediate existence within it. The determination of labor-power as the principle of the expansion of commodities and of value hinges upon its conception in relation to, and in relation of opposition to, capital.

The method employed in the analysis of labor-power is not, then, that of choosing, from among a group of existing factors – factors already posited within the general conception of commodity exchange – that one which happens, by chance, to fulfil the need of capital to expand. Misunderstanding of the theory of value always stems from the notion that labor-power has its specificity fully developed in the elementary conception of the commodity and especially of its use-value. This misunderstanding is tied to the conception of labor as simple use-value having the capacity to fulfil a particular need the specification of which has nothing to do with the concept of capital. The conception of labor-power, as nothing more than a particular commodity already given as an element of the commodity circuit, and therefore also of the circuit of capital, has the effect of depriving labor-power of its specificity. To be sure, labor-power has a use-value and in this sense its conception exists implicitly within the most elementary notions of exchange. Furthermore, as the basis for the production of commodities, labor-power exists latently within the most abstract conception of the commodity relation. What is lost in the subsumption of labor-power into the elementary conception of the commodity is the specific determination of labor-power, and therefore its real conception. While labor-power is a commodity, its conception is not synonymous with that of the commodity. The real emergence of the conception of labor-power, in its specificity as a determinate relation to capital and therefore to the production of commodities, is only made possible on the basis of the conception of capital as self-expanding value, having as its objective the production of commodities and therefore the production of value.

Every concrete specification of the commodity relation involves a further determination of that relation which goes beyond the elementary notion of the commodity. The conception of labor-power can no more be reduced to that of the commodity than can the concept of money. Just as within the expanded form of exchange-value money has no existence and is not one among the particular equivalents, so also within the circulation of commodities and money, labor-power has no existence since that need which it fulfils is only allowed to emerge with the development of the capital circuit.

Thus, if we consider commodities in the elementary form, there can be no basis for the conception of a universal equivalent since it is characteristic of the equivalent in the elementary form to be particular. Money does not, then, pre-exist the conception of the money form. It will not be found waiting there, already fully developed, to be chosen from among the particular equivalents existing in the more abstract forms. Money is first established as such only with the development of the general and the money forms, since it is only these forms which first establish the conditions necessary for the conception of money.

This distinction, which may appear to be purely formal and definitional, in fact goes to the heart of the conception of economic life. Were the money commodity to be presumed prior to the development of the general form, its conception would be posited as immediately given outside of and independently of the logical content of the theory. The conception of money would become an *a priori* condition of analysis rather than a product of the conceptual development. It would, then, become impossible to provide for the money relation any theoretical account. Money, taken simply as a commodity, would not have the qualitative features which establish the conception of money except by accident. In order, then, to consider the money relation in its specificity it would become necessary to introduce a series of *ad hoc* specifications, with no theoretical justification, in the form of a set of empirical or intuitive qualities. The real qualities of the relation, rather than established as such by a systematic argument, would appear at random, and the conception of money would be made unintelligible. Economic analysis always grasps the specificity of economic relations (of money, labor-power, etc.), but always refuses to consider the inner necessity which establishes that specificity in a systematic way, thereby reducing the necessity of the specific determinations to accidental and random attributes. The idea that money is *just* another commodity, which is equally characteristic of classical and of modern economics, excludes any conception of money and leaves aside any possibility of a satisfactory theory of money.

This result holds equally in the case of the conception of labor-power. Economic analysis always tends to the constitution of labor as a natural condition which may be taken as a presupposition of the conception of economic life. Labor is considered to be a 'factor of production' among an indefinitely large set of factors, having no innate connection to the self-expansion of value. As such a presupposition, labor has no specifically economic conception. The problem becomes, in this case, that of the choice from among the already existing empirically or naturally given factors of production, and not that of the conception of labor and of its relation to labor-power. Where labor-power exists prior to the conception of capital, for example within the elementary notion of commodity circulation, its specific conditions elude the concept of capital and remain external to it. To remain external to the conception of capital is tantamount, however, to remaining excluded from the conception of economic life. Capital is not simply one element of the theory of economic relations, it is the self-subsistent unity of the economic process. It is economic life established within a movement governed by the law of self-determination through self-renewal. The exclusion of labor-power from its determination in relation to this process is equivalent to its exclusion from any determination within the conception of economic life, and therefore to its constitution as a natural condition.*

In the analysis of economic relations there is no place for production taken without regard for its specificity, and in particular for the exigencies of the circulation of commodities. Production, as an activity undertaken on the part of capital, is encompassed by the movement of capital. Capital, however, is a commodity circuit, so that its incorporation of production requires that it extend itself beyond the sphere within which it is originally identified, in order to engage in the activity of commodity production. In order to realize its self-expansion, capital must also be that activity of commodity consumption which is also the production of value. Capital is labor-power and commodities united in the process of commodity production. Capital is a form of commodity movement through exchange, and capital is the movement of commodities through their production process. It is simultaneously a movement of commodities and a production of commodities, a movement which creates the conditions necessary for production, and a production process which makes possible the movement of commodities. The formula for capital reveals the connection between the movement of commodities within the sphere of exchange and their consumption within the process of commodity production.

---

* The economic conception of labor as having a social determination begins with classical political economy and most effectively in Adam Smith's analysis of the division of labor and its relation to exchange. The implicit content of the 'labor theory of value' is always that of the conception of labor as a social relation. This implicit conception is first made explicit in the mature works of Marx (see especially, *Grundrisse*, tr. M. Nicolaus [Harmondsworth: Penguin Books, 1973] p. 259). Even here, however, the argument and manner of exposition retain elements of the typically classical confusion between labor as the substance of value and labor as a purely material condition (see especially the first volume of *Capital* and the 'Marginal Notes on Adolph Wagner's *Lehrbuch der Politischen Okonomie*' of 1879–80). For a critique of Marx's treatment of this problem see R. Winfield, *The Social Determination of Production* (Ph.D. dissertation, Yale University, 1977), part III.

Here, the equality of commodities and of commodity owners is also the basis for the distinguishing of commodities and of commodity owners, between capital and labor, which distinction provides the starting point for commodity production. The series of exchanges, which realizes the equality of commodities, is the origin of the movement of commodities into production where the equality of commodities and of their values is first produced in the production of value and simultaneously overcome in the expansion of value.

PART THREE

Production

CHAPTER FIVE

Labor

I The immediate production process

1 Commodity production

The consumption of labor-power by capital is the process of commodity production. When this process is considered in general, and without regard for the concrete conditions bound up with its full determination, it is termed by Marx the immediate or direct production process. The immediate production process is the process of commodity production conceived without consideration for its specificity to this particular commodity product or to the activity of this particular unit of production. In the investigation of the direct production process all those relations which mediate the productive activity of the concretely determined unit of capital are left aside. Abstraction is made from all specificity of the producing unit as regard its level of development, concentration of capital, or distribution of capital among its particular forms.

The abstraction involved in the investigation of the immediate production process does not involve any isolation of the particular producer. On the contrary, abstraction from the particularity of the producer makes explicit its universality and therefore the underlying unity which links it inseparably to the system of producers. The general conception of commodity production contains within it the principle of particularization of the system of productions, but only implicitly. That principle is given in the conception of the direct production process and of the universal qualities which stamp all particular productions as commodity production. These general features make intelligible the particularization of production by connecting that particularization to a necessity implicit in the general notion of the commodity and of its production process.

To begin with the system of particular producers would be to take the principle which underlies their opposition as fixed independently of the specifically economic relations into which they enter. In order to constitute the particular production process as an instance of commodity production, however, it is necessary first to investigate the general qualities which distinguish commodity production and its product. The theoretical starting point is neither the totality of particular producers taken as a logical construct, nor the presupposed empirical actuality of divisions and oppositions among existing commodity producers. While the general qualities which characterize commodity production are shared in common by all particular producers, the conception of those qualities is not a matter of empirical generalization, but of establishing conceptually the distinctive features definitive of production in economic life. Such a conceptual investigation must necessarily precede the determination of the distinguishing qualities of real particular producers which make of them particular instances of capitalist commodity production by distinguishing them one from another in accordance with the particularity of their product, of their market, of the mode of investment of their capital, of their distinctive histories, nationalities, etc.

Commodity production eventuates not merely in a product but in a commodity. For the commodity to be posited as a result it must develop out of a process within which its distinctive qualities exist in their process of generation. The commodity is, then, a determinate product and its production is equally determinate. Since the specificity of the production process is connected to the specificity of the product, the process of commodity production is the process of the production of value and of use-value. The value and use-value as intrinsic properties cannot be attached to the product arbitrarily but must be incorporated into it in a systematic manner. Otherwise, the product, in becoming such, remains indifferent to its commodity character, which is not itself produced but only added on subsequent to its production. This would not be commodity production but simply the production of a product, an activity to which the commodity relation of the result is a matter of total indifference. Were this the case the production process could be left out of account in consideration of the commodity since it would be inessential to it. The effect of this would be that the commodity relation, since not produced in any determinate production activity, must remain the contingent effect of accidental factors. For commodity production, by contrast, the qualities which stamp the object as a commodity are produced and not attached subsequent to the act of production. The life of the commodity outside of its production, while not immediately given in that production, is inseparably connected to it as the necessary expression and realization of the inner force already present within and definitive of the production process.

2 The labor process

The acquisition of labor-power by capital is the unification of wealth with the activating principle of its own generative process. Wealth contains within it the capacity for its own growth and development. The sole object to be achieved in the consumption of labor-power is that of bringing to life that productive potential latent within the wealth. The consumption of labor-power, labor, is the activating moment of commodity production, and commodity production is, in this sense, a labor process. To consider commodity production to be a labor process does not imply any full determination of the process and its product on the side of the laborer or his labor-power. On the contrary, the distinctiveness of the process of commodity production as a process of laboring derives from the unique ability of labor-power to set in motion the productive capacity of the wealth existing as capital. When capital acquires a given quantity of labor-power, it, in effect, acquires so much of its own productive existence: labor-time.

The labor process is the productive phase in the process of the self-expansion of value, so that when labor-power activates wealth it thereby brings about the self-generation and expansion of wealth in its quantitative determination as value. Thus, the object in accordance with which labor-power activates wealth is the production of value, and laboring, or the labor process, is the process of value production.

Labor-power, in its consumption, is no longer the antithesis of capital, but the vivifying principle of its self-expansion. From the standpoint of the purchase and sale of labor-power, the two are opposed: on one side the labor-power, on the other the capital in the form of money. With the purchase of labor-power this opposition gives way and the two principles are united into capital as elements of its process: on one side there is wealth existing as capital, on the other side there is labor-power, as the activating force within production, also existing as capital. With this unification, wealth is constituted as the objective basis for its own realization as wealth through its expansion without limit. This constitution of wealth in its self-generative process is the process of capitalist commodity production.

The abstraction which constitutes labor-power as a productive principle indifferent to the particularity of the use-value of the product establishes the labor-power in opposition to the system of particular use-values – wealth. This particularity exists, then, in the wealth which confronts labor-power as capital. It is the specificity of the wealth consumed in the labor process which enables that process to produce commodities. While it is the labor-power which provides for wealth its life-giving force, it is the wealth which provides the means by which laboring produces the objects of need. The wealth which confronts labor-power as capital existing within the production process is the means of production, the instruments and materials by which laboring produces the means to the satisfaction of particular needs and thereby produces wealth; and labor is the active force which makes wealth productive of wealth.

The means of labor are capital existing as particular use-values. These existing use-values are also the requisite conditions for laboring. It is the consumption of particular use-values within the labor process that gives to the latter its specification to the use-value of its own result. Where all such specification exists within the system of particular commodities and not within the laboring capacity, the specification of the production process to the use-value of its product resides in the consumption of particular commodities within the labor process. Labor-power can only produce commodities when it does so as an element of capital. Labor-power only becomes active, becomes labor, when it has first become capital. In this sense, it is capital alone which is able to produce commodities and which is alone capable of accounting for the value of the product. The unity of labor-power with capital is the starting point for commodity production. For the latter, labor-power has already become an element of capital, so that the production of commodities and values is by means of capital and the expansion of capital in production is the self-expansion of capital.

So long as consumption is the production of commodities, it differs from the abstract act of consumption in that the materials, equipment, etc., are not simply consumed – destroyed – but are transformed. To the extent that capitalist production is a transformation of commodities and value, it preserves through transforming, so that the product is connected to the consumption of the means of its production by its retention of the qualities of the means of production in a new form. The consumption of commodities is simultaneously the production of commodities, so that the act, taken as a whole, is the transformation of commodities. Within this change of form, there are retained the essential qualities brought to the production process. The specification of the means of production to the use-value of the product is equivalently the use-value of the means of production, so that the use-value of the product exists already, latent within the use-value of the means of production. Production, by consuming the means of production, brings out the use-value of the product implicit within the instruments of labor, changing their form from that of an implicit idea, locked within the objective conditions of labor, to the explicit useful form of the product.

This constancy of substance through its transformation in production is characteristic of the capitalist consumption of commodities. It is in the nature of consumption that it (1) destroy the matter consumed, and (2) have a result. This is equally the case for consumption viewed as a material interchange as it is for consumption which takes place within society and as a social act. Consumption is never a simple elimination but is always ultimately a change of form; a transformation dictated by the material consumed and by the manner of its consumption. That consumption be production implies that the result fulfil certain conditions, and do so not accidentally, but precisely because of the peculiarity of the consumption act. There is always a result or product, but this may or may not be a commodity. The instruments of labor are consumed when they are destroyed by fire, or when they are allowed to spoil through disuse. Such consumption does not, however, eventuate in the production of a commodity. It is, then, not simply a matter of the material consumed; it is also a question of the manner or mode of consumption. In the case of commodity production, it is the simultaneity of the consumption of the means of production and of the labor-power which makes the product a commodity.

Indeed, from the point of view of society as a whole, nothing is, in principle, lost; it is produced, consumed, and in its consumption reproduced. The consumption of a given commodity is the production of another commodity, while the consumption of a third commodity is the production of the original commodity. To this degree, the consumption of the product is simultaneously an element of its own production so that its disappearance within production at one point in the process of production, taken as a whole, is a condition and result of its reappearance at another point. This holds for the system of capitalist production taken as a whole to be considered in the second volume of this work. At present this condition exists only implicitly, since the system of particular productions is not as yet taken explicitly into account. Still, within the immediate production process the mutual interdependence of productions can already be discerned and, as we shall see, the preservation through consumption which makes production only the transformation of the inputs depends, for its realization, upon the interpenetration of the system of productions.

The determination of the production process concretely as the process of the capitalist production of commodities is the determination of its constituent elements as elements of capital, and as thereby made adequate in their inner constitution to the production of commodities. The production of surplus-value involves the opposition of the worker and the means of production as co-ordinate elements of a single process of laboring. At the same time, the consumption of labor-power and of the means of production in the production of the commodity involves a concrete specification of the nature of the laboring and of the means of production. The theoretical investigation of commodity production cannot satisfy itself with the abstract counterposition of labor-power, means of labor and product. It must also consider concretely the inner nature of the labor-power and means of production determined as co-ordinate elements of the production process of wealth; and it must consider as well the concrete constitution of the product of laboring as the constituent element of wealth. The analysis of production must lay bare the manner in which the formal idea of production as a transformation of inputs into the product is constituted concretely in accordance with its substantive determination within the cycle of capital.

II Collective labor

For the production of wealth, the labor process is first considered from its quantitative aspect. This is the labor process as the process of the production of value and surplus-value. For this objective it is necessary that the laboring activity be deprived of all determination other than that of labor in general. This deprivation is, in the first instance, and especially from the historical standpoint, a negative quality of the labor, an abstraction of labor from all specific determination in the features of the particular product. But this negative determination, which results from a deprivation of the labor of any specification to the use-value of the product, is also a real positive determination of the labor with respect particularly to the constitution of the value as a qualitative characteristic of its product. The abstraction of labor is not only a deprivation of the work activity, but it is equally, and more importantly, an achievement on the part of labor which involves for the first time its real determination as *labor*. Production which is conceivable as laboring has a character intrinsically connected to the abstraction which is implied in the general idea of labor. This abstraction has also an existence as a qualitative determination of the product, so that the latter bears within itself a property inseparably connected to the fact that it is produced by labor. With this development, the abstraction of the labor becomes a real force within production.

The starting point for the abstraction of labor is in the positing of labor-power by capital as its antithesis, which develops originally in the purchase and sale of labor-power. The conception of commodity production as the consumption of labor-power brings with it the conception of production as a labor process whose extent is the quantity of laboring. Prior to the consumption of the labor-power, the latter stands in opposition to capital as the property of the laborer. In its consumption within the labor process this is no longer the case. Within the laboring activity the will of the laborer is no longer primary, and the development of the labor process is synonymous with the development of the capacity on the part of the laborer to separate himself from his laboring and to deprive the latter of all determination in his personality. The purchase of the labor-power makes the latter not only the property of capital, but also a part of capital, so that the objective realized in the consumption of labor-power is always that of capital and never that of the laborer. So far as capital is concerned, the laborer is himself left outside when he brings his labor-power into the production process. Once the worker has alienated his labor-power, it becomes subject to determination in accordance with the self-development of capital. The first step in the subjection of labor-power to this objective is precisely the severing of the labor-power from the laborer and its constitution as a principle independent of its original owner. With the incorporation of his labor-power into capital, the laborer leaves aside his individuality; or, more precisely, the labor-power realizes its own intrinsic independence of that individuality, entering the labor process as nothing more nor less than the capacity for laboring. This suppression of the connection of the labor-power to the particular laborer who brings it to production is essential. It is effected by capital, which produces commodities not with the intervention of the individual worker as active agent, but with the extraction of the labor supplied by that laborer, made independent of his personality, and made separate from any connection to his distinctive characteristics. Here, within production, the owner of the labor-power actually becomes a laborer. He ceases to oppose capital as an independent commodity owner, and exists within capital as labor-power in action. The starting point of capitalist production is, then, not the individual laborer in his relation to the means of production; nor is it the sum total of many individual laborers united together with the means of production. That starting point is, instead, a quantity of labor supplied indifferently by the consumption of the labor-power of any individual laborer.

So far as capital is concerned, it is the quantity of labor acquired in the purchase of labor-power which is fundamental. It is in this sense that the consumption of labor-power involves a separation of the laborer from his labor which, within production, adopts the form originally of the pooling of labor-powers and then of labors. Since the production process is indifferent to the specificity of the laborer it is the production indifferently of many particular laborers. Viewed from the standpoint of capital, production is the activity of labor, and the variety of particular laborers is of no consequence. Production is the collective laboring of many workers merged into a single connected activity whose determination is wholly without regard to its composition in terms of particular workers and of groups of particular workers.

For labor to be fully constituted in its abstraction as labor, the first step is the collecting of the laboring capacities of particular laborers and thereby the constitution of their activity as independent of their particularity. This aspect of production, which involves it in a merging of many labor-powers, is implied in the idea of labor and is essential not only to the historical development of social production, but also to its conception. The emancipation of laboring from its connection to the particular laborer begins with his integration into a total process of collective laboring. With the collecting together of the labor-powers of many laborers, each labor-power confronts its abstraction in the form of its equation with labor-power in general. For the labor-power to be merged into the laboring process, it must be equated with the labor-powers existing within production. This equation of different labor-powers realizes their indifference to the laborer who brings them to production, and realizes that indifference within the production process. The equality of labor-power with labor-power expresses and realizes the abstraction of the labor-power and of the labor. When labor-power is consumed within production, then, it is not the labor-power of this or that particular worker, but labor-power existing as such, and its consumption is not the laboring of this or that particular laborer but labor as such. Here, the limits of the labor, as regards its extent, are not given in the capacity of the individual laborer, but are overcome in the constitution of laboring as the activity of many laborers, and indeed, of laborers collected together without limit.

Marx considers this constitution of labor in the abstract within production from the aspect of the collecting together of many particular laborers, and terms it 'co-operation.'[1] The notion of co-operation, while grasping the indifference of laboring to the laborer, also retains the element of the opposition of particular labors, and considers the overcoming of their independence as a matter of their mutual co-operation. Such co-operation still requires the active participation of the laborer, and to that extent excludes the full emancipation of laboring from the personality of the worker. As a result, the unification of labors within production is unable to fully penetrate the inner determination of labor, so that the bringing together of laborers unites them externally (e.g. physically and temporally). Such unity is not yet made a requirement intrinsic to laboring itself. This external quality, which is connected to the unity within production effected by co-operation in the Marxian sense, restricts that principle of unification to a more primitive level of economic development than that characteristic of the collective activity of labor as such. The independence of particular labors implied in this conception of co-operation is overcome with the collective activity of labor which has achieved its full development.

Labor, considered in the abstract, also begins with the pooling of the laboring capacities of particular laborers. In this sense collective laboring is the most elementary form of abstract labor and provides the conceptual starting point for the constitution of labor's abstraction as an intrinsic quality. This external or formal equation of labors can, however, only provide the starting point for their substantive submergence into a single process to the degree that the equation of labors does not presuppose their prior concrete constitution as opposed types of labor. Instead, the formal merging together of the laboring capacities of separate laborers provides the logical basis for the concrete determination of the labor in terms of its object within production. Collective labor neither retains nor overcomes previously fixed differences of labor, but instead makes possible the systematic conception of the different types of labor in accordance with the idea of general abstract labor.

The idea of labor is not achieved in the external abstraction from a concreteness presupposed within the reality of laboring. The starting point is not the presumed primordial particularity and opposition of labors, but their elementary conception as abstract and general, therefore as labor. The abstraction of labor does not divorce the idea of labor from any empirically presupposed particularity, but grasps conceptually the reality of labor as it exists within the life process of capital. Any systematic conception of

labor must constitute the particular types of labor as particularizations of labor, which originate conceptually in the analysis of labor
in general. Indeed, it is the unity of labor-power with capital that
brings about its particularization, a particularization which originates not in the labor-power, but within the process of commodity
production.*

Thus, the theoretically necessary conception is precisely the
opposite of that which is most frequently to be found in the
analysis of economic relations. Instead of attempting to abstract
from an empirically presupposed condition of many particular
labors, the theory seeks to constitute that particularity as a condition derived from the investigation of the general conception of
labor. This allows the particularization of labor to derive its
necessity, and therefore its theoretical account, from the requirements latent within its general conception.

---

* This does not hold directly for the development of skills which are required
to precede the productive activity of the worker. Any skills directly connected
to a particular productive function must be developed within the production
process and therefore represent a particularization brought about in the manner
indicated here: by the actual consumption of labor-power on the part of capital.
Skills which are not job specific must develop outside of the labor process and
do not represent the direct particularization of labor-power by capital. As we
shall see, it is the objective of the capitalist development of the production
process to eliminate all dependence upon such extrinsically given attributes of
labor, and to make labor always 'mechanical.' The process of the constitution of
wage-labor as 'unskilled' labor is implied in the nature of the capitalist production of commodities. That this result develops unevenly does not imply that
it is ineffective. In particular, the emergence within the history of capitalist
development of new types of skilled labor need not be inconsistent with the
general argument presented here, especially in so far as the emergence of skilled
labor is also the prelude to its mechanization. It needs also to be borne in mind
throughout that labor refers here to a specific social and economic relation which
may not, and indeed does not, encompass all of those activities which are
empirically gathered together under the dual categories of skilled and unskilled
labor. Much of the phenomenon currently associated with the demise of unskilled labor either (1) is not labor in the strict economic sense, or (2) is itself
giving way to the process of its constitution as fully wage-labor (see H. Braverman, *Labor and Monopoly Capital* [New York: Monthly Review Press, 1974]
part IV). The general conception of labor always entails the idea of its full
specification to the product within its productive consumption. The formation
of skills necessary to the process, to the extent that this transpires outside of the
labor process, cannot be considered systematically upon the basis of the abstract
conception of commodity production, but only upon the basis of a concrete
investigation of the structure of the labor force. This investigation must form an
element of a general theoretical treatment of the uneven development of capital
as a whole.

With the merging of labor-powers, the amount of labor is no longer limited by the quantitative proportion between the purchase of labor-power and the labor acquired in its consumption. Instead, the limitations which exist for the individual laborer as regards his capacity for labor cease to be real limitations of labor. The transcendence of the limitations which restrict the laboring for the individual worker is made possible with the constitution of laboring no longer as the activity of the laborer, but as the activity of capital. The indifference of the latter to the particularity and limitations of the individual laborer makes the labor process, as regards its extent, effectively unlimited. The approach to the limit of the capacity of any given worker involves not an impassable barrier to the continuation of the laboring process, but only the replacement of one laborer by another. So far as the temporal extent of the labor process is concerned, it is now possible for that process to continue without disruption. This, in itself, marks a tremendous extension in the productivity of the laboring. At the same time, the merging of labors overcomes the limitations of the laboring of the individual laborer not only temporally, but contemporaneously. Labor is no longer the activity of the individual, but the activity of many workers working together. To the degree that each is working as a limited part of a connected process of labor, that labor is no longer reducible to the individual activities of separate workers. Laboring cannot be done by the individual, but presupposes a mass of laborers. The intrinsic quality of the activity transcends the limitations of the worker taken by himself. As a result, it is no longer possible for the laborer alone to labor. In this respect the activity of laboring is taken away from the laborer. Now only capital can labor, since it is only the merging together of the labor of many workers, working together and simultaneously within a single connected process, which can be fully considered to constitute laboring.

III Division of labor

The equality of labors implied in the concept of abstract labor exists within production as a unity of labors. Within this unity, differences and oppositions of particular labors and laborers are suppressed in order that all labors may act together within the single process of laboring. This unity of labor impresses itself upon the labor as an intrinsic quality, so that labor can only exist within a mass of labor extended in principle without limit. Laboring is thereby constituted as an undifferentiated mass, and the force of labor in production is not limited in scope to the power and capabilities of the individual, but develops instead as the unlimited 'power of masses.'[2] Since the laboring process takes the mass of labor as its unit, it constitutes itself no longer on the basis of the individual worker as its element. The process divides itself into its constituent elements in accordance with the logic of laboring with a mass of labor. This logic is fundamentally distinct from the logic of production, where that activity is fixed by the limitations of particular workers. The interdependence of the elements of the labor process, which makes of the whole a single act, is no longer the interdependence of different laborers (although this condition also follows), but the interdependence of the elements of the labor process defined without reference to the worker *per se*.

The process of commodity production is a unity of a sequence of phases made up of a complex of specified tasks necessary to the formation of the product. These tasks find their determination not in any presupposed skills or capacities of the particular workers, but in the object of laboring – the commodity – and in the means of production as the embodiment of a technique. In this sense the logic of the process as a whole dictates its division into elements defined independently of any particularity of the workers. For this mode of operation of the productive activity it is necessary that the concrete determination of the processes and tasks presuppose the availability of labor, but not of particular types of labor. On the contrary, it is precisely to the degree that labor-power is the general capacity to do labor of all specification that it becomes possible for that specification to pass over to the means of production. Once this transfer has been accomplished it is no longer necessary for commodity production to conform to a fixed division of labor (e.g. the 'handicraft division of labor' described by Marx) developed out of the opposition of types of skills. Instead, it is the labor which is made within production to conform to a division which is established in accordance wholly with the technical requirements of the production of commodities taken as a wholly objective process. This division is a division of labor in abstraction from the laborer, and is therefore emphatically a division of abstract labor. Such a productive activity is substantively the division of labor without qualification.

The unity of laboring on the part of a mass of labor imposes, then, a complex interdependence of the elements of the labor, so that there is also an element of difference within the labor process which serves to unite not only the individual workers, but also the elements of laboring. In this case, however, the difference relates not to the particular separate workers, nor to the specification of the task of the particular worker, but to the qualitatively distinguishable elements which together compose labor. The unity of laboring, which makes the mass of labor a power within production distinct in character from that of the individual worker, does not derive from the simple summation of the capacities of separate workers. Rather, the power which develops with their unity differs in kind from that of their independent, separate activities. The overcoming of the limitations imposed by particular laborers and their capacities within production involves not only the external combination of laborers which retain those limitations, but the development of a total labor process whose constitution is indifferent to such limitations. This development is not achieved with the elementary abstraction of labor, nor with the indifference of production in principle to the particularity of the laborer. It is achieved, rather, only with the constitution of the internal logic of laboring in accordance with a principle which defines the labor process, both qualitatively and quantitatively, in terms of the power of masses. This principle is the division of labor within the production process so far as that division derives from the logic of labor constituted as the activity of a mass of laborers.

The divisions which make of the labor process the unity of distinct elements and stages are defined in connection with the production of the use-value constituted as the element of wealth and determined by its contribution to the expansion of capital. These divisions are dictated by the intrinsic requirements of the labor process viewed as a process of commodity production. Such divisions have nothing to do with differences of laborers united within production. Indeed, to the extent that such differences are retained (as is implied, for example, in the notion of the 'detail laborer')[3] there can be no full development of a division of labor, since the unity of the process is always impeded by impassable obstacles derived from original differences brought into the production process, and not determined within it and in accordance with its intrinsic objectives.

While the development of the division of labor within production cannot be considered here, that development clearly hinges essentially upon the constitution of the differences of the labor as all intrinsic to the labor and not dependent upon any external factors. Historically, such factors predominate to a greater or lesser degree so that the division of labor is not simply a division of labor, but also, or even predominantly, a division of the sexes within the family, or a division of status groups within society. These are fixed differences connected to conditions within society not given within the logic of commodity production. To the extent that the inner divisions of the production process are determined by the sexual division of the species, the object of production is not the commodity, but the continuation of the concrete unity of the social organism conceived as a unity of the sexes, therefore as a familial unit. To this degree, the distribution of productive activities is not fully a division of labor since (1) the totality which emerges with the unification of the particular productive activities is not labor as such, but the laboring family, and (2) the divisions originate not only in the logic of wealth producing activity, but also in the logic of the family structure. Once the logic of family life is merged into the production process, that process must find its determinate limits not exclusively in the generation of wealth, but also in the conditions which must be met if the renewal of the family is to be accomplished.* By contrast, what is distinctive about the productive life of capital is that the sole logic determining the process is the generation of wealth. The laboring which produces wealth is, then, divided exclusively in accordance with this object. The resulting process is laboring as such, emancipated from any determination extraneous to its abstract constitution; and the division of this process is a division of labor.

To the extent that production is subordinated to differences whose logic has nothing to do with the commodity and its defining

---

* It is precisely this condition which makes the so-called 'sexual division of labor' not a particular instance of the division of labor in general, but instead 'nothing more than a device to institute a reciprocal state of dependence between the sexes' (C. Lévi-Strauss, 'The Family,' in A. Skolnick and J. Skolnick [eds.] *Family in Transition: Rethinking Marriage, Sexuality, Child Rearing, and Family Organization* [Boston: Little, Brown & Co. 1971]).

features, it is impossible to fully constitute production as a labor process, and the result of production as the commodity. By contrast, to the degree that such extrinsic differences are suppressed within production, the latter is subject only to its own intrinsic logic in the production of the commodity. Here, the product is neither more nor less than the commodity. Where production is limited and even determined by an intrinsic logic connected to divisions and oppositions which are arbitrary so far as laboring is concerned, the product is also determined to a greater or lesser degree by the logic imposed upon its production by these extrinsic conditions. The product remains something more, or at least something other, than a commodity, since there is retained in its production a principle distinct from that which defines and determines commodity production. The commodity is also, for example, a work of art defined not simply by the logic of the labor process, but also by the personality of the immediate producer. Or, where the character of production is given in natural differences, the product may remain a natural product or substance determined by and within nature. In these cases the production process lacks the element of universality connected to the commodity and to the concept of labor. The product is, then, something other than a commodity since it has the nature of its production determined by divisions and conditions unconnected to the production of commodities, of use-value and of value. By contrast, for the product to be neither more nor less than a commodity, it is first necessary that within its production the only logic be that of the production of the commodity, the unity of the production of value and of use-value.

The division of labor within production constitutes the divided labors as mutually dependent, such that each stage of the labor process can only subsist within the process as a whole. As a result, the unity of laboring becomes a quality innate within each of its elements. The abstraction of the labor process is embedded within the particularity and opposition of its elements since the logic of the division of those elements is the conception of the process as a whole and its division. This division is without regard to any particularity of *labor*, therefore to any prior division of that labor not emergent wholly within the labor process. To the extent that the division of labor makes the unification of that labor into a single process an intrinsic necessity of its elements, the abstraction of labor develops in and through the division of labor, so that division and unity are two sides of a single process. Here, the condition for abstraction is also division into the intrinsically connected elements of a single labor process, the unity of which is achieved to the extent that its divisions are divisions connected intrinsically to the labor itself.

There is no possibility in this case for the conception of labor as a unity of opposed principles thrown together without regard to their innate interdependence. The labor is no sum of disparate principles, but the unification of differences which contain that unity as an intrinsic necessity. At the same time, the mutual dependence of labors makes the opposition of the elements of the labor process the work of a general principle which can only develop with the development of abstract labor. Abstract labor is the activity which contains the intrinsic logic which underlies its divisions into a multitude of parts and stages. The separate parts derive their differentiation from the conception of the laboring, and are to that extent dependent upon the abstraction of labor as the activity originally subject to division. The division of labor makes the unity of laboring an intrinsic necessity of each element and phase, and thereby makes the abstraction of labor a living force within each separate and distinct element of the labor process. Just as laboring must constitute a whole out of the sequence of innately interdependent elements and stages which together constitute the labor, so must the whole divide into those stages and elements if it is to be a process which is singular and unified: the process of laboring.

The constitution of the labor process as a unity of diverse but intrinsically connected movements, determined not by the particularity of the laborers but by the intrinsic logic of commodity production, requires on one side labor-power – the capacity for the abstraction of laboring – and on the other side the means of production which embody the logic of the production of the particular commodity product. The labor-power brings to production its contribution to the mass of labor, whose force is the power which is alone able to set in motion the means of production, while the latter brings with it the potential to draw out of the labor-power the commodity-producing activity. The means of production take it upon themselves to divide the labor process into the elements requisite for their own total motion, and especially for their transformation into the product. The unity of the divided labors now exists within the means of production as the logic of the production of a single commodity product.

IV The extensive and intensive limits of labor

For the laborer, the production of particular commodities is a matter of no consequence. The separation of the laborer from his labor-power, implied in the constitution of the latter as a commodity, deprives the laborer of any determination on his side of his laboring activity. It is only to the extent that laboring threatens to absorb the whole of the existence of the laborer, and to deprive him of any life outside of production, that commodity production becomes a matter of direct concern to the laborer, and the activity of commodity production comes to be considered a part of his life as a laborer. In principle, however, the labor process takes part aside from the life of the laborer. As a result, from the side of the laborer the act of laboring is something separate, something which is indifferent to him and to which he is also indifferent. In this respect the labor is *purposeless, objectless* activity. Far from the conception of subjective laboring characteristic of social thought, for which the determinacy of the activity remains always in the conscious apprehension of its end in the mind of the laborer, the subjective element within the labor process is nothing other than that abstraction from the personality of the laborer required for the constitution of his activity as laboring. To be sure, this subjective aspect has as its presupposition the constitution of the laborer as a person, determined also in terms of his personality. But here it is the abstraction from that personality which, while retaining it as a presupposition, none the less leaves it aside in the constitution of the laboring. This result is especially evident when we consider the specification of the use-value of the product as a means to the fulfilment of need. Here, the qualities which define the use-value need have no relation to the personality of the worker. For the constitution of laboring as the production of the commodity it is not even necessary that the laborer know what it is that his labor produces. On the contrary, it is precisely the absence of such knowledge which most clearly stamps his activity as labor.

Once the laboring capacity is considered without regard to the laborer, the content of the activity is also subject to definition upon a basis distinct from that given in the personality of the worker. In the purchase of labor-power capital acquires the capacity for labor defined in relation to a given period of time. In effect, capital acquires so much labor time. What transpires during that time is determined, in principle, in accordance with the object of laboring: the subsuming of wealth into its generative process. Since laboring is the productive moment of wealth, the determination of labor is an element of capital's self-determination.

For the theoretical treatment of wealth and its production it is necessary to presume throughout that the right of the purchaser to the use of the commodity which he acquires is fully recognized in all cases, including that of the purchase of labor-power. That this condition is the result of a long and protracted historical process, and in this sense by no means given, does not allow for its violation within the logical treatment of economic relations. Capitalist commodity production can only be made intelligible upon the basis of the generation within the labor process of wealth and its increment. This generation can only be considered theoretically to the degree that it is not the result of the contingent configuration of 'class forces,' but the systematically necessary result of the logic of the capital-labor relation and of the social determination of the labor process. The logic of the labor process is that of its determination in accordance with the object of the growth of capital. The labor process is therefore a determination of capital and not of the laborer. The labor process begins where the laborer is left aside and his labor-power is given over to capital as its life-giving principle. At this point the conception of commodity production proceeds without further reference to the laborer, to his will and his desires, and considers only the single overarching objective of the production process – the expansion of capital.

For the right of capital to the consumption of its property to be fully respected, it is necessary that the labor-power be separated from its determination in the personality of the laborer. This separation is not, however, a physical act. The separation of the laboring capacity from the worker is, instead, an essentially mental function carried out continuously over the period of the wage contract. While the laborer plays no part in the determination of the content of the laboring process, he plays the logically prior role, which is temporally continuous, of providing the abstraction of labor as a force within production. The juridical separation of the labor-power from the laborer is not directly synonymous with its productive separation, although the latter is necessarily implied in the former.

The force of the laborer's personality and will within production is the force required to sustain the abstraction of his laboring. In this sense, the involvement of the laborer and his personality in production is essentially negative. It is this element which is missing in the work activity of animals, which is intrinsically incapable of achieving the abstraction required for laboring, and therefore the universality implied in the objective of the process of commodity production. The limit to which the work activity of animals may be extended is thus given physically. By contrast, the limit which is effective for labor is both physical and mental. While laboring can never transcend the physical capacities of the species, this physical barrier is never, aside from the most primitive stages of the development of the productive system, the real limit which defines the extent of the laboring capacity of the individual laborer. That limit is defined mentally by the fact that the laborer must sustain, by the force of his personality, the abstraction of labor. The laboring activity cannot be determined in such a way as to endanger the continuity of this abstraction which, as a mental and physical act, has determinate limits.

The limits which are effective for the abstraction of laboring on the part of the worker are both extensive and intensive. Marx considers the former under the heading of the determination of the length of the working day, and the latter under the heading of the intensification of labor.

The extensive limits to laboring on the part of the individual laborer are not fixed simply by that point at which the physical exhaustion of the worker is immanent and his ability to labor lapses. Instead, the real limit on the extent of laboring (the length of the working period) is not physical but mental, depending upon the preservation of a part of the life-cycle of the worker for the development of his personality. There can be no abstraction from the personality and will of the worker where that personality and will are wholly suppressed. The alienability of labor-power from the laborer excludes from the outset any purchase on the part of capital of the entirety of the waking life of the worker. Violation of this condition would be tantamount to a lapse into conditions of bondage and would make the juridical recognition of the laborer's original proprietorship over his labor-power purely formal. It is precisely to the degree that the laboring process requires the abstraction of labor, and therefore the participation of the personality of the worker in this negative sense, that the laboring process cannot be allowed to absorb the entirety of the active life of the worker. This necessity is expressed in the determination of the limits which govern the length of the working period.

At the same time that the development of the personality of the worker places a limit on the extent of the working period, the actual length, for example of the working day, is not immediately determined by this upper limit. Since the length of the working period is stipulated in the wage contract as part of the recognition of the laborer's proprietorship over his labor-power, the determination of the actual magnitude of the working period involves an opposition of right: on one side that of the laborer who owns his labor-power, on the other side that of capital to strike a bargain for the acquisition of that labor-power. As Marx points out, where equal rights stand opposed, it is force which decides. The implication of this is simply that the determination of the extent of laboring provided by the individual laborer must be considered to be indeterminate so far as the conception of capital is concerned. It is necessary, then, that the conditions requisite to the development of capital, its production and growth, be fulfilled where the length of the working period is taken as externally fixed. This does not, in general, represent a real barrier to the development of capital since limits on the working period are by no means synonymous with limits on the length of the labor process.* As has been previously established, labor is not the function of the individual laborer and its limits are not defined quantitatively by the extent of the labor time provided, in any given period, by any given worker. The labor which works as capital encompasses the activity of a plurality of laborers and thereby has no limit in the capacities of the individual worker.

The essential indifference of capital to the extensive determination of the laboring of the individual laborer contrasts sharply with

---

* Nor do limits on the length of the working day represent real barriers to the productivity of capital (which Marx connects to the proportion of the labor time which goes to renew the wages bill). The fallacy in the argument by which Marx considers extension of the working day to directly imply an increase in the 'rate of surplus value' is considered below, chapter 9.

the question of the determination of the 'intensity of labor.' While the force of abstraction required for the constitution of the worker's activity as laboring places impassable limits on the mode of consumption of labor-power, within these limits the determination of the intensity of labor is not a matter of the opposition of right, and is not, therefore, in principle an arena for the struggle of will. Once the consumption of labor-power commences there can be no opposition of right, since in the alienation of his labor-power the worker has given over to capital all rights regarding its consumption. The determination of the intensity of labor is equivalently the determination of the concrete content of the process of laboring, the specific tasks involved and the pace at which they are to be executed. Given the stipulations of the wage contract the amount of laboring which is acquired by capital is fixed. What is not determined in the contract is the productivity of that labor. Since the productivity of labor is also the productivity of capital, the mode of its determination is essential to the conception of capital. At stake, in particular, is not the concrete quantitative determination of that productivity,* but the matter of principle: is the productivity of labor determined by capital, by the laborer, or in the struggle presumed to ensue within production between capital on one side and the worker on the other?

The assumption that the concrete content of laboring is determined by the worker is evidently inconsistent with the constitution of the object of production as the unlimited growth of wealth. Indeed, the idea that the laborer determines directly his productive activity implies that commodity production be made a sphere for the realization of his personality. The product becomes, in this case, the objectification of the personality of the worker and not a commodity. Any contribution of this product to the wealth of society is purely accidental (just as the valuation of a work of art has nothing to do with the objective conditions, for example the

---

* The characteristic manner in which the productivity of labor develops in the course of capitalist expansion (which Marx considers under the heading of 'production of relative surplus-value') cannot properly be considered in the context of the abstract investigation of production in general. The way in which capital accumulation brings about an increase in the productivity of labor, and the effect which that increase has on continuing growth, can only be considered upon the basis of the conception of the system of economic relations as a whole (which constitutes the subject-matter of volume II of the present work).

costs, of its production). Thus to proceed on the basis of the determination of the productive consumption of labor-power by the worker is tantamount to the obliteration of the notion of labor-power, of the universality of laboring, and ultimately of the whole of the conception of commodity production. It is apparent that the conditions implied in the purchase and sale of labor-power are fundamentally irreconcilable with this conception of laboring.

The determination of the content of laboring must necessarily pass over to capital if the production process is to be constituted as the basis upon which the growth of capital is sustained. And, indeed, the productivity of the process, the quantity of commodities producible within a given period of time, is built into the means of production as a pre-determined magnitude, or, at least, as a magnitude which is fixed within certain objectively determinable limits. The part of wealth which exists as capital has a latent productivity (or productive potential) which it is the purpose of labor-power to realize in the form of a production process. Labor-power, then, brings to life this productivity but does not determine it.

Given the latent determination of the content of the laboring within the productive apparatus, the sphere which remains for conflict over the nature and pace of work is made strictly subordinate to the inner constitution of production in accordance with the objective of the generation of wealth. Any struggle which ensues, for example over the pace of work, does so upon the presupposition that the expansion of capital is the objective of production. The parameters of the 'struggle within the workplace' are therefore dictated by capital's determination of laboring. To this extent, the productivity of labor is not a proper object of struggle between the laborer and his employer. Indeed, were this productivity to be made contingent upon the counterposition of forces between worker and capitalist, the growth of capital which is made possible – and which is quantitatively limited – by its productivity, would be completely accidental. In particular, there could be no way in which capital could assure to itself the production of the means to its continued development, so that the production of those means could not be considered as subject to necessary laws which could be grasped theoretically. The theoretical standpoint with regard to the conception of production is always that of the determination of laboring within the self-generative process of capital.*

The participation of capital within the production process as a subjective agency ('management') responsible for the direct exercise of the rights obtained in the wage contract is not necessitated by any opposition of right existent within production. The problem of management is not, in principle, a matter of the struggle over control of the labor process (which, aside from specific historical conditions, is not at issue), but a question of the concrete manner in which capital exercises its right to determine the mode of consumption of labor-power.† The abstraction required on the part of the worker if he is to sustain his laboring activity has its only purpose, so far as the worker is concerned, in the fulfilment of the wage-contract. The extent of the struggle over the conditions of work rests, therefore, not upon the primordial and inviolable right of the laborer to the purely subjective determination of labor (which is implied in the notions of the 'alienation' and 'degradation' of labor), but upon the extent to which both worker and capitalist fully acknowledge the substance of the contractual obligations which sustain the system of property rights. To the extent that the buying and selling of labor-power alone makes possible the grounding of property within its own characteristic production process, the recognition of the contractual obligations entered into in the wage-contract is the condition *sine qua non* of the subsistence

---

* Thus, the idea that the production of commodities, and especially of surplus-value, is directly a matter of the 'control' exerted by capital (in the form, for example, of 'management') over the will of the laborer excludes any theoretical treatment of the production of wealth, replacing the theoretically necessary conception with the indeterminacy of an empirically presupposed struggle of wills.

† The problem of 'scientific management' is essentially one of establishing historically (1) the concrete content of the laboring process and therefore the nature of the commodity acquired in the purchase and sale of labor-power, and (2) the right of capital to the full determination of laboring. This also entails the historical and practical determination of the physical and mental limits which bound the abstraction of laboring on the part of the worker. The real limits which restrict the intensification of labor are not given physically and must therefore develop historically. This historical development, and the struggles which it entails, do not however impinge directly upon the conception of the production process and cannot be adequately considered at the present level of abstraction. For a descriptive account of the historical role played by scientific management in the realization of labor's innate universality, see H. Braverman, *Labor and Monopoly Capital* (New York: Monthly Review Press, 1974).

of the relations of civil society. The conception of commodity production proceeds, therefore, upon the presupposition that property rights are recognized and contractual obligations met.

There is nothing in the abstract conception of capital in general which makes impossible the fulfilment of the wage-contract. In particular, there is nothing in the conception of the laborer which is violated by the idea of the purchase and sale of labor-power. On the contrary, to the extent that the only property owned by the worker is his labor-power, its alienation in exchange is essential to his constitution as a property owner. This holds so long as that exchange accepts the limitations, both extensive and intensive, of the separation of labor-power from the laborer. Were the full development of capital to be intrinsically impossible within these limits, then, indeed, capitalist development would stand in opposition to its own productive foundation. This possibility cannot, however, be considered at the level of analysis of capital in general. For the latter the problem is solely to ascertain the determinate limits directly implied in the idea of commodity production. These limits pertain to the extensive and intensive development of laboring but do not in themselves constitute absolute barriers either to commodity production *per se*, or to the self-development of capital.

CHAPTER SIX

The self-generative
process of wealth

I The productive unity of capital

1 The means of production

The division of the labor process in accordance with the concrete requirements of commodity production originates neither within the personality of the laborer, nor within his labor-power. It is, instead, capital which divides the labor in accordance with the necessities bound up with the production of wealth. The whole of the specification of the commodity to the fulfilment of a particular need resides neither in the mind of the laborer, nor in his labor-power, but in the wealth which stands in opposition to the laborer. The idea of the product resides not in the mind of the laborer, but in the objective mechanism which he confronts as the productive means. This mechanism embodies the idea of the product in the form of a sequence of determinate movements brought to life by the mass of labor collected together in production. This objective mechanism, the means of labor embodying the idea of the product, is the machine. In the opposition of machine to labor-power, which precedes their unification in the labor process, there is also an opposition of labor-power to the conception of its product. For the constitution of labor in its full indifference to the particularity of the use-value which it produces, it is necessary to displace the specification of the laboring to the use-value from the labor-power to the means of production. This displacement brings with it a polarization: on one side is the labor-power, deprived of any specification to and conception of the particular product; on the other side is the machine, which contains as a potential latent within it the specification of the production process according to the stages and elements requisite to the production of a particular commodity.

The unity of labor-power with the means of production in the activity of commodity production requires that the general capacity for laboring be integrated into the process of the production of the particular commodity. This integration is not determined on the side of the labor-power by its self-constitution in accordance with the elements of the production of the use-value. The total laboring process is, instead, specified to the generation of the particular commodity product by the inner determination of the means of production, especially the machine. The machine identifies the laboring with the particular commodity product. There is, then, no division of the activity of the worker in accordance with the twofold determination of commodity production (i.e. into 'abstract' and 'concrete, useful' labor).* To the extent that the idea of useful labor implies that the labor-power provides its own concrete deter-

---

* Marx first considers useful labor simply in terms of the two-fold nature of the commodity which, he correctly argues, must reflect itself within the commodity's production process as a two-fold determination of that process. At the same time, however (see especially *Capital* [New York: International Publishers, 1967] vol. I, pp. 41–6), Marx tends to consider the two-fold determination of the process of commodity production wholly on the side of the laborer. Indeed, Marx presents the duality of the laboring (as 'concrete useful' and 'abstract' labor) prior to any conception of the determinacy of the means of production and their contribution to the commodity product. This discovery of the concrete specification of the labor within the labor taken without regard to the determinacy of its relation to capital, provides the basis for the notion that abstract labor develops out of the generalization from, or the averaging of, particular useful labors. Labor in general is thereby made derivative of an empirically presupposed particularity of labors. Furthermore, labor, since it provides for the determination of the use-value independently of the conception of the machine, must do so as a result of its specification to the intentions of the laborer. As a result of this, useful labor becomes the purposive activity of the worker, forming the materials of labor into the product in accordance with his own subjective intention rather than according to the idea already embedded in the objective mechanism of the machine. Once, however, the specification of laboring on the part of the means of production is fully grasped, the notion of useful labor becomes redundant since it simply repeats the determination of laboring in accordance simultaneously with the value and use-value of the product. This simultaneous determination is already implied in the idea of the labor process so long as that is the idea of the unity of the labor-power with the means of production and not of the subjective activity of the laborer.

mination to the production of the particular product, that idea violates essentially the conception of commodity production.

The purposelessness of the laboring for the laborer (whose own purpose in laboring is the purely external one of fulfilling the wage-contract) is implied in the indifference of his labor-power to any specification of the particularity of the commodity product by the worker's own act. For this abstraction to be achieved, however, it is not sufficient that the laborer be deprived of the means of labor and confront in the market the proprietor of the means of production as an independent commodity owner. While this condition is necessary to the full development of social labor, it remains purely formal until the production process is itself determined intrinsically in accordance with its capitalistic character. Within production, capital confronts labor-power as one of capital's own elements. It is necessary, in this case, given the abstraction which effects the separation of the labor-power from all specificity to a particular commodity product, that the labor-power, in order that it produce commodities, be united with the principle which by consuming labor-power concretizes commodity production and connects it to the particular commodity product. This principle resides on the side of the means of production to the extent that those means of production embody the idea of the commodity in all its complexity. The means of production which work with labor are, then, no mere tools or implements of labor, but the total mechanism necessary to the specification of the labor process in terms of the production of the commodity. For the latter, the purpose of the laboring resides neither in the consciousness of the laborer nor in the consciousness of the owner of the capital, but within the capital itself, so far as that capital emerges in the form of a labor process uniting labor-power with the means of production in the form of machinery. This makes the object of the labor process wholly internal to it, rather than a matter of external imposition or of subjective intention. The nature of production is severed equally from the subjective intentions of the laborer and from those of the owner of capital. For the constitution of the process in its full integrity neither personality need intervene.

The labor-power, by activating the productive mechanism, draws out the productive potential latent within the part of wealth existing as capital. The means of production, on its side, by contributing to the process of production its concrete determination to the commodity product as a use-value, gives to the laboring its specific form, its determinate divisions and phases, and the sequence and pace with which the materials are transformed into the product. In this sense, while the labor-power brings out the inner productive capacity of the machine, the machine draws the laboring activity out of the laborer and makes that laboring activity its own productive existence. Thus, as Marx points out, the machine extracts the labor from the worker and, in effect, provides for laboring its concrete determination as a specific set of movements. The labor-power activates the machine, but, at the same time, the laboring is nothing but the machine in its active life, so that it can be said that the machine also activates the labor-power by fixing the concrete mode of its consumption.

The objectivity of the productive mechanism is the reflection within production of its determination as the generative moment in the expansion of value. The potential for the quantitatively unlimited extension of the production process exists latent within the instrument of labor. The means of production are determined in their relation to the production of the particular use-value. But they are not determined in relation to this particular unit of that use-value. In this sense the relation of the instruments of labor to the use-value of the product is already abstract and possesses an intrinsic indifference to the particular unit of the product. This indifference is represented in the capacity of the means of production to produce the particular use-value over and over again. The instruments of labor are determined, then, in relation not to the particular unit of product but to the idea which determines that unit and which is to that degree abstract with regard to it. The idea of the product embedded in the use-value of the instruments of labor is able to realize itself not in this or that particular unit of product, but indifferently in an endless, or at least extended, repetition of the production of particular units of the product. In this sense the means of production produce not simply the particular use-value but the use-value as the element of wealth.

At the same time, the idea of the use-value, which is embodied in the instruments of labor, must realize itself in a sequence of particular products. The productive consumption of the means of production, therefore, entails the forming of a series of individual products. For this the instrument is, by itself, insufficient, since it brings with it only the potential for commodity production. This potential, in order that it find its embodiment in the particular unit of product, must be the governing principle in the production of a product which is separable from the means of production. This substance, which separates from the machine as its individual product, contains, in its singularity, a principle which opposes that which governs the construction of the machine. The substance which becomes the product is not an element of the machine, but an external material which passes through the mechanism of production and is formed into the product. These external substances which come to exist as the particular products by being formed in production are the materials of labor.

As the essentially passive substance which is made into the product, the material comes into the production process as a use-value which is more general in its specification than is the product. The productive consumption of the materials of labor is also their specification to the use-value produced. In this respect, the process of commodity production fulfils the useful potential within the materials. The original use-value of the materials is connected, then, to the latent potential which they possess to become the various particular use-values. Their original use is wholly their transformation into, and therefore their further specification to, the particular product.

The fact that the materials of labor can only fully realize their utility in their productive consumption does not imply that, prior to production, they are provided directly by nature. On the contrary, the higher the level of development of commodity production, the more the materials of labor are themselves produced with the specific end of their productive consumption, and further, the more the materials of labor come themselves to be made specific to particular production processes. Inputs of wood become inputs of specific types of wood treated in particular ways. Or, inputs of wood become inputs of metal or plastic of very detailed specification in accordance with their productive consumption in a single or limited number of production processes. With this development, the true 'raw material' becomes less and less adequate to any productive use and comes to be replaced in every instance with an input which is itself a commodity product.

The raw materials, to the degree that they are provided not by commodity production but by nature, contain no hint of the determination of the use-value. Were the raw materials, as the

products of nature, immediately useful, the production of commodities would be unnecessary. It would be nature which provided
directly for the needs of the members of society by providing for
those needs the requisite 'resources' which are, ultimately, alone
capable of their satisfaction. By contrast, for socially determined
need, the material substance provided by nature is wholly inadequate and ultimately useless. Since the use-value fulfils a need
not given directly in nature, neither can its production be provided
immediately within nature. The specification of the use-value
outside of nature takes place within the system of use-values and
particularly within the production process of the commodity.
Since the product is not given by nature, neither is its production
process naturally determined. The latter must be specified, so far
as the use-value of its product is concerned, not by any natural
principle or substance but wholly within the system of productive
activities. The means of production, since they also determine the
product as a use-value, cannot be derived immediately from
nature. Any direct derivation of the means of production, including
the materials of labor, from nature is the penetration of a natural
principle into the production process of the commodity. The more
the process of production is adequate to its end in the commodity,
the less can that process be the activity of the transformation of a
fixed natural substance. The retention of the latter is always the
retention of a natural principle within the process of production
and, therefore, also within the product.

A true raw material is provided immediately by nature as one of
nature's own elements. It is, therefore, necessarily of no use (it has
no use-value). Since the raw material is of no use it is also of no
value. A true raw material is, therefore, inherently without a
price. Only when it becomes a commodity does it take on a value,
and it becomes a commodity because it is *not* provided by nature
but produced (at the very least extracted from its natural condition). However, into the process of its own generation as a use-
value the raw material does not enter as itself an input. Thus, even
in the process of its own extraction and constitution as a use-value,
the raw material does not constitute a natural input into a social
production process. To be a commodity, the raw material must be
made into something useful. Since the raw material, taken by
itself, is neither useful nor valuable, it is not itself a commodity
input into any production process. Raw materials are, then,

excluded from the economic category of materials of labor.* They contribute to the determination of neither the use-value nor the value of the commodity products.

The specification of the use-value of the product is the consumption of particular use-values, the means of production. These particular use-values fall into two categories: the mechanism of production or machine, and the materials. The former is the embodiment of the idea of the product taken in abstraction from its realization in a series of particular commodity products, the latter is the embodiment of the individual units of the commodity product. Neither the machine nor the materials limit the production process to a fixed quantity of products. The machine is always the basis for the production of a multitude of the same product or of a limited range of connected products. The materials of labor, while their own units are specific to particular units of the product, do not in any way limit the scale of production as far as they are acquired in accordance with a determination of the magnitude of production, which is never given in the specification of the materials themselves. The materials of labor neither determine nor limit the scale of production (except under the most abnormal conditions), but are determined in their own consumption by the determination of the scale of production.

2 The factory and its product

The locus of the unity of the labor-power with the means of production is the factory, and commodity production fully developed as such is factory production. The factory considered not as an inert complex of equipment, but as a living entity, is the productive existence of capital. The commodity which is produced

---

* The determination of the price of the product in relation to the costs of the necessary inputs may involve, in the case of the constitution of the raw material as a material adequate to commodity production, the element of rent. This element is traditionally considered to reflect the original and irreducible value of the raw materials themselves, and especially their 'scarcity.' The real determination of the price of ostensibly 'raw materials' (which are, in reality, commodity products of an extractive process) does entail the element of rent under certain specific circumstances. It by no means follows from this, however, that the rent together with the price of the material produced (extracted) is determined by any primordial natural condition of 'scarcity.' This aspect of the system of prices will be considered in volume II of the present work.

by capital is also distinguished by this characteristic point of origin. It is not the labor-power or the machine which produces the commodity, but their unity. The full objectivity of the product, and therefore its universality as a commodity, is connected to its constitution as a factory product. The very idea of factory production is the idea of a product retaining no ties whatever to the intentions of its producer whether that producer is considered to be the capitalist or the laborer. Instead the producer is the total and objective mechanism of the factory.

For the factory, repetition of production without alteration of the product, and extension of production quantitatively, are intrinsic characteristics. Since the determination of the qualitative character of the product is the result of the objective mechanism of the factory, uniformity of production is raised in factory production to an entirely new level. This uniformity marks the product as a use-value in no way connected to the specific desires of its consumer as this particular individual. Just as production is disconnected from the intentions of the laborer, it is effectively disconnected as well from the intentions of the consumer of the product. Just as the product becomes objective and uniform as the result of the objectivity of its production process, that process develops into production for a consumer who is also objective and uniform. The consumer of the products of factory production is the consumer of products which are in no way tailored to his particular personality and uniquely defined whims. Needs fulfilled in this way display an objectivity and universality which determine the individuality of the needy individual in accordance with the total mechanism of capitalist production. Thus, the consumer must come to define his own needs as fully objective. The needs which substantiate the individuality of the consumer exist for him as the means to his concrete determination as an individual only through their objective social determination, which is without regard for his particular personality and his uniquely defined desires. Need takes on its fully objective, social determination, and determination of the need as of the means to its fulfilment are taken out of the hands of the producer on one side and of the consumer on the other.

The subjectivity of individual need as the pursuit of the self-constitution of the person in accordance with the dictates of his personality cannot express itself immediately within the commodity and its consumption. Indeed, the very contingency of individual need can only be realized in relation to a complex system of commodities produced without regard to the particular individual. The multiplication of needs and of the means to their fulfilment into an ever-expanding complex can alone make possible the individuation of consumption. The result of the multiplication of needs and commodities is that while each remains objectively determined without regard to the whims of particular individuals, the total system of commodities is established as the sphere within which the purely subjective elements of personality are able to find expression. Thus, the individual 'consumer' discovers in the market place an endless variety of objects which are produced by the wholly objective process of factory production, yet are provided as the material basis for the expression of the most subjective elements of his personality.

The need fulfilled by the products of capital have a real determination within the life-cycle of capital. This determination involves a universality which implies an expansion and multiplication of need without limit. Such needs are characteristic of civil society and mark the determination of the species as a social rather than natural condition. This multiplication and expansion of need and of the means to its fulfilment is not, however, the simple extension of needs and means already determined. On the contrary the needs are determined by their inherent multiplication and expansion; that is to say, the needs fulfilled within civil society are illimitable in so far as they are not tied in their specification to particular producers and particular consumers. On the side of production, the commodity products of capital are not determined by the subjective intentions of the producer, and are not therefore limited by the limitations of conception accessible to the individual producer. On the side of consumption, this objectivity is retained as an essential condition. It is reflected in the uniformity which is expected, by the consumer, of the products of factory production. This uniformity, far from violating the individuality of the consumer, is made the objective basis for the expression of that individuality. This condition, on the side of the fulfilment of need, makes it possible to produce commodities without immediate reference to their particular consumers. Even the most intensive market research, aimed at isolating the defining characteristics of the potential consumers of a particular product, rests originally upon the objectification of the consumer, and indeed, realizes that to the highest degree.

The condition that commodity production transpire without any immediate determination to the particular consumer is the condition of production for the market. The anonymity and objectivity of the market is reflected in the anonymity and objectivity of production. These conditions are realized in the determination of the use-value of the product, which is defined by this same anonymity and objectivity. These conditions also break down limitations in production derived from market limitations in consumption, and make the repetition of production without alteration of the product possible and necessary.

Factory production is production which is intrinsically for the market. Equally, production for the market can only fully develop as factory production. The development of wealth is tied, therefore, to a development in the intrinsic determination of need and its constitution as an objective social quality. This determination exists as a principle within production when production transpires without regard for the particularity of either producer or consumer. With factory production the illimitability of production and consumption – illimitability both in extent and in qualitative determination – becomes a real possibility. Production becomes, for the first time, fully determined in accordance with its objective in the generation of wealth. This qualitative determination of use-value within the factory makes that determination internal to the process of the self-development of capital. It is this condition which makes possible the whole development of capitalist production and its self-constitution in the form of a world market and a system of factory production for that world market.

II The production of wealth

I The illimitability of production

The active force within the labor process is capital existing as the labor-power and the means of production whose unity is made subordinate to the preservation and expansion of wealth. The labor process is the mode of existence of capital within the activity of commodity production, and the commodity is the product of capital.

For capital, the production of commodities has as its objective the expansion of value, and for this the production of a particular use-value is nothing more than the necessary means. The product as a use-value has the capacity for the fulfilment of a particular need, but not of the particular need which is the real objective of its production. The production of the commodity is the means to the acquisition of money, since in the transformation of the product into money capital makes possible the renewal of production and its renewal on an expanded basis. For the acquisition of money, it is insufficient that the product have a use; it must also be inter-changeable within the system of commodities. In its production the product must not only be endowed with a particular use-value, it must also acquire the value requisite to its making a contribution to the expansion of value. As a use-value, then, the product must be given a particular determination which opposes it to the system of use-values; as a commodity the product must also be indifferent to the fulfilment of particular need. The production process must, therefore, in order that it become adequate to its real objective, go beyond the production of the particular use-value. This overcoming of the limitedness of the particular product begins with the multi-plication of productions and particularly with the production of a multitude of particular products. The production process is, then, not restricted to the particular use-value in that it produces that use-value repeatedly, and therefore it is not limited to the com-pletion of the production of the single use-value. Commodity production conceived as a process of the production of wealth is the process of the repeated production of the use-value, and there-fore of the production of the use-value beyond its intrinsic limit.

This extension of the production process establishes the product as of no use to the producer except in so far as it becomes, for that producer, the means to the acquisition of wealth. In this respect the endless repetition of the production of the particular use-value is the production of wealth. The process as a whole has, then, the following aspects: First, taken as a process of the expansion of capital the production of commodities is production continued without limit. This entails the production of particular com-modities, but is not limited by the production of any particular commodity or by a fixed sum of commodities. For this end, the labor process must incorporate a mass of labor extensible temporally and contemporaneously in accordance with the objective of the expansion of capital The production of the particular commodity is only a quantitatively limited part of a process, the totality of which extends without limit. This extensibility without regard to its intrinsic divisions is not the contribution of the laborer to production, but the constitution of his laboring as an element of capital. Second, the labor process is a process of the production of particular commodities and cannot transcend the limits entailed in that production except by passing through the production of the particular commodity as its element. The illimitability of commodity production always presupposes 'the production of the commodity in its particularity. This is the same labor process conceived in terms of the elements of the laboring which make it also limited. It is the unity of these limited and determined elements which makes possible the movement of laboring beyond the limits given in the production of a particular commodity.

Production of commodities begins as production of use-values without limit. This capacity for unlimited extension of production is latent within the means of production. The realization of this potential requires that the means of production be employed for a period determined without regard to the production of the particular commodity. This entails the unification of the means of production with a principle which (1) activates the productive apparatus, and (2) represents directly the extension of its use without regard to the production of the individual use-value. It is essential, that is, not only that the productive apparatus be made active, but also that the principle which has this as its end be endowed with a universality which activates the means of production to the end of the limitless production of commodities. This principle is labor-power and its productive existence – labor. Labor is the determination, within the production process, of the extension of that process beyond the limit of the production of the particular use-value, and, ultimately, without any limit in the production of use-values. Labor-power, in its consumption, constitutes the production process as the process of the production of value.

The labor-power is intrinsically unconnected to the production of any given use-value, and is, therefore, related indifferently as the potential to produce a world of use-values. This potential reflects itself within the production process as a determination of that process without regard to the intrinsic limitations which define the production of the use-value. The labor-power is in this respect also connected to the repetition of the production of the product and therefore to the production of a continuous stream of products. For the labor-power, its consumption involves its connection to the process of the repeated production of a particular use-value. It is in this repetition that the real object of production makes itself felt and that, in particular, the indifference of production to the particular use-value is made explicit. The unity of the labor-power with the means of production is, then, a process which can be considered without regard to its divisions in accordance with the requirements of the production of the particular use-value. The labor process is the multiplication of the single production of the individual unit. This multiplication, in so far as its extent is unconnected to the fulfilment of need, reflects the inner determination of production according to a principle which goes beyond the particular unit. The production of wealth is, first, this going beyond the particular unit, which movement rests originally upon the determination of that unit as a use-value. The capacity for this movement beyond the limitations in the production of the use-value constitutes the production process in its full continuity and in terms of its real objective. This is the process of production as the process of the production of wealth without limit. The production process, considered as so much laboring extended according to the law of the increase of capital and not of the production of the use-value, is the process of the production of value.

Laboring produces value by producing use-values beyond any limitation in the use-value: first by repeated production of the use-value, and then by extended production of the use-value without any reference to need or to the particular unit by which it is fulfilled. The law of the production process which governs its extension is the law of the production of value and of capital. There is, in the production of commodities, no mysterious intervention of value production proceeding, as it were, alongside the production either of the use-value or of the product as a materially defined entity. On the contrary, the process of production, conceived as a social labor process, eventuates in commodities and only in commodities. In this sense, the laboring brings into existence the commodity and its determinate features. The labor process produces use-values as the means to the production of value and constitutes the use-value of the product as the unit of wealth, therefore as a value.

On one side, the value does not simply attach itself to the use-value which is produced within the production process as an extrinsic quality unconnected to either the use-value or its production. Indeed, the production of value is, in the first instance, nothing more than the repeated production of the use-value. At the same time the production of the use-value is determined by its existence as the element of wealth, so that the repetition of production is possible only because the use-value has an intrinsic character which is expressed in its multiplication and expansion. This intrinsic character is the contribution of the use-value to the wealth of society, therefore its value. The production process, considered in terms of the production of wealth, is laboring taken without reference to the limitations of the single unit of the product. The concept of labor is the concept of commodity production taken in the abstract, production considered in its full universality without consideration for any specification to *this* commodity product. In this sense labor time is time expended producing wealth in its full universality. This time includes the production of the multitude of use-values: it includes the generation of the use-value as the means to the fulfilment of need and as a component of wealth. But it includes that production indifferently, exclusively in terms of its contribution to wealth taken as a total.

The labor process viewed as the unity of the means of production and the labor-power, each considered solely as parts of the capital advanced and abstracted from the particular useful product, is the process of the production of value. Value, considered as a product or result, is value situated within its process of generation, therefore value existing as capital. The principle of production is value existing in process, the result is value existing fixed into the product. The value which is present as an active force within production is the unity of the means of production with labor-power. Labor-power in its consumption is the principle which activates the entire process without regard to any limit in the particular use-value and individual unit of product. The abstract unity of the means of production and labor-power constituted in this way is the laboring which produces the value of the commodity. This laboring is not the isolated activity of the laborer. It is

the unity of labor-power and the means of production both constituted as the active, productive life of capital within the process of
its self-expansion.

The production of the use-value breaks the labor up into
elements which correspond to the set of tasks which together
eventuate in the particular commodity product. The process is
itself measured in units which correspond to the bundle of activities
which constitute the use-value, one unit of the process corresponding to the production of one unit of the use-value produced.
Within the unit, the process is composed not of equivalent elements
measured quantitatively, but of discrete elements linked as separate
stages within a single unified process. Production of value, by
contrast, is indifferent to the qualitative ruptures in the production
of the discrete use-values, the units of the product. In contrast to
the production process considered in terms of the use-value of the
product, laboring considered as the production of value is indifferent to all aspects of its process which are inseparably connected to
the particularity of the use-value produced. Labor, in the production of value, is, in this respect, homogeneous. The value represented within production is the measure of the production process
taken without regard to its division into the separate functions
requisite to the production of the use-value.

The abstraction which determines the laboring activity as having
for its product the value of the commodity must also be considered
with respect to the means of production and materials. It is an
abstraction, that is, which affects not only what the worker does
immediately, but also the instruments with which he works. So far
as the labor process is considered purely 'n terms of its dimension,
the contribution of the means of production must equally be
conceived in abstraction from the use-value to which their production is specified.

Leaving aside the specification of the means of production
implies taking the instruments and materials of labor not in their
determination to the particular commodity product, but simply as
so much capital invested in the production of wealth. The means
of production enter into the process already fixed in their commodity character as a unity of value and use-value. As a use-value
the means of production are instrumental in the specification of the
relation of the commodity product to the fulfilment of a particular

need. The consumption of the means of production translates the use-value into the product. At the same time this consumption, which consumes the means of production, is the consumption of their value. For the expansion of value this event must also be taken into account. The means of production, taken without reference to their particular use-value, enter into production as a fixed quantity of capital-value. This quantity is fixed in the relation of exchange which effects the acquisition of the productive inputs and which makes them part of the capital existing within the production process. The process of commodity production, as a process of the production of value, must be considered as a process not only of the consumption of labor-power but also of the means of production. The abstraction by which the process of the production of the use-value is made to transcend the limitations which define the generation of the particular product and its unit, affects both the labor-power and the means of production. The latter produces the particular use-value and in so doing is itself consumed. This consumption of the means of production is also the consumption of the value of the capital expended in their acquisition. In so far as the expansion of value is an extension of its preservation, the determination of the exchange-value of the product must also account for the consumption of the means of production and therefore not only for the commodity produced but also for the condition – the consumption of capital-value expended – which makes possible commodity production.

At the same time, the labor process conceived as the activity within which the means of production are productively consumed cannot directly account for either the value of the productive means or for the relation of that value to the value of the product. In particular, any presumption that by positing the value of the commodity product as a result of the labor process, that process also posits the valuation of the means of production (for example in accordance with a rule of labor time) is completely arbitrary. For the conception of the development of the product out of its production, the conception of the productive inputs is essential. This involves the determination of the nature of those inputs in accordance with the requirements of commodity production. The generation of the necessary inputs, and especially their valuation, is not, however, thereby made determinate. For the conception of the labor process it is the distinction between productive means and product which is essential. Any conception of the immediate valuation of the means of production obliterates this distinction and thereby undermines essentially the determinacy of the conception of the commodity production process.*

2 *Labor and value*

It by no means follows from the analysis of the labor process that the value produced is either proportional to the labor time expended or determined by that labor time. The production of the commodity must have, intrinsic to it, a principle of universality with reference to which the production of the use-value can proceed without limitation in the particular use-value. That process considered in terms of this illimitability is the production process as so much laboring, so much commodity-producing activity. The laboring which produces commodities is not, however, the production process conceived as the determination of the laborer, of his will and his subjective intentions. The labor process is, instead, the productive unity of capital considered as the process of the production of wealth without limit, therefore of value. In this respect, while labor produces value, in that laboring is capital's value-producing process, it is by no means implied that the quantity of value produced bears any fixed relation to the simple extent of the labor time. Such a result would only be implied where the sole aspect of its production which is relevant to the determination of the product as the component of wealth is the laborer's time taken in the abstract. This would place the determination of value in labor time by placing it within the laboring considered not as an element of capital, but as the work of the laborer. However, once laboring is considered as the productive moment of capital, it cannot be attributed to the laborer as his activity, and its pure extent cannot be the exclusive determinant of its productivity. The significance of the conception of commodity production as a labor process lies not in its immediate determination of the magnitude of the value of the commodity, but in the manner in which the determination of the distinctive features of production makes possible the determination of commodity production as a universal and extensible process.

---

* This aspect of the treatment of capitalist commodity production is considered more concretely below, chapter 9.

The significance of the labor theory of value taken in this sense was clearly grasped by Ricardo, who begins his analysis of value with the intimate connection between the illimitability of production and the possibility of increasing the product by extending the sum of labor expended. Ricardo begins, that is, with that conception of production implied in the notion that commodities may, through repeated production, be multiplied 'almost without assignable limit, if we are disposed to bestow the labour necessary to obtain them.'[1] This illimitability of production is embedded in the nature of the production process, and it is to the determination of the latter that the labor theory of value points the direction. At the same time, to equate value with labor time is to subsume the most concrete determination of commodity exchange into the most general conception of the commodity and its production. The failure of this conception is to be found not simply in the inconsistency of exchange-value and labor time, but in the impossibility of any concrete determination of exchange-value within the conception of the direct production process where the latter develops on the basis of the abstraction from the concrete conditions bound up with the circuit of capital and the total system of commodity exchanges. It is only within the conception of the system of economic relations as a whole that the full determination of the value relation can finally be considered.

III The theoretical analysis of value

1 Labor and property

The idea of value is connected originally to that of property rights, and value represents the quantitative measure of property taken as such. For this conception, any notion of the production of the value, and therefore of the real determination of its magnitude, is excluded. The advance which is marked by the Lockean notion of the origin of property in labor consists wholly in the development of the idea that property and value are determined by a process of generation. Out of this idea there emerges the notion of value as an intrinsic quality of the object independent of the whims of its owner. Property becomes objective to its owner in that it is connected to an objective process of generation. For Locke, however, this objective process of the origin of property becomes a purely subjective act on the part of the isolated individual.[2] In this respect Locke loses the idea, previously established by Hobbes, that the subsistence of property and of property rights can only be within a system of reciprocal recognition of rights, therefore within a social order. With the elimination of the connection of right to its recognition, the social determination of property and of the process of its generation is made impossible. Locke deduces the notion of labor immediately from that of the proprietorship of man over his body and over the work of his body, its physical functions. Proprietorship is thereby constituted as a physical function, and individuality is made also a physical condition. This makes labor objective only as a physical activity and subjective only in its personal aspect. The labor which is natural bodily activity separates its product from nature, making it the laborer's private property, and endowing the laborer with the right over it.

The inadequacy of this conception derives from its constitution of property as the unmediated relation of the individual to the result of his private laboring. What makes something property is not its embodiment of a purely subjective or purely physical laboring, but its recognition as the embodiment of the will of its owner, and therefore the simultaneous recognition of that owner as substantively a property owner. The laboring activity does, however, *make property* in that it makes that which is worthy of being appropriated. Locke confuses these two aspects, confusing that which *makes* property worthy of being property with that which *makes* property. He confuses, therefore, the most abstract conception of property rights with the conception of their concrete determination within an original process. Since this makes labor equivalent to the recognition of right and the embodiment of will, it also makes labor a purely subjective and personal matter connected not to the system of economics relation, but to the self-constitution of the immediate self-subsistent person. To this extent the Lockean notion of property and labor fails to establish the productive basis for the development of a scientific conception of economic life.

This failure is clearly established in the conclusion drawn from the identification of labor with the abstract relation of the self-subsistent person. For Locke, the principle of labor and property is shown to be not the principle of the full development of wealth, as in the *Wealth of Nations*, but a principle of the limitation of wealth. The reason for this is implied in the idea that right extends only to that which can be used immediately by the direct producer. This follows from the identification of wealth with the fulfilment of fixed, nature-given needs, and clearly betrays the absence of any concept of value. This limitation of right is then embedded in the labor so that right extends only to those substances provided by the immediate labor of the private and independent producer. This makes the connection of labor to property a principle of the limitation of right and allows Locke to circumvent the Hobbesian conception of the state of nature as one in which the rights of man extend over all things.

The implication of the Hobbesian standpoint is the more profound in that it is seen to imply that the limitation of right is not to be found externally, in the physical functions of the individual, but within the subsistence of right, which can only sustain itself in its self-renunciation. By taking the illimitability of right as his starting point, Hobbes is led to consider the renunciation of right as the only means by which right can be made determinate. The renunciation of the right to all things entails the recognition of the rights of others. It is only on the basis of this recognition that property rights are able to subsist. Otherwise the right of every man to all things must immediately imply the reciprocal denial and violation of right. The illimitability of the right of each entails a mutual opposition of right such that the negation of right is always implied in the form which it adopts. Thus for Hobbes, the recognition of property rights is established as a substantive end in itself in that it is implied in the sustenance of the system of relations of freely contracting persons. By contrast, for Locke right is limited not by the rights of others (at least not explicitly) but by need and labor directly. The right is limited by the need of the individual who has the right to appropriate only that which he can himself produce and consume. Property becomes the means to the satisfaction of fixed needs, given independently of the system of reciprocal recognition of property-owning persons. As a result, the laboring connected to property becomes the principle not of the unlimited extension of need and wealth, but of their limitation. With this notion Locke has made impossible any conception of the type of need characteristic of civil society and of the inner nature of the wealth which is the substance of its satisfaction. The Lockean conception fails to establish the possibility and necessity for an economic science in its denial of the illimitability of need and of the connection of property to its concrete determination within civil society. Locke fails to grasp the connection of the idea of property to the conception of the mutual dependence of commodity owners and producers in the provision of a system of needs which is multiple and extensible.

For Locke, labor and the generation of the means to the fulfilment of need occur outside of society. This extraction of the provision of need from society makes impossible any development of an economic science. In order to advance beyond this standpoint, it is necessary to assert the specificity of laboring to the generation and expansion of wealth. This is the task of political economy. Prior to the emergence of classical political economy, the Lockean conception of labor remains predominant. At the same time, however, its formulation undergoes an important alteration.

This alteration is clearly exemplified by Rousseau. For Rousseau, labor also appears as the immediate ground of property and property as the means to the satisfaction of need.[3] None the less, in contrast to Locke, Rousseau begins to grasp the specificity of labor, and of the need which it fulfils, to society. Rousseau does not consider what man does to satisfy his wants in the state of nature to be labor properly considered. The reason for this is not only that the object of human activity in the state of nature is immediate and natural, but more importantly that in the state of nature human activity lacks the negative element which is distinctive of laboring. Laboring is the means by which man acquires the substances which fulfil needs which are unnatural and artificial. These are needs bound up with the mutual dependence of men within a social division of labor. As such, the needs which labor satisfies mark the subjection of man to a state of dependence. The implication which this notion has is that the pursuit of the needs characteristic of civil society is tantamount to the abandonment of freedom. The pursuit of these needs is the violation of the autonomy and freedom of the self-subsistence person within the natural condition. The negative element which attaches itself in this way to the concept of need, also marks the first explicit recognition of the social determination of laboring as the means to the satisfaction of needs. The negative element transposed to the laboring activity is essential in that it clearly establishes that, within civil society, work is the means by which man passes beyond the limits of the natural condition. This, more than the Lockean conception, represents a starting point for the Smithian idea of labor as synonymous with 'toil and trouble.' Labor, for Locke, is the immediate activity of the abstract person and develops out of his own inner drives and desires. It is directly self-constitutive activity, which is immediately implied in the self-subsistence of the abstract person. For Rousseau, and later for Smith, to labor is not to work immediately for oneself but to work for others, to work for one's own immediate ends only by working for others and therefore for external ends. This gives to the work that negative quality which makes it labor, an element which develops only within civil society.

Laboring is an activity whose limitedness and determination spring not immediately out of the subjectivity of the laborer himself, but out of the totality of his social condition. His labor, therefore, incorporates a limitation of his free self-determination. This makes the laboring distasteful to the immediate self-subsistent person in that it is a violation of his freedom. This violation is then constituted as an irreconcilable contradiction between freedom and the system of relations within which it seeks a concrete determination. By making the social determination of labor essentially negative, social theory simultaneously establishes laboring as a social condition while constituting the relation of the labor to social life as an extrinsic condition, eventually as the means to an end. The standpoint of classical political economy takes the violation of freedom in the system of mutual dependence as the sole means to the subsistence of freedom, and thereby gives to the notion of freedom a radical reinterpretation as the freedom of the market and its unlimited development. With this insight the science of economics begins its real development. It is this notion connected to the idea of labor, rather than that of Locke, which marks the inception of the 'labor theory of value,' and it is this notion which is able, for the first time, to establish property as produced and the worth or quantitative dimension of the property as connected to the laboring which creates it.

2 *The classical labor theory of value*

Prior to the development of classical political economy the idea that property was the result of a distinctive activity termed 'labor' was already established. This connection of property to labor was, however, established at the abstract level of the treatment of individuals not yet firmly situated within a system of economic relations. Even for Rousseau, who considers laboring to be entrenched within the system of mutual dependence, the conception of the system of relations within which labor transpires is at best poorly developed. Indeed, any real development of the conception of social labor is excluded by its attachment to the violation of freedom and equality within civil society. To the extent that laboring is connected to property, it is as the basis either (1) for a conception of the abstract person outside of any social condition, or (2) for a conception of the development of dependence and inequality. In either case any systematic connection of laboring to commodity exchange is inconceivable where the labor is either abstracted from the concrete conditions requisite for the conception of exchange, or situated within those concrete conditions at the cost of the constitution of mutual dependence in terms of the equality of commodity owners. For the development of the conception of the production of value it is essential that property be determined concretely as wealth so that its production can be determined in a relation to need which is not a violation of the substance of property as value. This determination of the notion of property is the project of economic science, and the development of the theory of value by the latter is the development of a conception of the production of property within a system of mutual dependence among concretely different individuals who are also, as commodity owners, equal. The theory of value has its real starting point in the effort on the part of classical political economy to connect value to labor and thereby not only to make labor productive of *property*, as in Locke and Rousseau, but also to connect labor to the determination of the exchangeable-value of *commodities*, so that the conception previously developed is made concrete without any repudiation of its underpinnings in the idea of freedom and equality.

The first definite statement of the concrete determination of commodity exchange in value appears in the *Wealth of Nations*. While the idea is not original to the latter, it is there clearly established for the first time. In his treatment of value, Adam Smith presents two distinct arguments for a connection between exchange-value and the labor time required in the production of commodities.* The first of these has to do with the division of labor, the second with the 'toil and trouble' requisite to the acquisition of the commodity 'from nature.'

In the first argument, Smith refers directly to the social division of labor, in effect taking the latter as an irreducible premise for the analysis of commodity exchange, and this even where he has already established that the division of labor is 'limited by the extent of the market.' By positing the division of labor in this way Smith is able to establish the necessity for interdependence in consumption and therefore also in production. In this respect, Smith takes the conditions of civil society as his starting point and constitutes the labor which underlies the value of commodities as the laboring necessitated by, and sustained within, the system of economic relations. The cost of this result is, however, a failure to establish the division of labor as substantively a division of *labor*, of a common principle determined in general. The starting point for this conception is that of division and difference, and is in this respect the starting point of all social theory prior to Smith: society composed of irreducible differences. Since this moment of concrete differentiation is taken as an *a priori* supposition, the determination of the differences cannot be an explicitly social determination which develops with the system of economic relations itself. As a result, the oppositions which ensue cannot be systematically connected to commodity exchange as a relation among elements whose differences represent the differentiation of a social principle. The equality embedded in exchange has no basis explicitly established in the differentiation connected to the division of labor. As a result, this argument cannot sustain the idea of the determination of value in labor time since value is the substance which constitutes the equality of different commodities.

Smith asserts, none the less, that with the division of labor the exchange of commodities becomes a necessity. This argument establishes, in however unsystematic a manner, that the exchange

---

* These arguments are presented consecutively in the first two paragraphs of chapter V of the *Wealth of Nations*. Subsequently, and indeed, even up to this point, these two elements of the Smithian theory of value present themselves, sometimes together, sometimes separately, as the occasion permits and requires, making the total treatment a confused combination of opposed elements. For a discussion of the treatment of value in the *Wealth of Nations* see D. Levine, *Economic Studies: Contributions to the Critique of Economic Theory* (London: Routledge & Kegan Paul, 1977) chapter 2.

of commodities is an inner necessity of their constitution as produced within a division of labor, and therefore that the differences sustained within civil society result from the differentiation of a social principle and are, thereby, the substantive basis of equality. What it is, within the division of labor, which expresses this universality of the laboring and thereby connects laboring to exchange is never clearly articulated. There is, evidently, nothing within the simple notion of mutual dependence which connects the products of production one to the other in accordance with the principle of labor-value. Mutual dependence, and the interchange of commodities through exchange according to their values, are not synonymous. While Smith attempts to deduce the latter from the former, he fails, and in this failure is driven to present another, distinct, argument for the identification of exchange-value with proportions of labor time.

Smith turns from the division of labor to the labor itself, taken without regard to its division into particular labors. The question which Smith addresses here is that of the common element in the division of labor which makes it a division of *labor*. Within the oppositions of particular production processes it is by no means evident that the universal element, labor, can account for the quantitative participation of each particular product in the exchange system. To the extent that the division of labor emphasizes directly the opposition of particular productions it is not possible to deduce from that condition alone the connection of labor to value, since the universality of labor remains only implicit. First, an abstraction must be made from the division of labor in order to discover the element in the production of wealth which makes that wealth valuable, therefore which makes it wealth.

According to Smith this element is the labor time required in the production of the commodity, the 'toil and trouble.' It needs to be emphasized that when Smith leaves aside the division of labor in order to consider labor he, in effect, roots out altogether any implication of mutual dependence in the laboring and constitutes the latter as self-sufficient individual activity, as the relation of the individual to nature. Smith discovers that man, in order to make nature into wealth, must labor, so that labor becomes the mediating process between nature and wealth. This laboring bears no necessary connection to the division of labor since labor is now determined as a relation neither pole of which is grounded within a social condition; instead on one side there is nature, on the other side the isolated individual. Labor, which begins as the common element in the division of labor, is now something quite distinct, bearing no necessary relation to the division of labor.

Smith proceeds to show that commodity exchange is grounded in the laboring of the self-subsistent individual. In this case, the exchange of commodities is governed by the rule that the value of the commodity acquired must equal the labor which its acquisition saves its purchaser. The implication which this conception has is that the laboring required to produce the commodity could be done equally by its seller and by its purchaser. This condition, however, excludes the specialization of labor implied in the division of labor. With specialization it is no longer possible for the purchaser of the commodity to do the same labor required for its production. It is, therefore, impossible for the purchaser to equate the value of the commodity acquired with the amount of his own labor from which he is released in its acquisition. The specialization of production makes the equation of commodities upon this basis impossible. Since it is this condition of specialization which necessitates exchange, by establishing the labor principle upon the basis that the purchaser saves his own laboring, Smith, in effect, excludes the necessity built into that labor which requires that its products be exchanged and be exchanged in determinate proportions. This leads directly into the economy of independent hunters of beaver and deer for which there is no division of labor but only labor. Within this economy, since there exists no mutual dependence in production, the exchange of commodities is a possibility built into the toil and trouble expended in the acquisition of consumable goods, but it is never a necessity built into a system of mutual dependence.

Smith begins with the necessity of exchange, which develops with the division of labor and the system of mutual dependence of producers and consumers. This starting point excludes, however, any conception of what it is within the division of labor which establishes the exchangeability of the products of particular producers, and which fixes the proportions of that exchange. The conception of the division of labor, furthermore, bypasses any fully general conception of the production of wealth as such, not as this or that particular element of wealth, but of the substance which defines all particular production as the production of wealth. In other words, Smith lacks here any conception of wealth as the product of a distinct process which accounts not only for the opposition of many particular productions, but for the general result that the product is given not by nature but, as wealth, only within a distinctive act which generates something over and above, even beyond, the nature sphere. As a result, Smith is unable, within this line of argument, to establish any systematic connection between wealth and labor which could provide the basis for a concrete analysis of exchange and include the determinate connection of exchange to the production of wealth.

Smith develops an argument for such a determinate, indeed proportional, connection but only at the cost of his original argument for the necessity of exchange and the grounding of the latter in differences associated with the division of labor and system of mutual dependence. The common element of the latter ceases to be a common element in the system of particular productions when those particular productions lose all interconnection based upon mutual dependence. Smith severs the necessity of the system of particular exchanges from what he argues to be the underlying substance of exchange, abstract labor time, and in the constitution of labor in the abstract loses altogether the concrete system of relations whose abstraction *is* labor time.

The Smithian notion of labor is only implicitly embedded in a conception of mutual dependence. With the assertion of an idea of labor as the element of a division of labor, the situation of laboring within civil society is clearly established and labor can no longer be the activity of the self-subsistent person taken in isolation. This quality of labor as working for others, and as a limitation of the freedom of the laborer, makes explicit the social determination of laboring. In order to exist within civilized society the individual, according to Smith, must sacrifice an element of his freedom: he must labor for others in order to work for himself. This social determination becomes attenuated when Smith passes over to the general conception of labor as 'toil and trouble.' Here, the division of labor becomes essentially external to the general conception of labor and the negative quality of laboring as a violation of individual freedom becomes the essential quality in its abstract determination as labor. Thus, Smith excludes all necessity of mutual dependence and makes the latter a matter of the free choice of the individual. This violates essentially the real social determination of the labor and reduces the latter to its Lockean form. None the less, even here Smith retains not only the negative quality of laboring which definitely establishes its, at least implicit, social determination, but he also connects this negative aspect immediately to exchange. What Smith is striving to grasp is the general social character of laboring and its connection to the production of wealth. He correctly discovers this character (1) independently of any immediate reference to the social division of labor, therefore in abstraction from that condition of particularization, and (2) as still existing within the laboring itself. But, when Smith abstracts from the social division of labor in order to consider labor in general, he sees this abstraction instead as the elimination of all mutual dependence, and the result is the explicitly stated exclusion of labor from civil society and the retreat to the Lockean conception of the relation of labor to property.

In this respect, Smith lacks a fully developed conception of the social determination of production and this lack is established most forcefully precisely where Smith approaches most closely to a conception of labor in general, where he abstracts from the social division of labor and considers directly labor as toil and trouble. By leaving aside the social division of labor, Smith is able to consider labor in the abstract. But, in leaving aside the social division of labor, Smith fails to really grasp the character of abstract labor, since he loses sight of the mutuality embedded in the most general conception of labor, retaining it only in a moral sense related to the distaste which the individual feels towards his laboring.

When Smith abstracts from the system of mutual dependence, the only basis which remains for the treatment of value is the isolated laboring of the abstract person; and when Smith considers the concrete conditions of commodity exchange, it becomes evident that the isolated activity of the self-subsistent individual, which Smith identifies with laboring, is insufficient for its determination. Yet, what ultimately connects laboring to value in the *Wealth of Nations* is the independent self-determination of the laboring activity, its immediate derivation from the subjectivity of the autonomous producer. For Smith, the abstraction of labor is synonymous with its isolation, and the determination of value in labor time is implied in the subjective determination of laboring as the objectification of the personality of the laborer. The derivation of laboring from the personality of the laborer makes labor independent of the system of mutual dependence. The determination of labor cannot, then, be a social determination which entails its full situation within civilized society. Instead, labor is made into the external determinant of wealth and wealthy society. Labor is the independent force which determines value and exchange. Since its determination of exchange is made possible by its own independent constitution (i.e. within the personality of the laborer), the labor governs commodity exchange as an extrinsic condition. This excludes any economic conception of laboring and sets up an impassable barrier between the concept of value as labor and the concept of the system of commodity relations within which the full development of the value relation is made possible.

The contradiction embedded within the classical theory of value of Smith and Ricardo – between labor as the determinant of exchange-value, and the conception of exchange within the system of economic relations as a whole – is characteristic of the whole of the development of classical political economy. The methodology of the latter always involves the idea that the determination of the system of economic relations necessarily entails recourse to an extrinsic, especially natural, condition or force which in its independent self-subsistence accounts for social life as a dependent form.

3 Ricardo and Marx

In general, the classical theory of value grasps the connection of wealth to a process of its production. Adam Smith presents the only argument for this conclusion explicitly articulated within classical thought. He is the sole author who dedicates economics to an investigation into the *nature* of wealth. Smith thereby requires of himself an argument which could link laboring to the production of commodities, and thereby link value and wealth to their process of generation. At the same time, Smith fails to establish the real link of laboring to its product when he isolates abstract labor from the concrete conditions of its particularization, constituting labor and division of labor as isolated and opposed spheres. Smith makes the concrete conditions within which commodity exchange is determined inconsistent with the general conception of the commodity, so that the concrete determination of commodity exchange is not able to develop as the concretization of the abstract analysis of commodities and commodity production.

Subsequent to Smith, even where the connection of labor to value is retained, it is retained for essentially subjective reasons, so that the intrinsic logic of the treatment of value is bypassed in the treatment of essentially quantitative problems. While Ricardo begins the *Principles* with the problem of the 'foundation' of 'exchangeable value' as a 'doctrine of the utmost importance,' his investigation of this doctrine preoccupies itself exclusively with the quantitative difficulties entailed in the effort to equate value and price. The only argument, extant within the *Principles*, for the grounding of exchange-value in labor time is taken, *in toto*, from the *Wealth of Nations*. Characteristically, Ricardo attaches himself to that argument in the Smithian discussion which is the most abstract. Leaving aside any consideration of the division of labor (a problem never confronted in Ricardian economics) Ricardo considers abstract labor directly upon the basis of the Smithian notion of individual toil and trouble. For Ricardo it is always the labor and not the division of labor which is essential, so that Ricardo takes that abstraction first fully achieved by Adam Smith as his starting point. To this extent the concept of labor within the *Principles* displays a greater unity than that of the *Wealth of Nations*. The cost of this unity is, however, the complete failure ever to investigate the nature of the labor which grounds the exchangeable value of commodities. Ricardo lacks even the rudiments of a conception of labor, which rudiments constitute such an important dimension of the contribution of the *Wealth of Nations* to economic theory.

With the decline of Ricardian economics the concept of labor dissipates into the concept of a naturally and empirically given factor of production lacking altogether that universality which makes of labor in classical political economy the activity innately capable of the production of wealth. The exception to this is Marx, who further develops both the concept of labor and the conception of the value which its activity engenders.

Marx takes the concept of labor as a starting point which serves as a presupposition of economic analysis rather than as itself an economic relation. He begins, then, his treatment of economic life with the essentially classical conception of labor as a natural *cum* individual activity. This leads Marx back to the classical theory of value, to the determination of exchange in an extrinsic condition (labor time), and to the implied opposition between the substance of exchange – labor-value – and its realization in the total system of exchange relations. This excludes equally the real determination of the exchange relation, and the full constitution of production as a socially determined process. Marx proceeds, none the less, directly to the derivation of that relation of opposition which underlies all real comprehension of the social determination of production – the separation of the laborer from his labor-power. With the emergence of a concept of labor-power this opposition can be grasped for the first time in a systematic manner. This makes the conception of social production and of abstract labor a real possibility; it is, therefore, in Marx that we find the first real development of a concept of labor adequate to the conception of the self-development of wealth.

CHAPTER SEVEN
Social production

I The social determination of production

The social character of the labor process is never the result of the mere summation of individual, independent, labors. For the labor process to take on a social character it is necessary that the worker, upon entering production, shed all trace of his individuality, appearing instead as nothing more than so much of the labor of society. The development of this condition is synonymous with the development of social production, which is the historical result of a process marked by the separation of the worker on one side from his labor-power, and on the other from the means of production. This separation brings with it the suppression of all innate connection which would determine the laboring capacity of the worker in its relation either to the personality of the worker or in its relation to the exigencies of the production of a particular commodity. Each phase in the development of social production involves the deprivation of the worker of his existence within production as anything more than labor, and thus also the constitution of the activity of the worker within production as nothing less than laboring. This constitution of labor in its full generality is simultaneously the full social determination of production and of labor.

Prior to the full development of social production, production for society remains subordinate to subjective factors connected to the personality of the laborer on one side, and to external natural conditions on the other. So far as the determinants of production are either outside of society altogether, as in the case of natural forces, or are within society but outside of the economic life of society, as in the case of the subjective factors connected to the personality of the laborer, production for society remains limited by conditions which exclude its full development. The imposition of these conditions as external, and even arbitrary, elements of the production process, curtails essentially the development of production and of its product. The multiplication and expansion of need and of the means to its fulfilment are fundamentally impeded by the fixity of the conditions out of which the generation of the means to the fulfilment of need emerge.

This fixity always begins as the fixing of production in accordance with accidental natural factors. The extent of production for society is determined not by the productivity of capital, but by the fertility of the earth. At the same time, the product is also determined in its composition by the materials made available to society by nature. This condition is necessarily implied where the product is lacking in the universality of a use-value and is, instead, the means to fulfil a fixed and limited need which exists for society as a given condition. The result of 'production' remains, in this case, an essentially natural product tied in its conception not only to its origin within nature, but to its material substance given by nature. The materials which sustain society are given to society by nature. Even where there is an element of the social transformation of the natural substance, the fixity of the product is retained to the degree that the conception of the product remains as a product of nature. Food consumption is not the fulfilment of *need*, determined within society, by a use-value generated within a social process and endowed with its determinate features by its social origin. Such consumption is, instead, the fulfilment of a species need made possible by a given and fixed natural substance, a product of nature (a grain, animal, etc.) which is given to society by nature. The natural determination of need, and of the means to its fulfilment, entails the conception of the substance which satisfies need as fixed within nature, therefore as irrevocably connected to a particular and given natural material. This restricts the multiplication and expansion of need to a limited sphere of objects of consumption already available. Under these conditions, the real determination of the product is in nature, in conditions of climate, geography, characteristics of the soil, etc. It is the force of nature which continues to govern production both qualitatively, as regards the nature of the product and its properties, and quantitatively, as regards the fruitfulness of production.

To the extent that the substance of the product and the need which it fulfils are given by a natural and contingent condition, the activity which generates that product lacks the universality of the commodity and its use-value. The need fulfilled in the consumption of the commodity is never connected to any fixed material substance, but always considers such substances as no more than transitory means to the constitution of a product capable of its real satisfaction. The production of the commodity takes place not within nature but within society, and the conditions which make possible that production, together with the active force within production, are determined by their social existence and not by any natural condition. Where the idea of the product is that of a natural substance, the process which brings it into existence is a natural process, and the means to its development are all given within nature. Food is immediately identifiable with the meat of a given animal, given by nature as a natural substance. The idea of food is synonymous with the idea of that particular substance and is strictly fixed by that identification. Its development is constrained by this fixity of the relation and of the means to its satisfaction. Where, however, the idea of the product is that of a social substance, in particular a commodity, the process which brings the product into existence must be a social process. The substance produced is never available within and to nature. It must be produced within society, so that society must supply to its own production process a means to the specification of the social determination of the product. Food is no longer a particular natural condition but now covers an expanding range of substances none of which are directly made available by nature.

In nature, the natural determination of the product is the natural determination of the means to its production – the soil and its composition, the natural renewal of the species, etc. In society, the social determination of the product is the social determination of the means to its production – the labor-power and the machine. The idea of the use of the product (in this case a use-value) is now embedded not in a natural process, but in a product of social production itself – the machine. Since the product is produced within society, this can only result from the social production of the means of production, and, therefore, from their constitution as capital.

In order to effect the social determination of the product it is necessary that the idea of the product be embedded by a social act within the means of production, so that those means of production must also be produced. Social production begins, then, not with nature, but with the production of the means of production within society, therefore with capital. The full emancipation of the product from any natural fixity requires the full emancipation of the means of its production from any determination within nature, and from any fixed natural principle. The fixity of production, together with the fixity of the product, stem ultimately from the absence of their full social determination and from the retention of a determination in natural and contingent factors which are not accountable to any objectively determined social laws.

What holds on one side for the means of production holds equally on the other for labor-power. Where the former must be constituted as itself the product of social production, so must the latter be established as an objective condition constituted within society; objective in the sense that all limitation in arbitrarily fixed factors is left aside. This condition is fulfilled with the separation of the labor-power from determination in subjective factors connected to the contingent personality of the laborer. On the side of the means of production, their full social determination comes with their production within society. On the side of the labor-power its full social determination comes with its separation from the personality of the laborer and its constitution as indifferent to his particularity. In both cases, the full social determination of the elements of the production process is synonymous with their intrinsic determination in accordance with the process of the self-development of capital.

In the absence of these conditions there can be no production, within society, of the means to the satisfaction of social needs. Without social production, however, it necessarily follows that the social determination of the product of an essentially natural process is an act which transpires subsequent to its production. Production must remain, to a greater or lesser degree, a process related to the social constitution of its product only by accident. Production, to the extent that its factors remain arbitrary and contingent for society, must hide its inner laws from society and appear to the latter as ruled by mysterious forces. That these forces are mysteries derives originally from their fixity with respect to social life. When production takes place outside of society, its full comprehension is withheld from society, and when both production and the production of society are taken outside of any full social determination, then neither production nor social life can be made fully rational. This implies as well the fixity of production which, since it is determined by factors which are for society irreducible, remains incapable of overcoming the contingent factors by which it is determined and therefore limited. Fixed conditions of nature, the knowledge developed and held secret within the guild, the traditions of form and composition evolved in the various crafts, these factors all serve to fix production and its product, limiting its content and scope, thereby depriving it of its full development.[1]

It is only possible to establish production on a sound scientific and technical basis when the conditions of production are not given arbitrarily, but are all themselves determined within a process which is governed not by arbitrarily given external forces, but by its own internal conditions and requirements. Production becomes fully rational within society when the laws by which it is governed possess the objective force within society that the laws of nature possess within nature. What distinguishes the operation of these laws within society is the universality of the objective to which they are subordinated, and particularly their determination in accordance with the social principle. For the latter, production must be constituted as the basis for the realization of the idea of social need in its full particularity. This ideal determination of production is realized in the form of a technology. Production as a technical problem is inherently rational in that it is the transformation of an idea into the form of a particular product. The idea existing as a technique is embedded in the machinery which is the objective existence of the technique. The idea is subsequently realized in the multiplicity of products of machine production. This result distinguishes production which is fully established upon the basis of capital from all pre-modern forms of production. Production is here made rational precisely in that the mechanism of production is itself the objectification of an idea. By contrast, in pre-capitalist economies, the ideal determination of the product and process is overlaid, and in certain instances obliterated, by its natural determination. Such a natural determination exists for social production as a complex of essentially accidental or contingent factors (of climate, fertility, etc.) which, since fixed arbitrarily, cannot be grasped rationally. This irrational element is then extended to the whole of the process which is considered, *in toto*, to be an extrinsically fixed condition.

It is only with its full social determination that production becomes finally a 'technical problem.' The production process comes to be analyzed objectively in accordance with its intrinsic stages and elements, and in accordance with the qualities of the product. Production in society becomes the technical process of the production of commodities by means of commodities, the transformation of use-value into use-value. It is thereby distinguished essentially from any natural activity as well as from any purely subjective activity on the part of the particular producer.

The system of concepts connected to the specification of the production process of the system of commodities constitutes the existing technology. The mode of generation of the product is first grasped ideally, as a logically connected sequence of alterations by which the materials of labor are transformed into the product. The entire process exists, first, abstractly, as the practical application of scientific concepts to a specific productive objective. The manner of production is formulated in abstraction from any actual productive activity, for example, as a blueprint or plan. This by no means implies that the actual development of the plan is independent of industrial practice, but only that the formulation of that practice abstractly, in the form of a general technique of production applicable in a variety of concrete situations, is an essential aspect of its determination. Technical knowledge is simultaneously general and specific since it always develops a practical result out of general knowledge of the laws which govern natural phenomena. Technology is both the practical application of general laws, and the abstract formulation of particular productive activities.

The objective mechanism of production, the machine and system of machinery, translates this knowledge into a continuous stream of commodity products. The idea of technology thus refers first to the purely ideal development of the productive mechanism according to universal principles, or general laws, and second to the embodiment of those ideas in the objectively existing productive apparatus. Indeed, it is the prior development of the idea of the process as a sequence of material transformations governed by objective laws, which marks production as a technical process and the means of production as the embodiment of a technique. Without this separation of the concept of the process from its specific, empirically existing forms, production could not be fully considered upon the basis of the idea of technology, as the application of a technique. The work of the artisan, for example, since it lacks this objectivity and universality, lacks also a fully technical quality. To the extent that the artisan is unable to formulate his productive activity abstractly, as the application of general principles, that productive activity is not fully the application of a technique. Similarly, agricultural production which is not firmly grounded in the application of scientific principles does not constitute the application of a technique. Primitive technique is also the primitive state of the development of production to the point at which it can be considered with reference to the idea of technique.

The system of interconnected laws together with their applications form the technology and are embedded in the system of machinery which produces commodities. The rationality of production is measured in the degree to which the laws by which it is governed are situated within the sciences and not within accidents of climate, geography, history and personality. The application of science to production develops with the development of social production. The latter must attain a degree of universality which can alone make possible its conception as a technical problem soluble by objective scientific and technical laws. The establishing of production upon a scientific basis imparts to production a universality corresponding to its emancipation from the constraints given in its determination by purely contingent factors.

For the social determination of production, it is necessary that the conditions of production display as well the universality implied in the scientific conception of their production process. This implies, on one side, that the means of production take the form of products, and particularly of machines, and that the labor united with those means of production be constituted as fully abstracted from any determination in the personality of the laborer and in the particularity of the product as regards its material or useful form. The machine, as the embodiment of the technique, contains within it the idea of the product and of its production, determining its specific construction and form. The notion of a technique is bound up with that of the machine as the objectification of that technique within production. The form of the product is no longer connected in any way to the particularity of the worker, but is wholly determined by the objective laws embodied in the machine, together with the idea of the product embedded in its total mechanism. Only out of this condition is it possible to begin to consider the technique as the 'means' to an 'end.' While this does, indeed, become the case, it is equally essential to bear in mind that the 'means' and 'end' are mutually determined, so that the end exists already embedded in the means to its achievement. The product is indelibly stamped as the product of machine production.

The embedding of the unity of the production process within the machine displaces it both from the mind of the particular worker, the craftsman, and from the external force of the natural process. Originally, the unity of the product is situated within nature, and the endpoint or result is fixed by the logic of the natural process out of which it develops. Here, the subjective element is wholly suppressed, as both product and its production process are exclusively determined by the inner logic of the natural world. So far as man intervenes it is only to appropriate a result already fully developed by and within nature, to gather materials already provided by nature. This condition is sustained to a lesser degree with the development of agriculture. With the latter, production is no longer exclusively natural. None the less, the idea of the production process and the unity of the whole remains within nature, and, indeed, the laws by which production is governed remain locked away within nature and inaccessible to society. This condition is overcome in handicraft production where the unity of the process is transferred from nature to the mind of the direct producer.

In handicraft production, labor retains the complexity connected to its own subjective determination of the specificity of the product, while the means which it employs remain elementary tools, simple implements. In this case the unity of the process as a whole is imposed upon it by the subjectivity of the worker, by his personality, and by the naturally given and unchanging properties of the materials worked upon. Since the unity of the product rests upon the unifying activity of the worker, the means of labor are not themselves determined in relation to a particular product except in the most elementary manner. To the degree that the laborer retains within his mind the concept of his product, the tools which he employs are means to his own end. Since they lack the determinacy of the particular product in all its complexity, they appear as simple and general implements of labor, as tools rather than machines. Here the worker works the tools and the product is the product of the worker's intentions and his subjective laboring.* The result has it stamped upon it that it is produced by this particular worker under these fixed conditions. Corresponding, then, to the complexity of the laboring for the worker is the simplicity and generality of his implements. Corresponding, symmetrically, to the simplicity of the labor is the complexity of the implements of labor, so that for the labor to be elementary it is necessary that the complexity of the product be shifted to the means of production. The development of tools into machines, by which the simplicity and generality of the tool gives way to the complexity and particularity of the machine, and the development of the worker from the complex locus of the unity of the production process to the elementary condition of abstract labor deprived of specification to a particular product, are the two sides of the development of social production. With the displacement of the simplicity and generality from the means of production to the labor, the laborer loses his connection to the particular production process, and is substantively severed from his connection to a particular means of production. With this condition the activity of the laborer takes on that peculiarly modern mode of existence as nothing more than so much labor. In effect, the producer exists for the first time as a laborer and his activity is for the first time

---

* This is the characteristically pre-modern conception of social labor which, while lacking the explicit basis for the idea of labor (the distinction between labor and labor-power), still grasps the subjective character of laboring activity. The main effect is to identify that subjective element with the personality of the worker. Thus, according to Aristotle, the product of handicraft is the producer:

> The cause of this is that existence is to all men a thing to be chosen and loved, and that we exist by virtue of activity (i.e. by living and acting), and that the handiwork *is* in a sense, the producer in activity; he loves his handiwork, therefore, because he loves his existence. And this is rooted in the nature of things; for what he is in potentiality, his handiwork manifests in activity [*Ethica Nicomachea*, tr. W. D. Ross, *The Works of Aristotle* (Oxford: Oxford University Press, 1915) p. 1168ª].

constituted fully as labor; for it is now nothing more than labor and, therefore, also nothing less.

II Social labor

The simplicity of labor marks the highest stage of its development, when it finally emerges fully constituted as labor. This simplicity presupposes a high level of development of society and of production. It is precisely because the activity of the worker loses all immediate purposive character that it comes finally to exist as labor. Since the conception of the product in its particularity exists within the machine, and within the totality of the labor process, the laborer does not consider his activity in relation to that determinacy. On the side of the worker there is only the idea of labor abstracted from the particularity of the product, labor as purposeless, endless activity, whose sole end and purpose is to sustain its own abstraction.

The simplicity of the labor appears to require hardly any intervention of a conscious element on the side of the worker. While the labor which develops appears as mindless, mechanical activity, it in reality presupposes a high level of comprehension of his work on the part of the worker. What is required for social production is labor, simple elementary labor divorced from any objective other than that of its own continuation, pure activity severed from any subjective grasp of its particular end and product. For the laborer, the particular product is of no consequence. Rather, the objective of the activity of the laborer is wholly contained within the elementary motions which compose his laboring. The simplicity of the labor, far from reducing its performance to the level of a pre-social, or even natural, condition, in fact raises that activity to the highest level of social development because the laboring is, for the laborer, severed from any instinctual end or gratification; it fulfils no immediate need of the laborer himself. In this abstraction, labor is constituted as an activity of a purely social character. Outside of society the abstraction required for the performance of labor could never be achieved.

Within nature, the work performed by animals or the forces of nature is never abstracted from its specific circumstances. For the species outside of society the activity is always connected directly to its end. In the case of instinctual behavior the behavior and the objective to which it is directed are irrevocably connected and subordinated to the particularity built inexorably into the biological constitution of the species. As a result, the animal is incapable of taking over the laboring within society since it can never, of the force of its own subjective existence, abstract from the immediate end of its activity and achieve the idea of laboring. Though the subjective element in the laboring does not involve a determination on the part of the intentions of the laborer, it is essential because it involves the abstraction of the labor from any immediate connection to the specification of its product.

Since it is not the purposiveness of the labor which is essential but rather its purposelessness which makes it labor, it follows that the labor is, for the laborer, motivated by no consciously grasped end connected to its real product – the commodity. This requires that the labor be conceived as such by the laborer, that there be present the idea of labor in all its purity. And, indeed, in the labor process it is this idea which is really at work. This ideal determination of the laboring activity is essential since labor is possible only where the idea of labor has developed to the point where its abstraction is the driving force within production.

The capacity for labor is, then, equivalent to the abstraction of labor. This abstraction is simultaneously from the specification of the particular production process in its complexity and as a connected movement, and from the specification of the particular laborer as regards his personality and the whole of his existence outside of the laboring process. Labor is separable, in principle, both from the means of production and from the personality of the laborer. This condition is fulfilled with the emergence of the capacity to labor as a commodity which, as such, is alienable from the laborer and, at the same time, as the property of the laborer, is separable from the means of production, bearing within its make-up no hint of the particular production process within which it will be expended. This separation of the laborer from his labor-power is, then, the condition *sine qua non* for the constitution of production on a modern basis, while the latter is the development which makes production intelligible as the proper subject-matter of economic analysis.

The abstraction of labor is grasped, if only implicitly, very early in the development of economic theory as the necessary basis for any scientific treatment of wealth. At the same time, however, that capital is grasped as the real basis for the full development of labor, the laboring which transpires within the life-cycle of capital is considered – precisely because of that abstraction which makes it labor – to be a violation of labor. Indeed, the separation of labor-power from the laborer, which makes the consumption of labor-power neither more nor less than labor, is considered to be the origin of labor's 'degradation.' Thus, since Adam Smith, the emancipation of labor is always that act which places it most irretrievably into bondage.*

The classical conception originally considers laboring as the subjective activity of the laborer forming the material into the product in accordance with a complex idea realized in the form of skill, dexterity and ingenuity (the three aspects which, for Adam Smith, define laboring).[2] It is this activity which when divided produces wealth, and it is the conception of wealth produced by a division of this subjective laboring which makes wealth the product of, and therefore reducible to, 'labor.' But this division of labor is immediately grasped by Smith to be also a deformation of labor since it tends to the elimination of the link between labor and the skill and ingenuity of the laborer. This development of labor is its deformation, however, only because it is the process which shakes off the inadequacies of form which are falsely identified with labor.

The full development of labor is its development away from its original determination in the personality of the laborer. This full development of labor is its integration into the process of the self-development of capital. As a result, the production of wealth becomes something other than labor, so far as the laboring is considered to be the subjective activity of the individual, and laboring ceases to be determined by the individual laboring subject, so far as labor is constituted as the productive moment of wealth. This connection of the idea of labor to the object of the production

---

* The idea that the integration of labor into the process of the production of wealth implies its degradation is typically connected to the contrast between the laboring activity of the independent producer (identified immediately with labor) and labor as it exists upon the basis of capitalist production. This is the position of Adam Smith, who never succeeds in distinguishing the general conception of labor from its pre-capitalist handicraft form. It is also the theme of much of modern analysis of the labor process, which draws the same contrast that motivates the Smithian analysis in order to arrive at the same result. See, for example, H. Braverman, *Labor and Monopoly Capital: The Degradation of Work in the Twentieth Century* (New York: Monthly Review Press, 1974).

of wealth inevitably undermines all attempts to grasp laboring as
the activity of the individual *per se*, and capital's laboring process
as a deformation of labor. The concept of labor in general is not
the deformation of labor, but the fulfilment of its productive
potential.

The abstraction of labor is connected to the mechanization of
production both logically and historically. Logically, the fully
elementary conception of labor requires that the 'skill,' 'dexterity,'
and 'ingenuity' be provided to the labor process by capital in the
form of a complex productive apparatus. Historically, this connection is brought about by a process within which the skills are
practically separated from the worker and embedded in the
mechanism of production. Labor-power is conceived in principle
to be independent of any skill connected to a specific aspect of
commodity production. Laboring, on the side of the worker, is no
longer the performance of a skill, but the essentially mechanical
performance of a set of movements conceivable independently both
of the particular worker and of the particular production process.[3]
In effect, the mechanization of the means of production also makes
the labor mechanical. Once laboring is analyzed into its constituent
movements, each step grasped as a separate component of the
worker's contribution which is in no way connected to any determinate attribute of the laborer, the performance of the specified
function by the laborer ceases to be compelling. As the labor is
made more and more to realize the idea of labor, it thereby in equal
measure becomes unnecessary for the laborer to execute the required task. Historically, the abstraction of labor is never a finished
task until the required activity is given over wholly to the machine.
The opposition of labor-power to the machine leads inexorably to
the replacement of the laborer by the machine. Those aspects of
the labor process which originally require the activity of the worker
cease to do so when they have become purely mechanical movements which, as such, can always be more effectively performed by
a machine. In this sense, the machine performs labor; but only that
labor which has become mechanical.[4]

Machine production is production fully emancipated from all
fixity of the product, qualitative and quantitative. Multiplication of
products and expansion of the scale of production are now defined
not as conditions dependent upon the caprice of nature, but as
scientific, technical and economic problems. There follows an

economic determination of the product not only as regards its qualities and the need which it fulfils, but also as regards its contribution to production as a continuing and unlimited process.

On the side of the means of production the expansion and multiplication of production is only limited by past production of means of production together with their productivity, and by the capacity of society to conceive of new methods of production and new needs to be fulfilled through social production. On the side of labor, the merging of labor-powers makes possible the overcoming of all limitations of production connected to its identification with the capacities of the individual worker. The two sides of the social production process are, then, each inseparably linked to the object of social production – wealth. The multiplication of needs can only achieve its full development on the basis of machine production, since intrinsic to the notion of wealth is that illimitability which can only be realized where the means of production appear in the form of a system of machinery worked by a mass of elementary labor.

III The alienability of labor-power

The abstraction by which the laborer's activity is constituted as labor presupposes a highly developed social condition whose primary requisite is the separation of the laborer from his labor-power. The implication of this separation is the emergence of the labor-power as intrinsically indifferent to either the personality of the laborer or the specificity of the commodity production process within which it is consumed. The laborer must be able to dis-associate himself from his own laboring activity. This requires that the laborer be endowed with the capacity to grasp in thought the abstract quality which inheres within his laboring activity. In order that he be able to separate himself from that activity it is necessary (1) that the laborer be capable of conceiving of his own activity in a manner which is fully general and purely social, having nothing to do with his own personality and particularity, and (2) that the laborer retain, in opposition both to his labor-power and laboring activity, that personality as an independent moment of his own existence. The separation of the worker from his labor-power requires on one side that the labor-power not be absorbed into the personality of the laborer and marked by the particularity of the latter, and on the other side that the personality of the laborer not be absorbed into his laboring activity and dissipated wholly within the sphere of production.

The constitution of labor-power as fully abstracted from the contingent and limited conditions of production which were characteristic of pre-modern economic formations is simply the other side of the constitution of the laborer as a *person*, who, as such, is not reducible to so much laboring activity. The freedom of the laborer, and his development into an independent individual (especially into a commodity owner), forms the basis for the development of the universal element in his laboring activity in that it first makes possible and necessary his separation from his labor-power, and then makes possible the constitution of that labor-power, and the activity attendant upon its consumption, as fully universal, therefore as elementary, general, laboring.

The universality of the laboring activity is translated into the product within production and constitutes the latter as a social substance not only defined within society, but also produced within a social production process. By contrast, where the laborer and his laboring are equated, the existence of the laborer as a person is obliterated and he is reduced to the status of an animal. The merging of the laborer with his labor-power brings with it as its corollary the merging of the laborer into the means of production as one element in those means not distinguishable in principle from the tools and the materials which are formed into the product. The implication of the suppression of the independence of the laborer is twofold. On one side, where the equation of labor with labor-power brings with it the suppression of the personality of the worker, the work activity has an essentially natural character. On the other side, where this suppression does not obliterate the personality of the worker, the product must be indelibly marked with that personality and inseparable from it. The first instance is connected to a lower level of social development and is character-istic of unfree labor and especially slavery. The second involves the explicit recognition of the worker as a person, and is characteristic of handicraft production.

The slave has, in principle, no personality of his own, and his existence is the existence of so much working activity for his owner. In the purchase and sale of slaves, the laborer is as much exchanged as is his laboring capacity. As a result, under these conditions there is no explicit separation of the worker from his laboring activity and capacity. The laborer is his labor. The unity which eventuates from this equation constitutes the slave as a natural and even material condition of production to the degree that the slave possesses no personality which he can either impose upon or abstract from his productive activity and its product.[5] Slave production is, therefore, characteristically agrarian in that the relation of the working activity to the objects of work is essentially the relation of natural principles whose interaction requires neither the immediate intervention of personality nor the original abstracting from the personality of the worker necessary for commodity production.

To the degree that the slave is considered to be simply the property of his owner, his existence is exhausted by the concept of property. This abstraction reduces the slave to a condition equivalent to that of the other property recognized as such (e.g. cattle). This is, indeed, a real abstraction upon the basis of which the slave economy is constructed. At the same time, however, it is fundamentally false to reduce the concept of a slave to that of property, since the implication of this reduction is also the equation of the most abstract relation of social life with the most concrete historical condition. The latter cannot be understood in any immediate equation with the elementary notion.

Indeed, it should be evident that the abstract idea of property is wholly incapable of directly accounting for the concrete conditions which are required to sustain the master-slave relation. Not only is the nature of human property irreducible to the simple notion of property, it is in certain fundamental respects inconsistent with the idea of property. To consider the slave as mere property is to suppress the social character of the master-slave relation, and while that relation entails the development of social life only to a limited stage it is, none the less, a stage in that development.

At the same time that slave production involves the total suppression of the personality of the producer as a matter of principle and constitutes the slave as wholly objective, the subjectivity of the slave remains as an implicit condition for the relation. Thus the slave is distinguished from the other property of the master by the implicit humanity of the slave, who is human property recognized, in however contradictory a way, to be possessed with a personality. The compelling condition, in this case, is not that the slave is born human, possessed of the requisite number of fingers on each hand and of the stamp of a like biological origin with his owner. Rather, it is the social condition which makes the slave not only property but also human, 'human property.' Thus, the fact that the slave is the one piece of property with which the owner can converse is not an accident, but is built into the master-slave relation. It is not the basis of the social relation of master to slave but the result, or expression, of that relation. The master converses with the slave, enters into various unequivocally social relations with the slave, precisely to the degree that the master considers the slave not only as his property, but also as his equal. The master, that is, recognizes in the slave that human substance by which he is himself determined and seeks from the slave the constitution of his own humanity.

While the relation of master to slave suppresses the personality of the slave, merging it into the will of the master, the condition for this relation is its opposite: the implicit constitution of the slave as an independent personality. The contradiction embedded in this relation makes it possible for the activity of the slave to bear the quality, to a greater or lesser degree, of labor. The existence of the personality of the slave presupposes that the slave is able, to that degree, to separate his existence from his working activity, to exist independently of his work, and to grasp in thought the abstract quality of his work. In this case labor is possible in the absence of the wage-labor relation to the degree that the logical basis of that relation is present implicitly, to the extent that the separation of the laborer from his labor-power, which is fully realized with the buying and selling of labor-power, exists also latent within the slave's activity, in however limited and distorted a form.

Even for unfree labor, to the degree that the laborer is able to grasp an abstract quality within his activity and even to abstract himself, to whatever extent, from that activity, the production of wealth is a real possibility. And, indeed, the laboring of unfree labor retains the production of wealth as its motive force even where the full development of wealth is excluded within the constitution of production. Agricultural production, on the basis of unfree labor, eventuates in a product which, while limited by its natural setting and natural conditions, is by no means a simple natural product. At the very least, the laboring which transpires under these conditions has as its objective the enhancing of the fertility of the earth and to that extent the subordination of the natural condition to the production of wealth, for example in the form of a net product. Here the product does not emerge without the intervention of the social condition, and the activity of laboring bears within it this social quality. Here also, the worker labors not for his immediate ends or for any satisfaction in the direct consumption of his product. The laborer works, rather, with the end of the production of a surplus destined not for his own consumption, but to enhance the consumption of others. Where this is the direct result of the ownership of the laborer, the whole of the product belongs not to the producer but to the owner of the direct producer, and the whole of the slave's laboring is for another. Where the freedom of the laborer is more highly developed the labor may itself be divided between that part destined to remain with the producer and that part which is owed to the 'owner' of the natural conditions of production. In either case the object of production has a social character and the productive activity must, in order that it achieve that object, deviate from the elementary appropriation of nature.

The suppression of the personality of the slave in the explicit constitution of the relation of master to slave, makes his working activity particularly appropriate to remain within a natural sphere, especially of agricultural production. His products are, in this case, sharply delimited by the natural conditions within which he works, and the full development of need is excluded since the fulfilment of need must always be with reference to fixed natural conditions. This limitation is as severe as regards the master as the slave, and the whole of the slave system is subject to a restricted development, restricted especially by the unfreedom of the worker. By contrast, in handicraft production the personality of the worker is primary, and the merging of the laborer into his laboring has the effect not of depriving the labor of its subjective element, but of connecting that subjective element to the personality of the worker. Thus, the development of craft production must bring with it a degree of emancipation of the worker, and the full development of handicraft production brings with it the development of the freedom of the worker, since the constitution of his personality within production is the primary basis for the specification of that activity. Even where handicraft labor is formally unfree, the character and requirements of its activity bring with them a development of substantial freedom for the producer. As a result, his laboring activity achieves, in this respect, a higher level of development than that characteristic of slave production, at the same time as it fails to fully achieve the universality of abstract labor. Handicraft production is the higher form in that it represents the displacement of the unity of the production from nature to a further point, and the greater development of an explicit idea of production which is restricted to a social condition. With the artisan the activity of production becomes explicitly different from the activity of nature. The subjective element, which sharply opposes the fixity of the natural condition, becomes raised in handicraft production to primacy.*

The unity of production on the part of the slave exists still within nature. The laws which govern the determination of the product are all natural laws only poorly understood within society. The objective conditions of production are natural conditions, and the idea of the product remains locked within nature. Here, even the worker remains an objective natural condition, and is unable to abstract himself from his own activity to the point of achieving a real conception of that activity and of its innate laws. Within handicraft production the unity of the process is transferred from nature to the mind of the artisan. While the process remains

---

* The first conceptions of labor are connected to the activity of the artisan, and it is the subjective element in the latter which is explicitly grasped as the principle of difference which separates it from the life of the species within nature. Thus, according to Aristotle:

> All art is concerned with coming into being, i.e. with contriving and considering how something may come into being or not being, and whose origin is in the maker and not in the thing made; for art is concerned neither with things that are, or come into being, by necessity, nor with things that do so in accordance with nature (since these have their origin in themselves) [*Ethica Nicomachea*, p. 1140ᵃ].

For Aristotle, social production is distinctive in that it is an 'art' and therefore is neither (1) purely instinctive activity for it requires a 'true course of reasoning,' nor (2) a science, since the reasoning is that of the artisan himself which concerns not fixed natural laws but the constitution of the artisan. Aristotle is unable, given this conception, to grasp the unity of science and production which subordinates the latter to objective laws. As a result he considers production within society to be a limited and particular activity. All social production is immediately particular, and any notion of abstract labor is impossible.

governed by laws which are only poorly understood, the unity of the process is raised to the level of an idea in the mind of the producer. It is for this reason that the personality of the producer is essential to production, since within that personality there remains the whole of the idea of the process, and the imposition of form on the materials of production is also the imposition of that personality upon the product. Under these conditions, there is retained a real opposition of the subjective and objective conditions of production – the worker as the subjective condition imposing his personality and idea upon the materials, and the materials and tools acting as essentially passive elements subordinated to the objectives of the producer.

This merging of the personality of the worker into his work activity has also the effect of limiting strictly the scope, both quantitative and qualitative, of production. Production is always limited by those factors accountable for the formation of the particular personality, factors whose determination is, so far as that personality is itself concerned, mysterious and external. The product is to this extent both contingent upon these accidental factors of personality, environment and history, and limited by those factors as by the limited capacity of the individual mind and the individual body. The laboring activity is always particular, each element irrevocably connected to the particularity of the product, while the particularity of the product is not essentially that of a particular use-value which is inherently universal and objective, but that of an historically and accidentally fixed form connected to traditional modes of production. Within artisan production, then, there can be no full development of social production since the universality of production is always suppressed and the conditions requisite to the abstraction of the working activity have not developed. So long as the laboring is not fully separable from the particular personality of the laborer, that activity cannot be constituted fully as labor and the productive activity cannot be fully developed into commodity production.

To the extent that the artisan produces a use-value he is not an artist, in that his product lacks that universality which characterizes a work of art. To this extent also the artisan does labor and the product bears that universality peculiar to laboring and its result. This ambiguity of process and product is the defining quality of handicraft production. The more the work of the artisan is subordinated to the production of use-values, and especially commodities, the more it becomes laboring and the less the craft form remains essential. Where the handicraft form has been made inessential it comes into conflict with the substance of the activity and acts as a fetter to the full development of production. For the development of the productive potential of the artisan, so far as wealth is the object, to be fully realized, handicraft production must give way to wage-labor.

Paradoxically, while the artisan and his activity are unable to provide a satisfactory basis for the conception of social production, it is, none the less, the work of the artisan which provides the prototype for the idea of labor throughout the history of social theory. This result derives from the element of freedom which is explicitly connected to the work of the artisan, while it is excluded from any explicit recognition in the case of unfree labor. The activity of the artisan appears emphatically to be (1) that of the worker himself and the expression of his personality and rational faculties, and (2) in no sense a simple natural process. This does, indeed, grasp the higher level of development of the work of the artisan which more fully realizes the idea of social labor. At the same time, the elemental character of the work of the slave entails a natural simplicity of activity which foreshadows the abstraction of labor to a higher degree than does the work of the artisan. For the latter, the complex unity of the process is in the mind of the direct producer. For the former, it remains outside. And while the external unity of the production process exists for the slave in nature, his work is in this respect only a step away from social production. What is required is that the unity of the process, existing outside of the worker, be transferred from nature to capital, a transfer which must affect as fundamentally the laborer as it does the means of production. It is this necessity which makes the equivalence of slave labor with wage-labor illusory; and makes a seemingly small historical step in actuality an entire epoch of social development.

In the slave economy both the worker and the means of work remain, to a great extent, objective natural conditions, and the conception of the process and of the product remains locked away within the as yet unknown laws of nature. In handicraft production there develops a real opposition of the subjective and objective conditions of production. The laborer and his personality are the essential subjective conditions of production in that the idea of the product is grasped first in the mind of the producer. Thus the activity of the slave and the activity of the artisan mark two levels of development of social labor. At the same time, historically these two forms subsist side by side and, indeed, represent mutual conditions. The agricultural work of the slave, transpiring within a natural sphere, provides an external condition or support for the development of the division of labor within society which is always considered as a development of the work of the artisan. In pre-capitalist forms of production, labor existing within society is especially the work of the independent producer, the artisan, while the work of the slave represents the provision of a natural condition necessary to the sustenance of social life.

The reason for this rests ultimately on the inability of pre-capitalist social formations to constitute the conditions of production as themselves the result of social production. For both the artisan and the slave the conditions of production are essentially fixed. To the artisan, these conditions are given by accidents of geography, history, and personality. To the slave, these conditions are provided ultimately by nature. This fixity of the productive basis of society outside leads inevitably to its conception as a natural condition, and moreover to a condition whose natural determination is synonymous with the absence of its subordination to rationally conceptualized laws. This is so even in the case of the artisan, where the subjective element seems paramount. The productive basis of the work of the artisan is itself grasped as a fixed, even natural, condition. Conceptually then, the natural process, which is made inclusive of the work of the slave, is grasped as the productive foundation of the work of the artisan. The social element is not self-sustaining since it does not posit itself as the origin of the conditions which its sustenance necessitates. As a result, that sustenance becomes dependent upon an external condition – the work of the slave in the provision of a natural subsistence.

In modern production, where the social character of production and of the product are fully developed, the opposition of the subjective and objective conditions characteristic of handicraft production is overcome. On the side of the worker, the separation of his labor-power from his personality constitutes that labor-power as a subjective condition endowed with a universality and

abstraction which makes it uniquely capable of commodity production, of contributing to the unlimited production of wealth. On
the side of the means of production we find not the passive and
inert tools of the handicraft producer, but an objective condition,
the machine, endowed already with a subjective character as the
embodiment of the idea of the product as a particular commodity;
the machine not as a passive implement, but as an active force
capable of producing commodities. Such production transcends all
limitations tied to fixed natural conditions, to the personality and
mentality of the individual worker, or to the physical capacity of
the individual laborer. The overcoming of all such limitations
constitutes the full universality of social production as the production of wealth and the full determination of the products as
elements of the self-development of capital.

The natural unity of the production process characteristic of
unfree labor excludes any proprietorship over the means of production on the part of the worker. Since the worker can never fully
separate himself from his immersion into the objective conditions
of production as one of their elements, neither can he stand in
opposition to the means of production as their owner.

Even for the owner of the land proprietorship is limited by the
constitution of the land as a fixed presupposition.[6] The land can
never be made fully the embodiment of will where the relation to
the land is the precondition for the constitution of its proprietor
as a personage within a social order. The proprietor derives his
own social status from the land, which precedes him and is still
considered to be given by nature independently of him. The land
is in this respect the active element which accounts for the social
determination of its owner. Since the landowner is tied to the
land so far as his social status is situated essentially in his relation
to the land, the land cannot be considered exclusively as the
embodiment of his will. The personality of the land owner, since
not independent, cannot fully oppose the land as its proprietor.
Instead, the land appears also as the origin of personality, and both
proprietor and laborer become inseparably connected to a natural
condition which is hardly reducible to mere property.

This condition differs fundamentally from that of the artisan,
whose production is not immediately natural and who, therefore,
works not with implements given by nature, but with tools which
he has himself produced. Since his implements are simple tools,

there is no difficulty entailed in their direct production, and the artisan is the free proprietor of his own means of production. The artisan is free since (1) his productive activity is not an element of a natural process, and (2) his property is not made up of natural means, but of produced implements. His means of production do not account for his personality as does the land for that of the landowner. The result of this is that he may oppose his productive means as their active determining force.

At the same time, the immersion of the artisan within, and his dependence upon, a natural productive cycle as the source of his own subsistence, together with his own lack of proprietorship over the land, make him dependent upon the landlord and therefore bring with them the subordination of his personality to that of the landed class. Where the real foundation of status is the land, the artisan, who by his nature does not own land, must subordinate himself to that class which derives its primacy from its relation to the natural condition. In this respect, the artisan is never really free, and his personality is limited in its development. Indeed, his direct production of, and proprietorship over, his productive means makes impossible the emancipation of his productive activity from limitations implied in its identification with his personality. The artisan is as much the slave of his craft as his craftsmanship is the objectification of his personality.

In wage-labor, the proprietor of the means of production stands fully opposed to them as their owner. The means of production are commodities, fully produced and determined within society. The laborer does not own the means of production and does not represent their limitation to his singularity and particularity. Neither, however, is he inseparably immersed within them as a purely objective element. The emancipation of the worker and the social production of the means of production eliminate all extrinsic impediments to the growth of wealth, making wealth the productive basis for its own generation and unlimited expansion.

The productive foundation of social life is now fully a part of the social process. All of the conditions for the production of wealth are themselves formed and determined within society. The living principle which is active in the production of wealth is wealth itself. The complex unity of the process resides no longer in nature as a condition given to social production from outside. The unity of the production process is now capital existing as the productive basis for its own development; capital existing within production as an active process, and emerging out of production as its determinate product.

PART FOUR

The circulation of capital

> The circulation of capital
> is its becoming, its growth,
> its vital process.
>
> Karl Marx

CHAPTER EIGHT
The circuit in general

I The unity of production and exchange

The nature of commodity production establishes as an inner necessity that the commodity product pursue, subsequent to its production, a strictly determined life-cycle. This life-cycle is simultaneously the realization of the product as a commodity and the realization of the production process as the process of commodity production. Further, since commodity production is equivalently the capitalist consumption of commodities, the realization of the product as a commodity is also the means by which the capitalist character of production is fully established, and by which the product of capital is constituted also as itself capital. The origination of the commodity within a determinate process of production establishes the mode of existence of the commodity product as intrinsically determined in accordance with a complex set of conditions. The life of the commodity product is the life of the capital existing as a product and moving outside of its production process. This condition makes essential the full development of the conception of the characteristic form of motion of the commodity product.

On one side, the existence of the commodity is nothing more than the working out of those qualities which have their origin in commodity production. The whole of this existence is already given in the act of commodity production and asserts itself as the living force embedded within the product. Thus, the life-process of the product emerges in its production as a potential needing only to realize itself in an active movement. Commodity production is the generation of this potential as a force, capital, which is implicit within the product, and which becomes explicit in its life-cycle. Indeed, this potential becomes explicit *as* the life-cycle of the commodity product.

At the same time that the existence of the commodity subsequent to its production is the realization of a potential already established as latent within the product, that existence is also the full realization of commodity production as such. The failure of the product to establish itself outside of its production process as a commodity can always be traced back to a failure of that production process to fully realize the idea of commodity production. Concretely, this failure takes a variety of forms connected to (1) the technique employed and the resulting costs of production, and (2) the adequacy of the product to fulfil needs and therefore to exist as a use-value. Failure in these respects is the failure of the product to be a commodity, and as such is equally a failure of its production process to fully establish itself as commodity production.

Within the concrete conditions of economic life this failure with respect to the quantitative and qualitative aspects of commodity production adopts a variety of distinctive forms. The realization of the value of the product, and therefore its realization as a value, rests upon the existence of a buyer, and the latter depends both on the useful characteristics of the product and upon its price. Where the relation of the costs incurred in its production to the price at which the commodity can be sold is such as to preclude the expansion or even the renewal of the capital, the production process is demonstrably inadequate to the end of the production of commodities and of capital. This inadequacy reveals itself either in the complete inability of capital to realize the value of the product, or in its inability to realize the product as the embodiment of expanded value. There may, for example, exist a technique for which the consumption of labor-power and means of production is the production of a particular product at a given cost. But, where the identical product can be produced at a fraction of that cost, the latter stands head and shoulders above the former in its commodity character; indeed it is to such a quantitative extent more of a commodity that it becomes qualitatively distinguished in its ability to realize its production process as a process of commodity production. And this qualitative difference expresses itself as a vital force in the further development of the respective production processes.

This same condition holds with respect to the ability of the product to fulfil a determinate social need. The use-value of the product is fixed originally within its production. But the latter is successful in the generation of a commodity only in so far as the product discovers in the market an appropriate needy individual with the requisite purchasing power, so that the transformation of the product from the commodity form to the money form may be effected. Where this is impossible due to the absence of any need for the product, therefore due to the absence of any effective demand, the production process has created a product which is incapable of realizing itself as a use-value in its consumption. To this extent, production is not the production of a commodity since it cannot establish itself as the origin of a product which is able to establish itself as a use-value by existing concretely as such.* Thus, while it may be possible to purchase labor-power and means of production and in their consumption to produce a pair of pants with three legs, there has not thereby been a use-value, let alone a commodity, produced. The conditions requisite for the production of commodities are, then, by no means given immediately in the conception of the production process. On the contrary, the conditions of commodity production are also conditions of commodity exchange. The latter is the process of production extended into the life of the product and realized there, while the life process of the commodity is the satisfaction of the conditions which exist only implicitly in the production process.

The movement of the commodity outside of its production is nothing more than the outward expression of a condition already implicitly established within commodity production. None the less this outward movement is as essential to the full determination of production as production is essential to the origin of the commodity and of the entirety of its movement. It is possible to discern already within the production of the commodity the

---

* '. . . thus the product, unlike a mere natural object, proves itself to be, *becomes*, a product only through consumption' [K. Marx, *Grundrisse*, tr. M. Nicolaus (Harmondsworth: Penguin Books, 1973) p. 91].

totality of its life process outside of production. However, this totality is discernible here only as a potential. The realization of this potential, its transformation into an active movement, is equivalently the full determination of the process of production as a moment in the self-constitution of capital. The full development of the life of the commodity outside of its direct production, and the full development of commodity production as such, are, therefore, two aspects of a single connected process – that of the circulation of capital. It is not within the immediate production process taken by itself that the determination of the commodity is accomplished, but only within the totality of capital's circular movement.

The realization of the product as a commodity entails the fulfilment of two conditions intrinsically connected to its commodity character: the realization of the commodity as a value in the sale of the commodity for money, and the realization of the commodity as a use-value by the purchaser of the commodity who gives up the general form of value for the specific embodiment of value in the particular use-value produced. The single condition embedded within the production process, which originally establishes the necessity of the alienation of the product from its point of origin and which, therefore, thrusts it outward into its characteristic cycle, is the separation of the production of the commodity from its consumption. This is the elementary condition for commodity circulation, and it must equally be fulfilled where the commodity is made explicitly to circulate as capital. However, within the circuit of capital the opposition of production to consumption has its origin built into the process of the production of the commodity, so that the separation of production from consumption is implied by conditions built into the system of commodity interaction. This excludes any attribution of the implied separation to the accidental configuration of individual consumption needs taken as an *a priori* condition. The opposition of production to consumption is an opposition latent within the distinction between the need which is directly fulfilled by the product and the need whose fulfilment has the production of the commodity as its means. The need of the producer is that of capital. This is not the need for the direct consumption of the product, but for the expansion of value and thereby of capital. From the standpoint of capital, this general need confronts that of the purchaser of its product, which appears as a particular need connected to the specification of the use-value produced. Here, it is a matter of no consequence whether the purchaser of the product is also capital. Even where the purchase of the commodity is as a productive input for capital, that purchase has, for its rationale, the fulfilment of a need which is specific in terms of its connection to a particular use-value. Thus, the purchaser of the commodity product, whatever his point of origin, represents for capital nothing more than particular need. The object of the purchase is the acquisition of a particular use-value, and the purchase makes possible the fulfilment of a need connected to the specification of the commodity product in terms of its use.

The opposition of need implied in the inner character of capitalist production is reflected in the form of the exchange which eventuates. Capital acquires money, which makes possible the fulfilment of its objective of expansion, while the buyer acquires the use-value capable of fulfilling a particular need. On one side there exists the universal equivalent capable of fulfilling no need, but of acquiring the means to the fulfilment of all needs as well as the means to the expansion of wealth. On the other side, there exists the particular use-value irrevocably connected to the particular need. This opposition develops out of the inner process of capital which produces particular commodities as the necessary means to the expansion of value, and therefore as the means to the emancipation of capital from its specification to any particular commodity. The capitalist production of commodities first necessitates and then sustains that opposition between production and consumption which establishes the basis for the realization of value and of value existing as capital.

The chronic inability of economic theory to grasp this elementary condition of economic life derives from the absence of any concrete investigation of the intrinsic requirements of commodity production, with regard both to the direct production process and to the situation of that process within the totality of the life-cycle of capital. It is characteristic of economic theory to ignore the opposition embedded within the nature of commodity production between the object of production and the need fulfilled directly in the consumption of the product. Leaving aside any consideration of the determinacy of the production process in this sense, the theory is incapable of considering the system of commodity exchange on the basis of the necessary laws by which it is governed. Instead, economic theory considers both production and exchange in the abstract, without any consideration for the concrete conditions eventuating in the development of a market system which is the necessary expression of conditions intrinsic to production. This excludes any conception of a process of production which is itself the necessary expression of the object of production: that object being the acquisition of command over the totality of a market system of production and exchange. To abstract from the opposition of different commodities, and to consider production in terms of a single commodity (as is implicit in the Ricardian as well as in the modern treatments of production),[1] is to make the exchange of commodities unnecessary. Similarly, the typically Ricardian notion that the conditions requisite for the consumption of the product are posited immediately in its production is equivalent to the elimination of any distinction between the objective of the production process and the need fulfilled by its immediate product as a particular use-value. The capitalist character of production is altogether obliterated, and production becomes instead the immediate provision of particular, even naturally fixed, needs.

Commodity production is connected to the circulation of commodities not by chance, but in accordance with the intrinsic implications of its capitalist character. The development of a concept of value is simultaneously the development of the idea of production whose object is no longer the direct fulfilment of immediate needs. Prior to the development of classical political economy exchange is not perceived to be a relation which is intrinsically implied in the product, and the product is not properly an object of exchange in that it 'is not *made* to be an object of barter.'[2] In modern society the object has an intrinsic value because it is produced for exchange, and therefore because the conditions of its production can only be fulfilled with the completion of the exchange.

The complete suppression of the idea of circulation, together with the constitution of commodity production as a process independent of the movement of its product, provides the foundation for the idea that it is labor time which fully 'determines' the exchange-value of commodities. The result of this conception is that the exchange of the commodity is fully developed within the conception of its production, so that production and exchange are, in effect, directly equated. This equation suppresses the necessity that the product be exchanged on one side, and the determinate character of production on the other. The only movement which is essential to the treatment of the commodity is its coming to be. The constitution of commodity production is wholly independent of the life-process of the commodity. Thus, for Ricardo, the expression of value in exchange is unnecessary to the determination of value, so that its existence becomes abstracted from any concrete life-cycle. Smith and Ricardo consider the 'toil and trouble' necessary to produce the object to be its value *to its direct producer*. It is the quantity of his inner substance which is objectified in the product of his subjective laboring. The value of the product relates exclusively to the production process and especially to its subjective character. In effect, it is not required for the full determination of the value of the product that that product be exchanged as a commodity. None the less, both Smith and Ricardo consider the market to be the arena within which the value of the commodity reveals itself. This requires, first, that commodity exchange be governed by the rule of labor-value. If the commodity is exchanged, then that exchange must be expressive of its prior valuation within production. Although labor-value is not required to reveal itself in the exchange of the commodity, if the commodity is exchanged it must be in accordance with its original valuation within production.

For the classical conception, all conditions specific to the process of commodity exchange and the circulation of commodities are not only latent within commodity production, they are fully developed within production. Thus, value not only develops out of production, it is fully determined in production, and the character of the product as a value is fully independent of any conditions which are developed subsequent to its production. Exchange is the inessential expression of the essential relation which grounds the exchange and fully determines its qualitative and quantitative character.

By contrast, the definitive characteristic of the circulation of capital is the reciprocal interrelation of production and exchange. This overcomes the opposition of essential to inessential and constitutes a process of movement which determines each element within a totality. Thus, within the circuit, ground and its expression are made to reveal their real unity as a mutual necessity connected to a total process within which each is no more than a

247

limited moment. Without production there can be no logical basis for the determination of commodity exchange with regard to its intrinsic necessity, its qualitative character and its quantitative magnitude. Equally, without commodity exchange the production of the object must be wholly disconnected from any interaction of commodities and value. It must, that is, be disconnected from any reality as a living process and acting force. Circulation is the mode of existence of the commodity and of capital, which establishes the movement of the commodity as the externalization of the intrinsic conditions of its generative process – commodity production – and which establishes the full determination of that process in the totality of the circuit.

II The phases of the circuit

1 Preservation through expansion

The explicit constitution of production as a moment within the circuit of capital establishes the character of production as the production of capital, and establishes the moment of consumption made possible by the exchange of commodities as a sustaining moment of the circuit as a whole. Thus the materials provided to the circuit are intrinsically determined in accordance with the self-movement of capital. The circulation of capital differs formally from the elementary circuit of commodities and money in that the consumption of the commodities acquired through exchange is now also a moment which is explicitly within the circulation process as a whole. When the consumption of commodities is the production of commodities, consumption does not deprive the circuit of its necessary materials; instead, it provides to the circuit the material basis for its continuation. The concrete determination of commodity consumption within the circuit makes the latter a sequence of commodity movements through exchange and production (P). The form is no longer simply:

$$\ldots M—C—M'\ldots$$

It is now:

$$\ldots M—C—P—C'—M'\ldots$$

These two formulas are not the formulas for two distinct circuits, but the formula for the identical circuit which is considered in the first case in abstraction from the inner determination of its moments, and in the latter in accordance with that inner determination. The distinction is therefore a matter of the degree of abstraction which specifies the elements of the circuit on the basis of the concrete differences by which they are distinguished (as in the case of the commodities advanced (C) and the commodities produced (C')).

The circuit of capital is its metamorphosis, the sequence of forms adopted by a single entity, indeed by a single sum of value, in order that it may both sustain itself and expand. The capital is the totality of the sequence, and not any of its particular elements taken in isolation. Capital is money, it is labor-power, and it is means of production. Capital is the commodity products and the money which their sale provides. And capital is none of these. It is the process of movement within which each of the moments is constituted not as an isolated entity, but as a phase in the process of the whole. Each element has its determination within the totality of the motion made up of the sequence of moments. Each element is, therefore, a particular form adopted by a single principle, capital; the movement as a whole is composed of a sequence of transformations. Capital is the principle which remains the same within the totality of the movement. It is the substance which establishes the unity of the process as a single connected movement. As the capital is transformed through the sequence of its metamorphoses, it is sustained in its integrity by its continual changing of form. To this degree, the capital, even as it expands, still remains the same. The more capital increases the more it becomes, therefore remains, what it is originally: capital. What remains fixed within the movement is the motion itself, and its intrinsic law of endless expansion. The capital is the total motion realizing that inner governing principle of endless movement.

The movement of capital is in all cases its transformation, and never merely its quantitative increase. The circuit is the changing of forms, and is composed of the totality of the different forms. The transformations are themselves determined intrinsically by the nature of the circuit as a whole. Since the circuit is conceived as the mode of existence of capital, the transformations which represent the movement from point to point within the circuit are determined by the twofold principle of the existence of capital: preservation through expansion.

The preservation of the capital refers not to its particular form but to its existence as a sum of value which is maintained quantitatively unchanged throughout the cycle. The movement of the capital which corresponds to the preservation of value is that movement which begins and ends with a like sum of value. Such a transformation is characteristic of commodity exchange within which a sum of value changes only its useful form. The preservation of value within exchange may be connected, for the capital, to two alternative changes of useful form within which the value is embodied. These alternatives correspond to the two poles of the exchange – the purchase and the sale. Movement through exchange transforms capital from the money form to the form of particular commodities, and from the form of particular commodities to the money form. The circuit contains this form of movement in both its aspects – that of purchase and of sale. Capital in the money form purchases commodities – labor-power, and the means of production; and capital in the form of commodities – commodity products – is sold for money. Both of these exchanges effect the preservation of the value existing as capital. The first preserves the value by changing it into that form within which it is alone capable of producing value. The purchase of commodities makes possible the production of value, and of new value, and preserves the value advanced in a new form which is also its expanded form. The second exchange, the sale, preserves the capital by realizing the value of the commodities produced, thereby realizing the products of capital as also values.

Commodity production is the second mode of the transformation of capital, and it is also the mode of its expansion. The production of commodities begins with the capital in the form of productive inputs: of means of production and labor-power. These inputs are first transformed into the production process itself, and the capital exists here as the process of commodity production. The production process is completed with the emergence of the capital in the form of the commodity products. The process, then, is the transformation of the productive inputs into the commodity products. Within exchange there is a transformation of the use-values in which the capital-value is embodied, from commodities to money and from money to commodities. In production there is also a transformation of the useful form of the value, in this case from the commodity inputs into the commodity products. This latter transformation also includes the transformation of the value itself from the active principle of production to the principle of a produced substance existent within the product. Within exchange, the value is always a fixed substance whose form is altered in the purchase and sale. Within production, there is not only the alteration in the useful form of the value, there is also the bringing into existence of value as a fixed substance. Its transformation is not only from use-form to use-form but also from motion to rest. Just as the value is transformed from a state of activity to one of fixity, so also is the capital transformed from its existence as a production process to its existence as a fixed magnitude developed out of production. It is this dissolution of the fixity of the value which distinguishes the inner nature of production as the production of value and capital. In production the value dissolves and reappears, existing in the interim as the process of its generation.

Considered in this way, the phases of the circuit divide into those which entail an exchange, and therefore preserve the value advanced by changing its useful form, and that phase – commodity production – which produces new value and therefore expands the value advanced. However, each phase in the life-cycle of capital contains within it simultaneously the principle of preservation and the principle of expansion. Commodity exchange, considered as the purchase of the productive inputs, maintains the value advanced unchanged, while making possible the reproduction of that value within the production process. Commodity exchange, considered as the sale of the commodity capital which contains not only the original capital-value but also the surplus-value, simultaneously preserves the value advanced and realizes the produced increment to that value. Thus, in the case of the sale of the product, the exchange of equivalents brings about an expansion of value.

Just as exchange entails the moment of expansion together with that of preservation, so also the production of value entails not only the generation of added value, but also the regeneration of the value advanced as the capital investment. Within commodity production, the capital advanced is preserved by being changed into the form of the product. New value is produced only where existing value is also reproduced. While the movement of capital through exchange is identified with the preservation of the value, and the movement of the capital through its production is identified with the expansion of value and of capital, in fact each movement is determined by the objective of the circuit as a whole, which is the preservation of capital through its expansion. Preservation and expansion do not simply oppose each other as distinct objectives, they intermingle as two mutually presupposed conditions embedded within each element of the circuit.

The circuit of capital is composed of three phases. These phases are: (1) The purchase of labor-power and means of production with the money capital. This is the phase of what Marx calls 'money capital' and the circuit considered in terms of its advance and return is the circuit of money capital. (2) The unification of labor-power and means of production within the production process is the productive phase of the capital or the phase of 'productive capital.' This is the phase of the expansion of value in production. The circuit as a whole, considered with reference to the renewal of this phase, is the circuit of the productive capital. (3) The final phase of the circuit is the phase of the 'commodity capital,' of capital existing as the commodity products of the production process. Movement through this phase involves the sale of the commodity products, and the simultaneous realization of the capital-value advanced to their production and of the added value newly produced within the production process. This phase effects the preservation of value by changing it into that form which (1) establishes it explicitly as value in the universal form and which therefore (2) makes possible the renewal of the circuit by leading directly back to the first phase of money capital. The circuit as a whole considered in terms of the return of this phase is the circuit of commodity capital.

The three phases and the characteristic movement which corresponds to each may be represented as:

(1) Money capital (M): $M—C$
(2) Productive capital (P): $C—P—C'$
(3) Commodity capital (C'): $C'—M'$

The circuit of capital is made up of the sequence of its particular phases. Each of these phases is, in its turn, nothing more than the movement of the capital into the subsequent phase. Since the motion is already built into the form which the capital adopts within each phase, that form is not only the means to the advance of the capital, it is also a limitation to its full realization. The adoption by the capital-value of its three different forms – money capital, commodity capital and productive capital – represents simultaneously the advance of the capital from the previous phase, therefore the fulfilment of that phase, and the commencement of the subsequent phase. The circuit as a whole is, therefore, in principle a continuous and unbroken movement.

Just as this movement brings with it the renewal and expansion of the capital, it also implies a renewal and increase of the phases of the capital. The circuit can, then, be considered in terms of the manner in which it effects the return of the capital to each of its phases and forms. The three aspects under which the single circuit of capital can be considered correspond respectively to the renewal of money capital, the renewal of the production process, and the renewal of the commodity product. The circuit considered as the process of the return of the money advanced is the circuit of the money capital:

$$\ldots M\text{—}C\text{—}P\text{—}C'\text{—}M'.\ldots$$

The circuit considered as a process of the continuous renewal of production is the circuit of the productive capital:

$$\ldots P\text{—}C'\text{—}M'\text{—}C\text{—}P.\ldots$$

Finally, the commodity products considered as the objective end and original basis of the movement of value constitute the circuit in its aspect of the circuit of commodity capital:

$$\ldots C'\text{—}M'\text{—}C\text{—}P\text{—}C'.\ldots$$

Just as the circuit is the unity of its three phases, the circuit is also the continuation and revival of each phase. The total circuit is a unity of production and realization within which production is nothing more than the means to the realization of value and its increment, while the realization of value is nothing more than the means to the continuation of production.

2 Money capital

The advance and return of money is the most elementary aspect of the circuit, in that capital appears here in its elementary form of self-expanding value (M—M'). The object of the circulation of commodities and money is that of the acquisition of more money – M'. For the circuit of money capital, however, the expansion of value, while a goal, does not subsume the movement of the capital in its entirety. To the degree that the return of more money is considered as only one, limited, aspect of the complex of circuits, that return can no longer be directly identified with capital itself. For the whole of the circuit, the expansion of value in the form which is directly universal (money) is a single moment which does not exhaust the determination either of the particular phases or of the movement as a whole. The circuit of money capital, far from being an independent movement, must be firmly embedded within a total motion of which it forms no more than one aspect.

This integration of the expansion of the money advanced into the sequence of continuing movements is lost in the immediate equation of capital with the elementary condition of self-expanding value. The latter makes the advance of money and its return the exclusive basis for the determination of commodity movement as capital. It thereby leads inevitably into the idea that the most elementary form of the circuit is not the circuit of money capital as a limited aspect of a greater movement, but a particular cycle of an individual unit of capital, the circuit of financial capital advanced in the form of loans. This notion is, however, fundamentally erroneous in that it takes as its starting point the one-sided subordination of the circuit to a single of its component movements. Money capital is the form bound up with the general conception of capital as value which preserves and expands itself through its circuit. All particularizations of capital also move through the characteristic cycle of money capital, and exist at specified phases in their cycle in the money form. By contrast, the circuit of capital which is advanced as a loan (M—M') involves a deviation from the general conception of the circulation of capital, a deviation which is founded upon the concrete conditions sustained by and within the system of opposed particular units of capital. The deviation which results in the conception of the advance and return of money as the whole of the circuit has the production of commodities as its presupposition while, at the same time, it excludes that process from its own movement. To identify such a particular form of capital with its general conception is tantamount to making the production of commodities the inessential moment. This makes the primary preconditions for circulation, the commodity and money, accidental effects of external forces rather than conditions developed within the cycle of capital itself.

Capital-value in the form of money performs the functions of money, and is also capital only in so far as it subordinates those functions to the determinate role which they play in the constitution of the circulation process, and in the movement of commodities through the cycle of capital.[3] To this extent the functioning of money as capital depends essentially upon the condition that the money capital first adopt, then give up, the money form. Therefore, money capital is not capital which exists as money and exclusively in the money form, but capital which adopts the money form only momentarily as the means to its continued movement through the sequence of the phases of the circuit – productive capital and commodity capital. The shorter the period spent by the capital-value in the money form, the more does the capital realize itself as money capital. This is, then, not money capital in the limited sense of capital which exists throughout its circuit within the money form, but in the sense of that phase and movement of capital in general connected to its existence as money.

For the circuit of money capital, production appears as the means to the end of the expansion of value, and especially of money. The production of commodities is the means to the acquisition of more money, and the moment of production is explicitly subordinated to the movement as a whole, constituted as the mode of value expansion in the money form. This is, however, a one-sided conception which loses its primacy once the full continuity of the circuit and the totality of the movement within which each sub-movement is fixed are fully grasped. That aspect of the movement which is raised to primacy in the consideration of the circuit of money capital is the increase of value in a form which is directly universal, so that here capital is evidently self-expanding value. The circuit of capital is the movement from value to more value; at the same time, the movement from value to more value cannot be sustained exclusively within the sphere of commodity exchange. The expansion of value transpires originally within the process of commodity production. The circuit of money capital must, therefore, be considered with reference to the production of commodities and becomes, in this respect, the means to the production of commodities.

3 Productive capital

The circuit of capital as the provision of the means to the production of commodities and capital is the circuit of productive capital. Considered as the circuit of productive capital each of the moments, or phases, of the process comes to be subordinated to the objective of the continued production of commodities. The sale of the commodity products is now no more than the necessary means for the purchase of the productive inputs, and therefore for the renewal and expansion of the production process. The phases of the circuit, which transpire within the sphere of exchange, are now determined in their relation to the production of commodities. The latter, however, is no fixed end in itself. Within the circuit of productive capital, the production of commodities becomes also the means to the continuation of production, and to its continuation on an expanded scale. Originally, the purchase and sale of labor-power is no more than the prelude to the consumption of labor-power and of the means of production, which is the production of commodities. That production was in its turn the means to the expansion of value in the form of money. Now, with the explicit subordination of commodity production to the circuit of the capital, it is also the case that the consumption of labor-power is only the prelude to the exchange of commodities and ultimately to the purchase and sale of labor-power. Within the commodity circuit the production of commodities is the means not simply to the expansion of value, but also to the continuation and expansion of commodity production. Commodity production is both beginning and end, it is both goal and means. The production of commodities and of capital is not simply the means to the increase of capital, but the means to the increase of the production of commodities.

The circuit of productive capital, in contrast to that of money capital, cannot be grasped exclusively with reference to one of its phases. In the case of productive capital, there can be no elimination of the realization phase, as there is an elimination of the production phase in the case of money capital advanced as loans. The particular capital which corresponds to this form realizes the

notion of capital in general to a greater degree. This result
accounts for the characteristic confusion of the circuit of capital in
general with the circulation of 'industrial capital.'* This equation
has a rational basis in the manner in which industrial capital
typifies the unity of production and realization of value as capital.

Within the conception of the circuit of money capital, production
appears as an intervening moment that is a force in the continual
movement from money to more money. Within the conception of
the circuit of productive capital, commodity exchange appears as
the intervening moment in the continuation of the production
process. For the circuit as a whole both results are correct. It is
equally necessary that production disrupt the advance and return
of value in the money form, and that exchange disrupt the continuation and renewal of the process of commodity production.

4 Commodity capital

The circuits of money and productive capital take a given condition, the productive inputs or money advanced, and generate its
increment; their form is that of the increase of a fixed sum of value.
The movement, then, serves to realize the capitalistic character of
its starting point – the value advanced – and is, in that sense,
constituted formally as the process of the capitalization respectively
of value and of its production process. The final aspect of the
circuit is distinguished in taking as its starting point value posited
already as capital. This is the circuit C'—C', and has at both poles
a sum which is explicitly capitalized value, or value which has
expanded itself. Here the capital is not only the movement but also
explicitly the starting point and ending point.

---

* The notion of industrial capital, especially as it is used in the Marxian
literature, is characteristically ambiguous in that it refers simultaneously to a
special sphere of capital investment and to capital in general as it emerges out of
its productive phase. All capital which has fully subordinated production to its
own objective is characteristically industrial, and all spheres of investment which
are intrinsically capable of being fully brought under the sway of capital are
capable of industrial development. This follows from the conception of commodity production and is not an accidental attribute of certain historically
developed forms. Thus, even the so-called 'services' can be 'industrialized' where
the activity is fully rationalized in accordance with the objective of capitalist
expansion; see H. Braverman, *Labor and Monopoly Capital* (New York: Monthly
Review Press, 1974) chapters 4–5.

The commodity products of the consumption of the labor-power and means of production make up the commodity capital. It can be considered to be a sum of values and of use-values. The commodity products represent, directly within the circuit, the means to the acquisition of money as the requisite basis for the continuation of the spiraling movement. It is the quantitative relation of the value realized in the sale of the commodity capital to the value originally advanced which measures the degree to which commodity production has also been the production of capital and its increment. The capitalized value, which is borne within the commodity products, makes them the embodiment both of the renewal of production and of its expansion.

For the conception of the circuit of commodity capital, the uniformity of the product is an insufficient basis for the analysis of the life within the circuit of the product subsequent to its production. The commodity product, as a phase in the movement of capital, is itself composed of two elements whose opposition is essential to the constitution of the product as capital. For the commodity products to be commodity capital, their existence as value and as the means to the satisfaction of need, is not sufficient. It is further required that the commodity products be subordinated to the self-development of capital. The existence of commodities as commodity capital has, then, two aspects and the homogeneous sum of products and of value is intrinsically divided into two distinct elements:

(1) Each commodity product, and the sum total of commodity products, is subordinated to the total production, so that the realization of the products as commodities, and especially as values, is the realization of a part of the value of the capital advanced. The value which is realized is no longer simply the value of the commodity. It is now the value of the capital which exists in the form of the commodity product. The commodity is not only intrinsically a value, it is intrinsically a moment in the self-development of capital. It is a phase in a total movement whose conditions are given not in its direct exchange, but in the situation of that exchange within the sequence of phases. The realization of value is the realization of capitalized value. As such, it is both the realization of capital and the means to the further development of capital.

(2) The commodity products, as commodity capital, contain not only the capital originally advanced to production, but also the

increment to that capital. This differentiates the conception of commodity capital from the elementary conception of the commodity. Each commodity contains surplus-value, and is therefore measured relative to the original outlay of money. There is contained, within the commodity, a relation to the whole of the circuit. In the exchange of the commodity, it is essential not only that the value of the commodity be realized, but that that realization of value entail an increase in the value of the capital. The commodity capital is the first form of the expanded value. It is the first phase in the circuit within which capital embodies the surplus-value produced within the cycle. The exchange, then, not only realizes the product as a commodity, the embodiment of value, but it realizes the capital originally advanced to production as capital. This intrinsic character of the commodity product makes itself felt in the development of a proportional relation between the value of the commodity capital and the value of the money capital originally advanced to its production. With the constitution of the product as commodity capital, it is no longer simply a question of selling the particular commodity but of realizing the value of the capital previously invested plus the increment to that value, the surplus-value. Within the unified movement of a single sum of capital, there remains hidden a differentiated movement of the elements or component parts of the sum of the capital.

The circuit of commodity capital has, for its starting point, a sum of use-values. The first phase in the movement is the transformation of the sum of use-values into a sum of money. The implicit difference embedded in the commodity capital (as the bodily form simultaneously of preserved value and expanded value) is transferred to the money capital, whose homogeneity hides an inner differentiation. Here we begin to see the problem of the differentiation of M′. Within the circuit as already considered, the differentiation of M into labor-power and means of production reveals the intrinsic determination of the money advanced as capital. Money is the potential for the acquisition of productive means. It is therefore potentially capital. In this respect, the money as a phase of capital's circuit is already earmarked for the purchase of labor-power and the means of production. Implicitly, therefore, the money, as capital, is already divided. This latent division is realized when the money is transformed into the productive inputs. The differentiation is, in that respect, latent within the money so far as that sum of money is to exist as capital. Equally, the M′, as the last moment in the circuit of money capital, is not homogeneous. While for the conception of the elementary circuit of capital value the M′ represents a single, uniform, sum of money, within the conception of the circulation of capital the latent difference embedded within this sum makes itself felt. First, the M′ represents a sum of value which is the sum of two distinct parts – the value advanced and the increment to that value produced within production. This aspect of difference is already explicit within the most elementary conception of the self-expansion of value. For the M′ which is acquired at the finish of a single cycle of the capital, however, there exists as well a second differentiation connected to the constitution of that sum of value as the means to the acquisition of specific productive inputs, which make possible the continuation of the cycle.

The M′ is a further movement and development of the C′. The latter is made up of commodities which as a whole have a value realized in the form of M′. To the extent that this movement is the realization of capitalized, i.e. expanded, value, the single sum must be measured also according to the inner determination and differentiation of the M′ as capital which is produced. Here the fact that the C′ are not the same commodities as the original C (means of production and labor-power), but must be different, implies that their value must contain this moment of inner determination, such that:

$$M' = \text{labor-power} + \text{ means of production} + \text{surplus value}.$$

And, for M′ to realize itself as capital, this inner determination must be realized in a specific series of exchanges. These exchanges entail the movement of the M′ through a further cycle of the capital.

With the expanded value taken as the inception of the cycle, the circuit as a whole takes on a new aspect. Not only is the continuity of the circuit implied in the constitution of its product as expanded value, but the starting point itself becomes the result of the preceding movement and no longer an arbitrarily posited condition. Where the circuit is grasped as beginning not with money (M), but with expanded value (C′ or M′), the starting point is explicitly linked to the movement of capital. The beginning of the circuit is also the end of the circuit, and the conditions which make that beginning possible are the results of the prior movement. The three aspects of the circuit – the circuit of money capital, of productive capital, and of commodity capital – are now merged into a single movement, and the circulation of the capital appears as an endless process of the generation and regeneration of the conditions requisite for its perpetual motion.

III The time of circulation

1 Disrupted movement

The circuit of the capital is the sequence both of forms of the capital-value and of the changes of form which effect the transition of the capital from one phase to the next. Movement as a sequence of metamorphoses constitutes a total process which is made up of a series of separate phases, so that the movement as a whole is also a unity of distinct and opposed moments. The continuity of movement has, then, as its other side, the disruption of movement. The circulation of capital, in so far as it is grasped as a sequence of changes of form, is an interrupted movement. The interruption of the movement is the alteration of the existing form of capital. Thus, the exchange of commodities, while necessary in order to create and recreate the conditions for commodity production, is also a disruption of the production process, a movement of capital away from that process within which it is alone able to generate its increment. The capital, to the extent that it remains within the phase of exchange, cannot generate new value, but can only realize existing value. Indeed, the greater the proportion of the circuit given over to the exchanging of commodities, the less rapidly can the capital increase; the lower the rate of self-expansion, the less is the circuit able to realize itself as capital.

For capital, viewed as a process of the generation of new value, the existence of a part of its value within the sphere of exchange represents a break in its expansion. At the same time, however, the existence of the value within production also disrupts the circuit in so far as the form which the capital adopts within production is essentially particular and thereby inadequate to its universal character. Production intervenes between the purchase of the productive inputs and the realization of the value of the product. The product of capital can only exist as capital by transforming itself first into money and then into new productive inputs. The longer the stay of the capital within the process of its production, the more protracted the period which intervenes between the advance of the capital and its return. This fixes the rate and amount of expansion which capital is able to experience within a given period of time. Capital, within an existing production process, is capital which does not advance into the expansion of that process. The longer the capital remains within production, the longer the productive capital must remain fixed at a given level, and the less rapid and successful the expansion of production. Since the capital can only be realized as such in the relation of advance to return, that is, in the increased value embedded in the return of the originally advanced capital, the production process also disrupts the total movement of the capital. Even as it brings about the production of new value it also impedes the spiraling cycle of the advance of the capital through its phases.

Capital takes up its particular forms – money, production inputs, commodity products – only as the necessary basis for moving beyond each particular form. Money can only exist as capital if the capital which it represents ceases to be money. Productive capital can only be capital by disappearing into the commodity products whose constitution as capital is synonymous with the transformation of their value into the money form. The different forms of capital together constitute capital, and thereby constitute themselves as capital, only to the extent that each is subordinated to a total process of the continual changing of forms. This total process is the circuit, and the circuit is the characteristic mode of existence of capital.

The degree to which value constitutes itself as capital can never be measured by its mere magnitude. Since capital is a moving process and never a fixed quantity it must be measured by that measure characteristic of movement. The capital as it exists fixed into one of its forms is measurable as a sum of value, and as a sum of use-values. But the capital existing as the totality of the circuit is measurable not as a fixed sum of value, but as a sum of value which is circulating. It is no longer simply a matter of the amount of value, but of the motion which it undergoes through its particular forms. The motion is measured by the length of the circuit, so that capital in its characteristic life-process has its measure simultaneously as a quantity of value and as the length of time during which that given sum circulates. This latter is the time of circulation. The law of the circuit of capital is that of the preservation of value through its transformation and expansion. The time of circulation is the time required for the expansion of value, therefore for the return of the capital advanced, together with its increment.

The time required for the capital to negotiate its circuit is the sum of the time during which the capital must remain in each of its phases in order to accomplish the objective characteristic of each phase. The time of circulation is, then, the sum of its three elements: (1) the time necessary for the purchase of the commodities required to set in motion the process of commodity production (M—C); (2) the time required for the transformation of the productive inputs into the commodity capital (C—P—C'); and (3) the time required to realize the value of the commodity capital as money (C'—M').

2 The period of acquisition

The first phase (M—C) is also, under normal conditions, the most readily accomplished and therefore the briefest. This is the phase of the purchase of the productive inputs – the labor-power, the materials of labor and the means of production. The execution of this phase depends exclusively upon two conditions: (1) the availability of the requisite inputs in the commodity form and at the appropriate time and place, and (2) the presence of adequate capital-value in the form of money to effect the purchase of those inputs. The availability of productive inputs in the commodity form is not immediately posited with the appearance of sufficient money capital to effect their purchase. To the degree that the cycle by which the needed inputs become available is dictated by forces outside of their process of productive consumption, it may be necessary for the money capital earmarked for their purchase to remain, for a period of greater or lesser duration, in the money form. In addition, the availability of commodity inputs must be measured in the relation of their price to the capital-value which is to be laid out in their purchase. These considerations make it necessary that some part of the capital-value remain in the money form for a period determined by the determinants of the availability and cost of productive inputs. None the less, given that the possession of money is the possession of universal purchasing power, the purchase of the commodity inputs, to the extent that they are available and at the appropriate price, is immediately posited with the positing of the presence of sufficient capital in the money form. The latter condition is equivalent to the sale of the commodity products of the previous cycle of production and realization.* Under normal conditions, then, the first phase in the circuit makes the least substantial contribution to the length of the circuit.

Given the conditions requisite for the acquisition of the productive inputs – their availability at an appropriate rate of exchange – the time which the capital spends in the money form can, in general, be driven to a minimum. This result needs only to be modified where a separation ensues between the purchase of the materials and their delivery. The phase during which the capital functions in the money form is made up of the purchase of commodity inputs. Where the money is advanced prior to the receipt of the commodities and the purchase precedes the actual sale of the commodities, a period of time intervenes between the advance of the capital in the money form and the acquisition of the productive materials. This is the period during which the capital exists within the phase of money capital. This time must, then, be added to the time required to purchase the productive inputs in the market.

The rapidity with which the capital advances out of the first phase in its circuit makes especially clear the deficiencies of the equation of capital with money. While money, as the universal equivalent, represents the most general, and therefore adequate, form of wealth, wealth exists in the money form for a period the duration of which makes the least contribution to its life-cycle. The money represents for wealth a fleeting moment the necessity of which is related inversely to its duration.

3 The period of production

The time required for the transformation of productive inputs into commodity capital is the period of production. This period is the

---

* This conclusion needs to be modified where credit is taken into account. In that case, the capital-value advanced may differ from the capital-value produced and realized in a given period by the amount of the increase or diminution of the indebtedness of the unit of capital.

normal duration of the time which extends from the moment the productive inputs are acquired to that moment at which they emerge out of production as finished products capable of realizing their exchange for money. The period of production is only complete, then, when the following conditions have been fulfilled: First, the productive inputs, once acquired, must be united within the production process. Second, the production process must be itself completed. This completion entails the constitution of the product as a useful object capable of fulfilling a need.

So long as the availability of productive inputs is assured, their unification within production is given directly in the presence of sufficient capital in the money form to effect their purchase. This does not, however, lead immediately into the production process. The latter may be delayed by the time during which productive inputs are held prior to their productive consumption. Technically distinct inputs are required for production at various of its stages and must be available in appropriate proportions for the production process to proceed in a continuous manner. To achieve this result it is generally necessary that capital-value advanced to the purchase of productive inputs experience a delay between its acquisition and consumption.

The holding of inventories of means of production does not apply to all of the types of capital of which the capital investment is composed, but only to that part which is directly connected to unit production costs (the circulating capital laid out in the purchase of the materials of labor). The time during which this part of the commodity inputs are held as inventories of productive materials translates into an increment in the costs of production and in the scale of investment.[4] The period which intervenes between the acquisition of the commodity capital and its productive consumption is therefore of considerable significance to the expansion process of the capital. This period will, in general, depend upon the technical interrelation of the phases of the production process and of the productive inputs, the perishability of the inputs, the time which normally elapses between order and delivery, and the costs both of delivery of inputs and of the holding and storing of inventories of productive capital. The production period does not, then, begin immediately subsequent to the purchase of the productive inputs, but is delayed by the period of time during which those inputs are held in storage.

The period of production itself commences with the unification of the technically appropriate inputs. Since the objective of the acquisition of labor-power is that of bringing to life the productive apparatus, it is in particular the unification of the means of production with labor which marks the beginning of the period of production of the commodity. Where production is made up of a sequence of phases in continuous operation, the temporal starting point of the period of production of the commodity is identical to the beginning of the productive consumption of the materials of labor. The period of production is determined by the length of time required to transform the inputs of labor, materials and equipment into the commodity products. This is a function first of the technique employed, which dictates the nature and duration of the sequence of specific activities required for the production of the commodities. A given technique may, however, operate at different rates depending, in particular, upon the pace of work. The period of production depends, then, both upon the technique and upon the normal pace of work.

Technically, the production process involves the transformation of material inputs, and is divisible into distinct phases or stages during each of which an element of the total transformation is accomplished. These distinct activities may transpire consecutively or contemporaneously. The final product may be assembled at the conclusion of the process out of its constituent parts produced separately, or the finished product may gradually unfold through a sequence of temporally consecutive stages. Where the latter condition develops, as is the case in assembly line production, the period of production is the sum of the time during which the product in its process of production, or 'intermediate product,' passes through each of the phases or activities required to produce the final product. In the former case, the period of production is not the sum of the time required for each phase in that certain of the phases transpire simultaneously. The period of production depends upon the technique, then, not only in the determination of a total amount of time expended, but also in the determination of the distribution of that time within a given period.

Given the time required to transform the inputs into a finished product, and the distribution of that time, the period of production depends upon the pace of work or the rate of completion of each phase and the movement of the intermediate product from stage to stage of the total production process. The limits placed upon the latter derive first from the technique itself, which has embedded within it a maximum, and possibly a minimum, rate of advance from stage to stage. Where each phase in the production process uses as inputs the products of the previous phases, there develops a characteristic proportion between the phases. This is also the case where the parts of the product are produced simultaneously, and the finished product is then assembled out of its elements. The technical relation of the phases of production places a technically determined upper limit on the pace of work, and therefore a lower limit on the period of production.

To the extent that the production process is a unity of discrete phases connected either sequentially or by their different contributions to the development of the product, that process is not a uniform movement but the sum of separate processes. The time which the productive capital spends within the production process is not exhausted by the time of its actual consumption, but also includes whatever time is required for the intermediate product to advance from one stage of its production to the next. The total period of production is the sum of the period during which the intermediate product is being actively transformed by labor into a form appropriate to its advance to the next productive stage, and of the period which elapses between stages. The former is the working time or time required to work up the materials of labor into the form of the product. To the extent that all changes in the working capital are brought about by the application of labor, the time which elapses between stages is determined wholly by the pace of work in the different stages and in the process as a whole, together with the physical and temporal proximity of the separate stages of the process. The closer the proximity of the stages, the less the time of production differs from the working time.

The period of production is itself determined by the total amount of labor required to transform the inputs into the commodity capital and by the distribution of that labor. The more it becomes possible for the different stages of production to be pursued simultaneously, the shorter is the period of production, given the total labor time required for the immediate production of the product. The closer the proximity of the separate stages in the production process, the less is the difference between the working time and the period of production, and the more reductions in the working time translate directly into a shortening of the period of production.

The time required for the intermediate products to advance from one stage of the production process to the next depends not only upon the proximity of the different stages, but also on the extent to which the time of production is made up of time during which the product is either being directly worked upon by labor, or being moved from work-place to work-place. Where the transformation of the product is not exclusively the result of laboring, the working time will differ from the period of production not only by the time required for the displacement of the product of one stage to the next stage, but also by that time other than laboring time required for the production of the product. This is the period of the maturation of the product which is, in general, connected to material transformations effected by natural forces. This period is normally greater the more dependent the production process is upon nature, and finds its extreme forms in agriculture and in the maturation of its products (the aging of wines, the growing of trees, etc.). The time of maturation will also depend upon the level of technical development and upon the degree to which the natural forces are made to work at a pace consistent with social production, rather than at that pace dictated by their fixed natural ends.[5] Various methods are developed to accelerate the process of maturation artificially, so that the limit of this process is by no means given, but a matter subject to a radical development. The alteration of the period of maturation is a primary objective of technical advance in agricultural production because it is in this sphere that the period of maturation makes itself most acutely felt as a dominant element in the time of circulation of capital. At any given level of the development of the social production process, the period of production has a technical limit also connected to the time required for the maturation of the product within each of its stages.

Given the technical limits on the rate of advance of capital through its production process, the latter is further limited by the capacities of the labor which works the means of production. These capacities are flexible within the limits governed ultimately by the mental and physical capabilities of the species. The change in the pace of work, so far as that change entails an increase in the speed by which the operations of laboring must be accomplished, is synonymous with an increase in the intensity of labor. Given the technique of production, increases in the intensity of labor and reduction of the length of the production period are synonymous. For any given technique, and therefore regardless of the technique, the limits of the capacities of the laborer to do labor present themselves to capital as a lower limit on its period of production. To overcome such limits is to eliminate their source, so that, ultimately, increase in the pace of production must entail reduction in the dependence of the production process upon the limited capacities of the laborer.

The products of labor are by no means limited by the fixed capacities and potentials of the worker. All limits of production relating to speed of work, precision, duration of working time, etc., which are connected to the physical and mental capabilities of the worker, are overcome in the replacement of labor with machinery. The conception of the product and of its production is determined, independently of the capacities of the worker, by the general level of development of technology and of the capacities built into that technology. From the standpoint of the conception of production as a technological process, the fixed capacities of the worker represent extrinsic impediments to the development of the mechanism of production and its product. Production confronts the fixed abilities of the laborer as contingent conditions unconnected to the intrinsic character of the production process and overcome in its characteristic mode of development: mechanization, or the replacement of handwork by the work of the machine. The machine has built into its mechanism the ability to produce with greater uniformity of product, greater precision, greater speed and greater continuity. The machine is also capable of accomplishing tasks which the human form is not simply less well adapted to, but intrinsically inappropriate for, connected for example to the application of force, of chemical processes, and to precision of working. In all of these areas the limited capability of labor makes it a bottleneck in the development of the product through its production process and, to the extent that the laboring remains essential, places a lower limit on the period of production.

The normal period of time required to produce a commodity with a given technique will, within the limits fixed by that technique, depend upon the intensity of labor. Increases in the intensity of labor proceed up to the normal physical and mental capabilities of labor. This limit, then, establishes the length of the time required to produce the commodity. The period of production is the sum of the working period, the time required to transfer the intermediate product from stage to stage of the total process, and the period of maturation of the product.

The period of production encompasses the whole of the time during which labor-power and means of production are consumed in the direct production of the commodity. For the general conception of circulation, the specific function of the differences in the types of laboring and of means of production required at different points in the production period are of no consequence. Consumption of commodity inputs is part of the period of production equally in the case of their direct material transformation and in cases where their material form remains unaltered. Thus the movement of the product to the point of sale and the transportation costs incurred are also elements of its production since they presuppose consumption of labor-power and means of production within the total process of the formation of commodity capital.

The time and costs of transportation derive directly from the spatial separation of the producer from the consumer. The spatial separation of producer from consumer is measurable along two dimensions: the time required to bring the product to its purchaser, and the cost incurred in transporting the product from its point of production to its point of purchase. The time required to transport the product to the location at which it can be sold depends first upon the location of the production process relative to the market for its products and second upon the level of development of the means of transport.

Given the conditions of transportation, the period of production will be positively correlated with the distance between producer and consumer. The greater this distance, the greater will be the length of time during which the capital remains fixed in the form of intermediate product. Similarly, given the location of producer relative to consumer, the duration of the period of production will be greater the lower the level of development of the means of transportation. This latter, in its turn, is a function of the speed of transport, the frequency of its availability, and its capacity.

The level of development of the means of transport will express itself not only in the duration of the period of production, but also in the magnitude of the capital which must be expanded during this period on the costs of transporting the product to the point of sale. To transport the commodity products to the point of purchase, or to the consumer himself, entails the incursion of transportation costs. Capital must, therefore, be advanced to the purchase of the means of transportation or to the payment for their services.

The forces which determine transportation time and costs act simultaneously in two opposing directions. Given the size and location of the market, the drive of capital is always to reduce the time and costs incurred in the movement of the commodities to the market in order to accelerate the growth of the capital. At the same time, an increased expenditure of time and capital in transporting the product may be the necessary basis for expanding the scale of production. Thus, while lower transportation time and costs may mean a more rapid advance of the capital, the greater the time and capital expended in transportation, the greater is the market available to capital, and the more rapid its growth.

4 The period of realization

The transportation of the commodity capital to the point of purchase does not, in itself, complete the realization of the capital-value in the sale of the product for money. The separation of producer from consumer is not simply spatial, but is also connected to the status of producer and consumer as independent principles. While the producer brings his product to the market he does not, by that same act, also bring the consumer of the product to market. On the contrary, there is nothing given immediately within the production process, or within the circulation of capital, which could assure that there will appear in the market consumer demand in the appropriate quantity and form. To be sure, the circuit of capital generates within it consumption needs and therefore demand for the means of production, labor-power and materials which it requires to sustain and renew itself. What the circuit does not directly engender, however, is the demand for its own products. Even on the assumption that the commodity products can be sold, it is possible for a lapse of time of greater or lesser duration to separate their availability for sale from the actual sale itself.

Once the capital has been transformed, via production, into

commodity capital, the completion of the circuit requires only the time necessary to realize its value. The time which elapses between the completion of the period of production and the return of the capital in the money form is the period of realization. The separation of production from consumption, which we have seen to be implied in the idea of social production, makes itself felt directly in the determination of the duration of the period of realization. This separation is predicated upon the absence of any immediate temporal equivalence between the completion of the production of the commodity and the beginning of the commodity's consumption.

The period of realization is limited by the length of time during which the finished product is able to maintain its value.* This limit may be connected either to the depreciation of the use-value, i.e. spoilage, or directly to the alteration in the exchange-value of the product in the market. The longer the use-value is able to maintain its integrity, the longer is the potential period of sale, and the longer may the products remain awaiting the appearance of their purchaser. For such products there is a final period during which they are stored up prior to their sale. The distinction between the pace of production and the pace of development of consumption demand necessitates that the product be available ahead of the demand, and therefore that inventories of finished products be generated. Given the depreciation of the use-value of the product, the limit on the building up of inventories is a limit connected to the effect of the growth of inventories on the expansion of capital. This effect is two-fold, having to do, first, with the extension in the period of circulation implied in the increasing of the stock of inventories, and, second, with the costs incurred in storing inventories of finished products. Thus the period of realization possesses both an upper and a lower limit. The lower limit is implied in the necessities of marketing and the necessity that the products be available at the pace dictated by the expansion and contraction of the market rather than by the pace of production. The upper limit is implied in the reductions in the growth of capital and in its rate of advance implied in the growth of stocks of produced commodities.

---

* The period of production, since it includes the transportation time, may also be limited by those factors which fix the temporal limit on the period of realization.

The sum of the period required to purchase the productive inputs, the period of production itself, and the period of realization is the total time of circulation. This is the time required for a given sum of capital-value to pass through all of the phases of the circuit and return once again to its starting point. This time is, in its turn, a critical measure of the ability of the capital circuit to accomplish its end of preservation through expansion.

IV The costs of circulation

The values of the commodities consumed within the circuit of capital make up the costs of circulation. The incursion of these costs is distributed temporally along the period of circulation, and marks out the limits of the period of production. Since the consumption of commodities and labor-power is equivalently the process of commodity production, the temporal limits of that consumption define the period of production. It is a matter of no consequence, for the general conception, whether the commodities consumed are turret lathes, transportation services, or advertisements. The capitalist consumption of commodities is always a part of commodity production. The sole object and rationale of capital's consumption is the production of wealth, and costs are incurred exclusively to that end.* Since the capitalistic consumption of commodities outside of the production process is excluded in principle, it is not the limits of the period of production which define the productive consumption of commodities, but the productive consumption of commodities which defines the limits of the period of production. The costs of circulation are, therefore, equivalently the costs of production.

The logical status of the costs of circulation, especially the extent to which they represent 'real' costs of production, becomes ambiguous[6] only when production is falsely identified either with the material transformation of the inputs, or with the formation of a product the utility of which is presumed to be determined inde-

---

* This need not hold for the owner of the capital whose object in consumption may be the fulfilment of private need. Such consumption is, however, intrinsically 'unproductive' in that it is not inherently capitalistic. The capitalist's consumption is always clearly distinguishable from consumption on the part of capital.

pendently of the total process of the self-development of capital. So long as the object of investigation remains the inner logic of bourgeois economy, however, the only necessity which is analytically relevant to the determination of cost is that of the self-regeneration and self-expansion of capital. Those costs necessitated by this process, and implied by its continuation, are necessary costs. Since they are incurred with the single object of sustaining the productive cycle of capital, they are costs required for the production of capital.

To be sure, were the object of production to be defined otherwise than as the self-development of capital, for example as the generation of the material requirements for the fulfilment of species needs, the necessary inputs, or 'costs,' would be defined differently. Similarly, were it possible to define social needs independently of capital, the costs incurred in their fulfilment would also be determined differently than those determined within the life-cycle of capital. Such requirements would hardly even be 'costs' to the extent that the object in accordance with which they are defined is made independent of the specificity of the system of economic relations as relations within which the life-cycle of wealth is sustained.

In general, however such (biologically necessary, or 'socially rational') costs might be defined, they can have no relevance to the theoretical investigation of the system of relations of bourgeois economy. Such considerations can only become relevant where the relations of bourgeois economy are argued to be in some sense expressive of, and therefore determined by, the independently defined 'real' requirements of production. Indeed, the idea that the capital relation provides nothing more than the 'form' within which a pre-determined productive activity seeks out its development underlies all attempts to distinguish between the 'real' costs of production and those costs incurred which are connected inseparably to the form which production adopts when made subordinate to capital. While such a conception may provide the basis for a moral indictment of bourgeois society, for the theoretical conception of economic relations the determination of production costs must be embedded within the conception of the life-cycle of capital, and based exclusively upon the exigencies of that life-cycle. The question of the limits which define the costs of production, and therefore the costs of circulation, is equivalently the question of the limits of the capitalist consumption of commodities,* limits which only become determinate within the growth process of the total capital.

Since production is only one moment in the circuit, production is strictly defined in accordance with the totality of the circuit. It is this determination of production which expresses the mutual dependence of production and exchange. The inner determination of production is not, then, independent of exchange. The dependence of production on exchange expresses itself both in the determination of the nature of the use-value in accordance with its market destination, and in the incursion of production costs associated exclusively with establishing the marketability of the product (e.g. the 'sales effort'). What needs to be emphasized is that the sales effort, so far as it requires the consumption of labor-power and commodities, is also an element of the period of production and entails costs of production.

Even advertising costs are, under conditions of capitalist commodity production, costs required for the constitution of the commodity as a use-value. Since use-value is not a material property of a physical substance, its generation is not completed with the material transformation of the inputs. The limits of its production are not, then, defined by that material interchange. It is also necessary that the social constitution of the commodity as a

---

* This problem is linked analytically to the distinction between 'productive and unproductive labor.' The correct resolution of the issue was already grasped by Smith, who defines productive labor simply as that labor which works for, therefore as, capital (*The Wealth of Nations*, book II, chapter 3). This identifies production with the capitalist consumption of commodities and not with any primordial natural or material interchange. Once having established the necessary standpoint for the conception of capital's productive consumption, Smith proceeds to corrupt his original conception by attempting to subsume the idea of productive labor into that of labor's participation in the generation of a material product. Subsequent to Smith the problem of unproductive labor, where it is not directly predicated upon the capitalistic character of its consumption, always refers to a quality of the labor (its 'necessity' for production) presumed to be independent of capital. Only costs necessary for the formation of the product independently of its destination as an element of capital are truly part of production, and only that labor which is necessary in this same abstract sense is productive. This idea inevitably excludes any systematic conception of necessary costs and therefore of productive labor. For an attempt to deduce the laws of capitalist development upon the basis of a conception of the rationality of production defined independently of capital in precisely this manner, see P. Baran and P. Sweezy *Monopoly Capital* (New York: Monthly Review Press, 1966) chapter 5.

use-value be pursued by its producer. The commodities consumed towards this end represent real costs of production so far as capital is concerned, and are directly relevant to the deduction of the general laws of capitalist development. In this sense, the entirety of the process of commodity production finds itself absorbed into the sales effort and there are no costs incurred at any stage of the generation of the commodity which are unconnected to the constitution of the product as a saleable commodity.

It by no means follows from the foregoing that the idea of real costs of production becomes arbitrary or purely subjective. So far as the particular producer is concerned, the costs, even though they are not defined in a purely material manner, are still fully determinate; and they are determinate regardless of whether the individual producer grasps them in his own evaluation of what is required in the way of costs in order to ensure the preservation and expansion of his capital. The determination of the socially necessary costs of production takes place within the interaction of the system of particular capitals taken as a whole. The activity by which each pursues his object of limitless expansion eventuates for the system as a whole in a determination of necessary costs which are both objective and real, existing for each individual producer as an external coercive force. The investigation of the economic determination of the necessary costs of production cannot be pursued at the present level of analysis, but can only be considered in the course of the investigation of the system of economic relations as a whole, and of the laws by which it is governed.

The conception of the sales effort, and of the costs and time which are normally devoted directly to the marketing of the product, requires a concrete analysis of the development of the market system and of the laws which govern its intensive and extensive growth. The pace at which the market as a whole expands is not only discontinuous, but is also made up of both the differentiated growth of its distinct elements, and of the particular markets of which it is composed. This complex process of development represents, for the unit of capital, the condition for the realization of its products. This condition, and particularly the pace at which the market develops, is not given immediately in the conception of the production process. The period and costs of circulation are determined by the relation of two distinct principles: on one side that which governs the growth of the production process and the rate at which it overcomes its internal impediments; on the other side that which governs the growth of the market for the products of the production process. It is intrinsic to the nature of the circulation of capital that these two principles become, at crucial points, opposed. This opposition forms the primary basis for the determination of the characteristic mode of development of capital.[7]

The total costs of production are distributed along the production period in accordance with its intrinsic specification to the commodity product. The manner in which these costs distribute themselves within the circuit provides the basis for the distinguishing of the component parts of the capital investment and, therefore, for the conception of the concrete determination of the circuit and of the unit of capital.

CHAPTER NINE

The component parts of the capital

I The differentiation of the capital

Up to this point, the circuit of capital has been considered as the form of movement of a single sum of value. This sum has been taken to circulate as a whole, and the resulting movement to constitute a single circular process. The circular process of capital is the complex of its phases marked by its different forms and by the different modes of development which connect the different forms. There exists, however, no necessity that the cycle of alternating phases be experienced in the same manner and at the same pace by all of the capital investment. On the contrary, the very conditions of the circuit entail the development of the capital into its different forms and therefore the breaking apart of the total capital-value into its component parts. For the conception of the circuit it is necessary to consider not only the movement of the total capital-value taken as a unit, but also the different patterns of movement of the different elements of that total.

The distinctions between forms of movement of the capital are the basis for the differentiation of the capital into its component parts. The circuit is not a single undifferentiated movement, but the complex of interconnected movements of the different parts of the total capital. The circuit is the unity of a system of circuits, and the capital which unifies these composing movements is the unit of capital.

The basis upon which the differentiation of capital is established is intrinsic to the conception of the circuit. These differences must all be encompassed implicitly within the general conception of the circulation of capital. Just as in the conception of commodity production the whole of the capital advanced is differentiated in accordance with the objective of its consumption, so also in the circulation of the capital the differentiation is in accordance with the objective of the circuit as a whole. The differentiation of the capital which is implied in the idea of commodity production connects to the opposition between labor-power and means of production, and to the different contributions made by each to the process of capitalist commodity production. Such differences are not imposed arbitrarily upon an already given production process, but are, instead, intrinsically implied by the idea of commodity production. The same holds true for the conception of the circuit of capital. Here, however, the distinctions are not determined exclusively by requirements given directly in commodity production. To be sure, the inner differences developed in the treatment of production are also reflected in the conception of the circuit. Differences within the circuit are differences connected to the inner character of production and to the opposition of the different elements of the capital as they exist within the production process. The differentiation of the capital, so far as the totality of its process is concerned, is not, however, given immediately in the opposition of elements intrinsic to the direct production process. The process which is the mode of existence of capital is defined equally by the necessity for the realization of value produced as capital, and therefore for the realization of the capital invested in the form of capital produced – i.e. the commodity product. The differentiation of the capital must subsume the differences which develop within production under the total movement of the capital-value and the requirements connected to the whole of that process. These are also differences of the productive capital, but differences raised to a higher level and endowed with a concrete determination in accordance with the whole of the circular movement of the capital.

In the first instance the sole distinction which develops directly out of the general analysis of the circuit and which is founded upon nothing more than the abstract idea of circulation is the distinction of pace of movement. Differences in the mode of circulation of capital are differences in the rate at which the different parts of the capital progress through the circuit. This rate of movement is measured in terms of the number of individual circuits which transpire between the advance of capital-value and its return. The individual unit of measure, the single period of circulation, is fixed by the time which elapses between the original advance of value to commodity production and the first return of value in the sale of the commodity product.

Differentiation of the capital upon the basis of its mode of circulation is, first, an exclusively quantitative differentiation measured by the number of individual circuits required for the return of the capital advanced. The investigation of this quantitative distinction leads, however, to the qualitative differentiation of the component parts of the capital according to its mode of circulation. In particular, the purely quantitative distinction between that part of the capital whose advance and return are separated by a period less than or equal to the period of circulation, and that part of the capital whose advance and return are separated by a period which exceeds the period of circulation, expresses a substantive difference with fundamental implications for the treatment of the self-development of capital.

Where the capital value is returned at the completion of the single circuit, the value advanced circulates as a homogeneous unit. Since the whole of the value advanced reappears in the product of the single circuit, that value has the form of a presupposition of the circuit and the circuit represents the mode by which the useful form of the value is altered. Where the value advanced does not circulate as a homogeneous unit, and the return of the whole of the value is not accomplished with the completion of the single circuit, the circuit no longer represents the simple transformation of the use-value within which the capital value is embodied. Since the use-value of the capital advanced is not obliterated within the single circuit, neither is the whole of the value consumed and returned. In this case it is necessary to differentiate the movement of the value advanced between that part which reappears in the product of the individual cycle and that part which remains behind still locked into the form of the use-value advanced to commodity production. The manner of this differentiation (the determination of the rate of depreciation of the capital invested for a period which exceeds the single period of circulation) is bound up essentially with the peculiar manner in which its valorization is accomplished. This valorization is no longer immediately given in the fixity of the value circulating as a single unit. Thus, the differentiation in the mode of circulation of the component parts of the capital is bound up essentially with substantive differences in the determination of the value of the capital invested and in the manner by which the expansion of that value is accomplished.

Where the whole of the capital-value advanced circulates as a unit, the form of its movement is identical to that of capital in general. This part of the capital advanced is termed the circulating capital. The value of the commodities which compose the circulating capital appear at the outset as a single sum of value. This sum of value together with its increment emerges at the end of the circuit still existing as a single unit. Where the whole of the capital advanced does not circulate as a unit, this implies that a part of that value separates itself off so that the different parts of the single sum move separately. Were none of the value invested to continue to circulate, that investment would cease to be capital and, indeed, where any part remains fixed permanently that part also ceases to exist as capital. Thus, the polar opposite of circulating capital is not capital which does not circulate, but capital which circulates in parts. The value which circulates in this way is the fixed capital. Capital, then, divides into that part which moves from the commodity inputs directly into the commodity products, and that part which is fixed for a period in excess of the time of circulation within the form of productive capital. These two component parts are the circulating capital and the fixed capital.

Circulation is the general mode of existence of capital, and no part of the capital-value can remain in the same form throughout the entirety of its life-process and sustain itself as capital. With regard to the component parts of the capital, the distinction between fixity and movement is not a distinction between movement and its absence, as is implied in the language, but between forms of movement. In this respect, all capital is both fixed and circulating, existing now in a particular limited form, now in its movement from form to form.[1] Thus, even at that point where the fixed capital, by depreciating, leaves the form of means of production and adopts the form of commodity capital, and later money capital, that capital remains locked within a circular movement which is peculiar to it as a moment in the life-cycle of fixed capital. The value of the fixed capital may, in this way, adopt the money form as a phase of its own circuit. For the continuation of the circuit, however, it is necessary that the money capital revert once again to the form of means of production, thereby realizing its implicit existence as a phase in the life of the fixed capital. Fixity is, thus, a phase in the circuit of a part of the capital advanced, and also, a form of circulation dictated by the passage of capital-value through that phase.

II Circulating capital

1 The concept of circulating capital

The most elementary component of the capital is that which corresponds directly to the most elementary and general form of movement of value through its circuit. The value which moves through this characteristic cycle is that part of the capital which sustains itself as a single sum of value throughout its cycle. This is the part which corresponds to the labor-power and materials of labor. The latter is composed of produced inputs so far as they must be purchased anew, *in toto*, for each production period and for each cycle of the capital-value.

This element of the capital investment, the circulating capital, includes all those productive inputs (and the money expended upon them and returned in the sale of the products) which are wholly absorbed in the production of the individual unit of the product. Since these inputs are wholly absorbed within the single productive cycle, they must be advanced to production in proportion to its scale, to the quantity of commodities produced within the given period of production. These, then, are unit costs which vary directly with the number of units of product produced per period of production. Both the use-value and the value of these inputs are wholly absorbed in the production of the particular products, and it is their movement along with that of the product which marks out a single production period and a single circuit of the capital advanced.

The renewal of the value of the circulating capital destined for absorption into the individual unit of product is the immediate basis for the continuation of the cycle of production. The existence of these inputs into production as circulating capital depends predominantly upon the relation which is sustained between their use-value and that of the product. It is this relation which establishes the characteristic form of motion of the value which they represent. The value of the circulating capital expended in this way proceeds through the circuit as a single sum because the whole of its use-value is absorbed into the product. Each quantum of the use-value which enters production corresponds to a quantum of the product. In the case of the labor-power, the production of the unit of the commodity product corresponds to a given quantity of labor time, and the scale of production in a given period corresponds to a proportionate total quantity of labor and therefore sum total of value – the wages bill. In the case of the materials of labor of given useful specification, a fixed quantity corresponds to a single unit of the product, and the scale of production is a multiple of the unit costs. To be sure, in the case both of the materials of labor and labor-power the efficiency of utilization may vary. Nevertheless, given the level of efficiency, there is nothing in the unit measure of this part of the capital which goes beyond the single unit of product and its production. To produce more, it is immediately necessary to purchase more, and the cycle of production corresponds exactly to the cycle of consumption of the circulating capital. In this respect, the commodity purchased, be it labor-power or the materials of labor, does not in itself go beyond the unit of the product.

The composition of the circulating capital is not, however, exhausted by those inputs which are directly related to the production of the individual unit of product. The costs of production and circulation include all costs incurred in the movement of the product through its cycle. These costs are inclusive of all capital expended in the determination of the marketability of the commodity product; both in the direct production of the unit of product and without regard to the formation of the unit of product (e.g. in marketing and product development). To the extent that labor-power, in particular, is expended without association directly with the production of the individual unit of product, that labor-power represents circulating capital which, while returned with the completion of the individual circuit, is not substantively attached to the particular unit of product. This distinction within the circulating capital, while relevant at the level of the analysis of the growth of capital, is of no consequence for the conception of the circuit. For the conception of the circuit, all labor-power and materials consumed return *in toto* with the completion of that circuit in the course of which they are advanced. Capital expended in this way is circulating capital regardless of whether the labor-power and materials are consumed in the immediate production of the individual unit of product.*

The circulating capital has as its specific form of motion the unbroken development of forms of a given quantity of value advanced. All of the capital-value advanced as circulating capital during a given production period emerges at the end of that period embodied in the use-value of the product. Given the value invested within a fixed period of time, the value of the product which results from the consumption of this investment must include a part which corresponds to the whole of the value of the materials used up. This is the condition required for the preservation of the capital and therefore for its expansion. The emergence of a value part which renews the labor-power and materials of labor is the preservation in a new form of the capital originally absorbed into the production process. Taking the materials cost within a given cycle of the capital to equal M, and the cost of labor-power consumed to equal W, then it is clear that the level of these costs is a function of the unit costs of the materials and labor, and of the quantity consumed. Taking the total value produced to equal G, the condition which must be fulfilled for the circuit of capital to sustain itself, given the costs of circulating capital, is:

$$G > M + W.$$

This also implies that the value of the individual unit of the product, g, be determined in such a way as to fulfil the condition:

$$g > m + w,$$

where m and w are respectively the wage rate and the unit cost of materials. This is the condition that the value of the product contain a part which corresponds to the consumption of the circulating capital. This condition must be fulfilled if the circuit is to be allowed to continue, and if the renewal of the capital and of the production of commodities is to be accomplished.

---

* The costs of circulating capital should not, then, be confused with unit variable or prime costs. Prime costs include only that part of the circulating capital directly absorbed into the particular unit of product, and depend for their determination upon the conception of the growth of the unit of capital.

The value laid out in the purchase of the materials and labor-power is money advanced not simply to commodity production but also to its own expansion. To the extent that the value expended upon the materials and labor power is (1) advanced in this sense, and (2) returned with an increment of surplus-value, that value proceeds through the characteristic cycle of capital, and the materials and labor-power exist as the embodiment of so much capital. Under these conditions it is required not only that the value of the product contain a part which corresponds to the renewal of the circulating capital consumed, but also that the value product contain an additional element which corresponds to the expansion of the circulating capital.

2 The payment of the costs of circulating capital

The exchange by which the materials and labor-power are united with the means of production in the form of fixed capital is a two-sided relation which, as in all exchange, is composed of two separable elements whose unity need not imply that they are immediately contemporaneous. On the contrary, it is implied in the idea of exchange that the two moments, the purchase of the commodity and the payment of its money equivalent, may be separated in time. For the general conception of exchange and of capital this possibility has no immediate consequences since the time element plays no active role. For the conception of the circuit, however, the time element is critical, since the span of time which elapses between the acquisition and the payment is no longer represented by time in the abstract, but now by the time of circulation. With the concrete conception of the circuit, the self-expansion of capital has an explicitly temporal element. It is therefore a process determined, both qualitatively and quantitatively, by the temporal order and magnitude of the events which it subsumes. In the case of the circulating capital it is essential to consider the temporal order of the acquisition of the productive inputs, their consumption in the production process, and the payment of money equivalent to their value to their original owner.

To the extent that the payment for the materials is given directly in the acquisition of those materials, the money laid out is substantively a part of the capital investment in that it is advanced to the acquisition of a surplus-value, therefore to its self-expansion.

The circulation of capital

To this extent, and only to this extent, the value of the materials of labor and the labor-power is a component part of the capital investment. In this case, the cycle of the circulating capital corresponds exactly to the circuit of capital in general (M—C—P—C'—M'). The circuit begins with the money capital laid out for the purchase of the labor-power and materials. It becomes, subsequent to that purchase, capital in the form of the labor-power and materials, the productive inputs. In the consumption of those inputs the value advanced is transformed into commodity capital, and eventually into expanded value in the money form.

By contrast, where the acquisition of the labor-power and materials of labor precedes the payment of the money equivalent of their value, that value may or may not constitute a part of the capital investment. Assume that the period of production is equal to A, the period of realization of the value of the commodity capital is equal to R, and the period which separates the purchase of the materials and/or labor-power from the payment of their money equivalent to their seller is equal to q. Then W + M constitutes an element of the capital investment whenever

$$q < A + R.$$

If this condition does not hold, then the value of the materials and labor-power is not a constituent part of the capital and the circuit of the part of the circulating capital composed of materials and labor-power is inverted. Since the value of the materials is not advanced as capital, the money which returns subsequent to the sale of the product contains a part which corresponds to the value of the materials and labor-power, but does not contain any expanded value connected to the value of the materials and labor-power consumed. Instead of the movement from money to more money through the intermediation of commodities, the circuit now has the form of a movement from commodities (W + M) to commodities (C') to money.

In general, the question of the contribution of the circulating capital to the capital investment is a matter of degree, depending upon the period of payment for the different elements of the circulating capital, the total length of the circuit, and the point within the circuit at which the element of the circulating capital must be consumed (and therefore the related, although not identical, point at which it must be acquired). For the different elements of the circulating capital, the period which may normally elapse between acquisition and payment will vary. This difference holds especially for the opposition of the labor-power to the materials of labor, in that the forces connected to the acquisition and consumption of labor-power differ from the forces connected to the acquisition and consumption of the materials of labor. As regards the question of circulation, this difference reduces to a difference of quantity in that it concerns only the time which elapses between acquisition, consumption, and payment. As a purely quantitative difference it may be left aside in the consideration of the general circumstances. Ignoring differences in the period between acquisition and payment for the different elements within the circulating capital, the general conditions have the following form: Let n represent the period of payment, c_i the amount expended upon circulating costs in period i, and t the sum of the period during which the commodities are held in inventory, the period of production, and the period of realization. The investment in circulating capital (K_c) is

$$K_c = \sum_{i=0}^{t-n} c_i \ .$$

The latter is the sum of all c_i for which $q_i > n$, where q_i is the length of time which the c_i spend within the circuit prior to its return in the money form.

If the sum of the period of production and the period of realization is greater than the period which elapses between the purchase of the materials and labor-power and the payment of their money cost, then, so far as the conception of the circuit of capital is concerned, the whole of the value so invested becomes a part of the capital advanced, and there must correspond in the value of the product a part which is the increment to the capital advanced as circulating capital. Thus, so far as the value of the circulating capital is concerned, there must under all circumstances emerge an element of the value of the product which corresponds to the value of the labor-power and materials consumed. This is required for the preservation of the value within the circuit. Further, where the period of production and realization exceeds the period between the purchase of, and the payment for, the labor-power and materials of labor, there must also emerge, in the value of the product, a part additional to that which replaces the value expended. This latter represents the increment to the value invested as circulating capital.

3 Labor-power and the circuit of capital

The circuit of the part of the capital paid out as wages is identical in substance to the circuit of the value paid out for the purchase of the materials of labor.* While these two elements differ in their concrete determination, and therefore in the concrete conditions which establish their specific patterns of movement, the two elements are indistinguishable for the general treatment of the component parts of the capital in circulation. Within the circuit, considered abstractly, the wages bill must be considered as an element of the circulating capital which is determined in accordance with the general laws of circulation. In general, the money paid out as wages is not advanced to the worker prior to the consumption of his labor-power, so that the acquisition of labor-power precedes by a fixed period the payment of the wage. The relevant period, in this case, is that of the cycle of wage payments. If the period of wage payment exceeds the period required to produce and market the product, then the money paid to the worker as the value equivalent of his labor-power is not a component of the capital investment. Here, again, while there must be a value equivalent in the product for the payment of the cost incurred in the consumption of labor-power, there will not in general emerge out of production a value sum which corresponds to an increment to the value expended in the purchase of labor-power.

What is distinctive about the labor-power is precisely that it is consumed more or less continuously throughout the period between its acquisition and the payment for its consumption. Unlike the materials of labor, which may be acquired independently of

---

* Since the purchase of labor-power is from the worker, while the purchase of the materials of labor is from capital, the concrete relation differs in ways relevant to the calculation considered here. In particular, when the normal period allowed for the payment of the costs of the materials is exceeded, then interest accrues to the supplier of the materials. This is not the case for labor-power, which cannot make a claim for interest payments upon the labor-power advanced. This accrual of interest makes more complicated the calculation of the price of the product and the rate of profit realized in its sale.

their consumption, the acquisition of labor-power is the acquisition of the use of the laborer's force over a fixed period of time, so that it is impossible to separate its acquisition from its consumption. It follows that, unless capital is to pay the wage continuously, it must either advance the wage to the worker or have the worker advance his labor-power prior to the payment of the wage. Here, it is not possible even in principle for the purchase and acquisition to be contemporaneous. In the case of the purchase and sale of labor-power, therefore, money must act as means of payment. Where money acts as means of payment (see above, chapter 3) the advance of the commodity and subsequent receipt of its money equivalent is in general implied. Thus in the case of labor-power it follows that the payment of the wage will in general be subsequent to the laboring acquired in the consumption of the commodity provided in exchange for the wage.

To the degree that the wage represents consumption on the part of the worker, the cycle of payment must be related to the requirements of that consumption. For the laborer there is no advantage whatever in extending the period which elapses between the consumption of his labor-power and the payment of the wage. To the degree that the wage is considered an element of capital, however, and more specifically, that the subsistence of the laborer is the outcome of the incorporation of his labor-power into the process of capital, the cycle of wage payments must bear a determinate relation to the expansion of capital. While the actual determination of the relation of payment to acquisition, in the case of labor, is subject to an opposition of forces, that determination must always subordinate itself to the exigencies of the self-expansion of capital.

Where the period of production and of the sale of the product is sufficiently short, and where the payment of the costs of labor-power and materials takes place subsequent to the realization of the value of the product, the value of the circulating capital is paid not out of the capital, but out of the proceeds or revenue forthcoming at the end of the cycle. In this case, the circulating capital is not part of the capital investment. Where the periods of production and of realization are so long as to exceed the period of the payment of the wage and material costs, then the value of the latter becomes a constituent part of the capital investment and the price of the product must contain a part which corresponds not only to the value of the circulating capital but also to the increment to that value. Money advanced in this way is capital and must realize itself as such by discovering in its product not only the means to its renewal but also the means to its expansion.

This necessity affects both the minimum capital requirement for production and the scale of production. The longer the period of production and realization the greater must be the total capital investment and especially the initial investment; the greater also must be the price of the product. Similarly, diminution in the length of the production period brings with it a diminution in the total capital investment required per unit of product and therefore in the value of the product. With the production period sufficiently short, the value of the product need not contain any part corresponding to the expansion of the circulating capital and may, therefore, be less by that margin.

For classical political economy, and for Marx, the implications of the circulation of capital for the value of capital invested, while of essential importance, were never fully developed. The capital investment was, in the case of classical political economy, taken to be precisely the equivalent of the wages bill, and in the case of Marx, to always include the whole of the wages bill as an element.

The logical basis for the classical conception is two-fold. First, the absence of any systematic treatment of the value relation of the means of production to the product expresses itself in the complete suppression of all component parts of capital other than the circulating capital, and then in the reduction of the circulating capital to the wages bill.[2] In this case the wages bill and the capital investment are identical so that any conception of the wage as not being advanced to its self-expansion would be tantamount to the suppression of the concept of capital itself. The logical basis for this result is in the reduction of the means of production to past labor time, and then in the equation of past labor time with the consumption of labor-power in the immediate production process. This abstract conception makes capital and labor identical, and eliminates all of the concrete conditions required for the full realization of the capital relation as a living process. Ricardo explicitly adopts this standpoint in his analysis of machinery in the *Principles*.[3] There he considers the introduction of the machine to be synonymous with its direct production by labor alone, so that machine production differs from non-mechanized production only in the length of the production process and its productivity. The period of production is extended by the time required to produce the machine prior to its own productive consumption. The machine, therefore, *is* so much labor time since it (1) is itself directly produced by labor alone, and (2) replaces, and therefore stands for, so much direct labor time.

The second basis for the conception that the wages bill is advanced prior to the realization of the value of the product is connected to the preoccupation of classical political economy with the land as the essential basis of the productivity of capital. The result of this standpoint is that the pace of production remains dictated by the natural cycle rather than by requirements directly involved in the expansion of capital. In effect, the cycle of capital (its circuit) is the cycle of nature so that its measure and extent must be dictated by conditions given within the process of the self-reproduction of the natural sphere. This is directly expressed in the classical extension of the period of production to incorporate the natural cycle of production, and the constitution of the product as a natural substance out of which the wage must be paid. The subsuming of labor-power into this condition is expressed in the determination of the period of payment of the wage in accordance with the natural renewal of the worker and with the pace and timing connected to that external natural process. Just as classical political economy considers the rate of expansion of capital to be an expression for the fertility of the earth, it also considers the concrete determination of the circulation of the capital to be its determination within the natural cycle. The implication of this conception is also that the wages bill is equivalently the capital investment, therefore that capital and labor are identical, and that the increment to the capital has necessarily the form of surplus-labor (even where this last conception is never explicitly confronted). This result makes the attribution of the value of the product to the labor time expended in its production, and of the surplus-value also to that labor time, a direct implication.

Marx's treatment of this problem is somewhat more complex.[4] Marx takes as his starting point the notion that the wages bill is a component part of the capital investment, and that the increment to the capital must be considered in its relation to the value laid out for the payment of the wage as well as for the value paid out for the remaining parts of the total capital. At the same time, however, that Marx considers the wages bill to be a part of the capital investment, its 'variable' part, he also insists that the laborer is paid for the use of his laboring capacity only subsequent to its consumption. And, indeed, Marx argues that the capitalist advances value to the worker only 'in appearance,' and criticizes the classical conception precisely on the grounds that the worker actually advances his labor-power to capital rather than vice versa. Given that this is the case, there can be no necessary justification for the assertion that the value returned at the end of the circuit must include a part not only to cover the renewal of the wages bill, but also to cover the increment to the capital advanced in its purchase. Only value invested as capital finds an increment to its magnitude in the value returned as the product. Where the worker is paid after the realization of the value of his product, there can be no part of the latter value which corresponds to the expansion of the 'variable capital.'

Given the productive consumption of the labor-power, the relation which its purchase and sale bears to the expansion of capital is only determinate on the basis of the conception of the mode of circulation of the value paid out in the acquisition of the labor-power (the wage). Just as in the case of the materials of labor, the labor-power is paid per unit of its use-value, in this case per unit of labor time. This result is no mystification of the 'real' relation within which the laborer is actually paid for the reproduction of his laboring capacity through the consumption of the wages goods. The consumption made possible by the wage bargain is determined both qualitatively and quantitatively not by any independently given subsistence requirements of the worker, but by the exigencies entailed in the process of the self-development of capital. The mode of payment of the wage is implied in the latter, particularly in the relation of the wage-contract to the production and circulation of capital. For capital, there exists a given relation between the labor time which must be acquired and the magnitude of the product. It is in this respect that the labor-power appears for the circuit as a constituent element of the circulating capital. Thus, when capital purchases labor-power it does so per unit of time, so that the quantity of labor-power purchased is determined by the amount of laboring time required, which is given by (1) the level of production, and (2) the productivity of labor. Any extension of the laboring time brought about by an increase in the scale of production entails the purchase of an additional quantity of labor-power. Thus, given the money wage rate established in the wage contract, and the technique employed, any increase in the scale of production entails an increase in the wages bill proportional to the increase in the amount of laboring required.

It is, therefore, incorrect to conclude that an increase in the length of the working period (e.g. the working day) will *ipso facto* increase the value of the product relative to the costs of its production. Indeed, the notion that increases in the length of the working period increase the rate of surplus-value (the proportion of the surplus-value to the value of labor-power) rests essentially upon the presupposition that the real wage remains fixed and, therefore, that the real conditions of the wage contract, the confrontation of capital in the money form with labor-power, can be left aside.* Without such an assumption, it is necessary to assume that, in general, the unit costs of production rise in proportion to the scale of production.

The commodity, labor-power, is the capacity of the laborer to labor during a specified period of time. The cost of labor-power is therefore intrinsically the cost of acquiring that capacity for a fixed period, and must be proportional to that period. So long as the laborer sells his labor-power, surplus-value can never arise directly

---

* Within the context of a developing system the idea of a 'real wage' is hardly even intelligible and would not be capable of providing a rigorously quantifiable measure relevant to the calculation implied here. In fact, the idea of a real wage is only applicable to a rigorous calculation where the wage is either represented by a fixed bundle of use-values, or by a vector of use-values expanding proportionately, whose growth leaves its composition unchanged. Theoretically, neither presupposition is justifiable, and, indeed, both conflict essentially with the inner nature of capitalist development. The idea of a real wage, whether intelligible or not, provides no basis for the deduction and calculation of the laws of capitalist development. In order to sustain the Marxian argument it would be necessary to have recourse to some such notion as the 'labor-value' of labor-power taken to be determined prior to the market interaction of capital and labor. Yet, not only are there essential difficulties in the calculation of labor-value, but it would need to be argued that the wage contract can legitimately be assumed to concern itself with this magnitude and to act as the mode by which this prior valuation of the commodity labor-power is made effective within the system of market relations, of the exchange of commodities at their money prices. So far as the immediate conditions of the wage bargain are concerned, the 'labor-value' of labor-power is completely irrelevant. In order to establish that something more than the money wage rate is directly involved in the wage bargain, a specific argument regarding wages, prices, and the market formation of prices is required. The intrinsic weaknesses of the argument required to sustain the Marxian conception of the determination of the 'rate of surplus-value' will be considered in the second volume of the present work.

out of an increase in the amount of labor-power purchased. Surplus-value could emerge in this way only if the commodity sold were not the laboring capacity for a fixed period, but the laborer himself. If the laborer is himself acquired in the exchange, then the cost of labor would be fixed independently of the quantity of laboring forthcoming. This is precisely the implication of taking the wages bill to be determined independently of the amount of labor acquired in the consumption of labor-power.

The logical basis for the idea of 'variable capital' is the attribution of the increment to the capital exclusively to the labor-power consumed. This idea depends essentially upon the notion that the total costs of the labor-power are fixed without regard to the scale of production, and therefore to the quantity of labor-power consumed. This assumption, together with that according to which commodity exchange is determined by the sum of direct and indirect labor time expended, makes the purchase and sale of labor-power and its consumption immediately equivalent to the expansion of the capital, and makes the increment to the capital investment the exclusive product of the laboring. This result cannot, however, be reconciled with the conception of the self-expansion of capital and with the concrete conditions entailed in that process. For the latter, the payment of the wage per unit of production period, and the determination of the exchange-value of the product in accordance with this condition, excludes any immediate specification of the increment in the capital to the labor-power consumed.

III Fixed capital

1 The concept of fixed capital

Neither the labor-power nor the materials of labor contain within them the specificity of the use-value of the product which eventuates from their consumption. In this respect, the elements of the circulating capital tend to exhibit a relatively higher degree of generality and simplicity than does their product. In the case of the labor-power this simplicity and indifference to specific useful form constitutes its essential defining quality. The materials of labor tend to be specific to the use-value of the product or, at least, specific to a limited range of products. Materials find in the production process a process of specification to a more strictly defined use, to the degree that their productive consumption involves their direct transformation into the product, and therefore their adoption of the attributes required in the specification of the product. In this respect the materials of labor, while not characterized by the generality of the labor-power, possess a simplicity relative to the product which makes them unable to determine its use-value by their own act.

This independence of the labor-power and materials *vis-à-vis* the use-value of the product underlies the distinctive manner of their circulation. For the production of the commodity, and therefore of capital, it is necessary that an additional part of the capital be laid out in the purchase of the instruments of labor accountable for the determination of the particularity of the commodity product. This condition is built into the nature of the fixed capital, whose specificity is to the idea of the use-value of the product and not to its particular unit.[5] This idea can never be realized in its direct identification with any single unit of product. Capital invested in this form is fixed capital in that its single unit acts to specify the use-value of the product without being in any way specific to *this* particular unit of that commodity product. The fixed capital attains this specificity to the commodity product, at the same time as it remains independent of the unit of that product, by incorporating the capacity to produce a multitude of the same product. The fixed capital, therefore, produces a product which is strictly limited in its complex concrete determination as this use-value, but it produces that product without limit. The illimitability of the productive potential of the fixed capital implies not that the capital investment is capable of producing an infinite quantity of the product, but that the quantity of the product which that investment is able to generate is not determined by the original technical specification of the capital. The indeterminacy of the productive potential of the machine is synonymous with its ability to produce beyond any limit connected to the single unit of product.

In order to sustain this result the fixed capital and its value cannot be absorbed into the unit of the product in the manner of the labor and materials. The fixed capital must remain behind as the circulating capital proceeds through its cycle. The value of the fixed capital, unlike the circulating capital, must always be advanced since its fixity implies that it is not immediately returned with the completion of the individual circuit.*

Fixity of capital by no means implies any absolute absence of movement, but only affects its concrete form. Indeed, the fixing of the capital into the form of a capital investment is the logical basis for all movement of capital through its cycle and for all expansion of capital. The fixed capital determines the productive potential of the capital. Fixed capital establishes capital as an objectively existing productive force, and the magnitude of the fixed capital investment corresponds to the magnitude of that force. The notion of fixed capital provides the basis for the development of the essential laws of capitalist expansion and, in particular, for the equation of the growth of the capital with the fixing of the capital into a particular form. The greater the fixity of the capital, the greater the productive basis for its movement and growth. The more the investment in fixed capital, the greater the potential for the repeated production of the commodity, and for its endless multiplication. In its characteristic function, fixed capital represents the productive existence of capital as an objective force and potential. To this extent, the identification of capital with fixed capital has a rational foundation.

The particular productive function of the fixed capital defines the distinctive manner of its circulation as a sum of value. The whole of the circulating capital which participates in the production process during a specified period disappears into the product, so that the renewal of the circuit requires that there exist in the product a value equivalent for the whole of the value of the labor-power and materials which are consumed. By contrast, the fixed capital is distinguished by the fact that its use-value is not tied to the individual unit of the product, so that it sustains itself beyond the limits of the single period of production. The continuity of the circuit does not, in the case of the fixed capital, require that the commodity capital contain a value part equivalent for the whole of the value of the fixed capital engaged in the production process. Indeed, it is possible, over a given period, that the production

---

* Although this result needs to be modified with the introduction of credit, the latter by no means overthrows the necessity that the capital be advanced, but only affects the relations between particular capitals as regards the origin of the capital investment and the distribution of the return.

process be renewed where the value of the product just succeeds in renewing the value of the circulating capital expended.

None the less, so long as the lifetime of the fixed capital is finite, it is necessary that the total value of the product of the productive life of the plant and equipment exceed the value of the circulating capital expended by a margin which covers the renewal, and expansion, of the fixed capital consumed. Were the lifetime of the fixed capital, measured in total productive capacity as a proportion of the output per period of production, to be taken to be given technically, then it would be possible to estimate the part of the value of each unit of product which must be devoted to the renewal of the fixed capital. If, for example, the fixed capital has a productive capacity of Y units per period over a span of T periods, and if the value of the fixed capital is K_f, then, for the simple renewal of the investment at the end of its productive life, the value of the unit of the product must exceed the value of the circulating capital expended by an amount equal to $K_f/(YT)$.

In the absence of technical change, and with the rate of devaluation of the equipment taken to be uniform over its lifetime, the mode of circulation of the value advanced as fixed capital appears in its most elementary form. This simplicity is connected first to the independence of the circuit of the fixed capital with respect to the determination of the price either of the equipment itself or of its product, and second to the purely technical determination of the depreciation of the equipment as an expression for the deterioration of its use-value. In contrast to the circulating capital, the value of which circulates as a single unit, the value advanced in the form of fixed capital splits apart, one part transferring itself to the product within the individual circuit, the other remaining behind in order to advance, bit by bit, into the product of subsequent production periods. Since the value of the fixed capital is not consumed within the individual circuit, it is not necessary that the result of that circuit be the renewal of the whole of the invested capital. With the investment of fixed capital, the value of the product ceases to exceed or even equal the value invested for production within the individual period. The value invested includes not only the part of the capital used up but also that part which remains behind at the end of the circuit in order to be advanced once again to production in the next period.

This result is clearly established in the elementary case, for which both the diminution of the value of the fixed capital advanced attendant upon its use, and the part of the value of the product attributed to the renewal of the fixed capital, bear a simple proportionate relation to the lifetime of the capital and its original value. The simplicity of this result derives from the assumption that the relation of the value of the fixed capital to the quantity and value of the product is technically fixed. It is not, however, characteristic of fixed capital that its lifetime be determined in this manner. In general, the fixed capital does not produce a fixed number of products given technically by its original specification. The capital produces instead an indefinite quantity of products over a determinate period of time. In other words, the total productivity of the capital is not the determinant of its lifetime; it is, instead, the lifetime of the instruments of labor which determines their total productivity, both of value and of use-values.

This result is directly implied in the idea of fixed capital. The fixed capital represents the productive potential of capital, and not immediately either its actual productive life or its product. In its original specification, the relevant determination of the fixed capital is to the continuous and repeated production of the product defined, in effect, without regard to its individual unit. The technical specification of the equipment is to a productive potential defined in relation to a fixed period of time (so many meters of metal pipe per hour). How much the investment actually produces depends, therefore, both on its technically specified productivity per period, and upon the length of its productive life. The productive life of the machine is not, within a developing system, directly determined by its original technical specification, and becomes itself an independent determinant of the total productivity of the equipment.

While the period during which the equipment can be maintained is not unlimited in relation to time in the abstract, it may be effectively unlimited in relation to the economic time which is specifically relevant to it. The limitation on the lifetime of the equipment is given not in relation to a quantity of use-values which it is technically able to produce, but in relation (1) to the development of the system of use-values as a whole and of the needs to which they are specified, and (2) to the productivity of labor and its development as that expresses itself in alterations in the value of the product and of the means of production. These factors are, in general, external to the direct production of the commodity. Given this quality, the physical 'using up' of the equipment is rarely equivalent to the depreciation of its value. The latter depends also upon the determination of the value of the equipment together with changes in the technique of production.

It is characteristic of the fixed capital that it oversee not the single period of production, or the production of the single unit of product, but a sequence of connected periods of production. For the circulating capital, the value of the product and the value consumed as labor-power and materials of labor remain fixed in relation one to the other. For the fixed capital, the relation of value advanced to value produced is a relation of two continually changing magnitudes, each varying over the lifetime of the investment. This variance finally becomes itself the determining force in fixing the lifetime of the equipment.

The depreciation of the fixed capital is its devaluation. This process involves developments both in the use-value of the equipment and in the use-value of the product. The original specification of the equipment and of the product is with regard to the production of a given commodity of a specified use. This use is not, however, a fixed material or technical property, but a quality itself dependent upon the complex of economic relations which as a whole makes possible the realization of the product as a use-value. Thus, the depreciation of the fixed capital can never be considered to be a matter settled at the level of its productive consumption. Given the distinctive circuit of the fixed capital, the rate at which the value invested diminishes and the rate at which that value reappears in the product are not fixed technically and by the original value of the equipment when new. Instead, that value undergoes an irregular diminution which is connected to the intensity of use of the equipment and the degree to which it has become economically obsolete. Economic obsolescence involves a depreciation of the value of the equipment which is connected to changes in its own costs of production and to the development of more productive and efficient alternatives. This productivity is, in turn, connected both to the calculation of relative costs and to changes in the technical specification of the product. The developing productivity of labor alters the product not only quantitatively, with regard to its value, but also qualitatively in that it alters needs while improving and developing the means to their satisfaction.

The circulation of capital

What passes for a use-value during one period of capitalist development is made by that development an object of no use in the
subsequent epoch. At the same time, the equipment specified to
the original use-value is devalued by changes in needs and by
changes in the conception of that use-value which is adequate for
their fulfilment. Over the lifetime of the equipment both the value
and the use-value of the commodity product may alter, and it is
this combined process of development which fixes the rate of
depreciation of the investment.

2 *The depreciation of fixed capital*

For the materials of labor and labor-power, their consumption is
also the active process of their devaluation. For the fixed capital
this is by no means the case. In the limiting case of long-lived plant
and equipment, the depreciation of the fixed capital is unconnected
to its productive consumption, therefore to the process by which
it is 'used up.' In this respect the long-lived plant and equipment,
which most fully realizes the idea of fixed capital, does not wear
out at all. The role of physical depreciation is also a matter of
degree. The shorter the duration of the productive life of the
equipment, measured relative to the period of production, the
more it approximates circulating capital in the determination of the
depreciation of its value. The fewer the productive cycles overseen
by the equipment, the less it is identifiable with the existence of
the capital, and the less it establishes the latter as an objectively
existing condition. The difference between the fixed and circulating
capital appears, in this case, to be a matter of degree. The purely
quantitative distinction between fixed and circulating capital
becomes, however, a qualitative distinction of the component parts
of the capital when the quantitative increase in the lifetime of the
equipment comes to express a qualitative alteration in the nature
of its relation to the product.

As the technically given potential lifetime of the equipment
increases, the process of depreciation changes not only quantitatively, but also qualitatively. The quantitative depreciation becomes proportionally less per period as the number of periods
which compose the productive life of the capital increases. After
reaching a certain point, however, the quantitative change in the
rate of depreciation becomes an alteration in the mode of deprecia-

tion and especially in the forces which determine the diminution of the value. At this point, the depreciation of the fixed capital ceases to be a technical process, becoming instead the reflection within the capital of the development of the forces of production within the system of economic relations as a whole. This makes the rate of depreciation nothing more than an expression of the prevailing conditions of the accumulation of capital at the level of the particular unit of production. The concrete analysis of the renewal of the value of the investment of fixed capital is, then, synonymous with the analysis of the concrete conditions of the expansion of the total capital.

The longer the equipment remains in use, the less is its original valuation relevant to the determination of its current value. Investments which are of sufficient durability in effect never wear out. This is the case especially for permanent and semi-permanent structures whose value changes with changes in the general economic conditions which develop around them. While depreciation of value may be considered the norm even for investments of this nature, it is also possible that, under certain conditions, their periodic re-evaluation will take the form of an appreciation of value.* Such a possibility is not excluded from the general notion of the periodic evaluation of the fixed capital. Whether the re-evaluation of the capital implies an increase or a diminution of its value depends not directly upon its technical specification and original cost, but upon the rate and nature of the development of the system of economic relations as a whole.

Marx emphasizes from the outset that the value of a commodity relates its exchange not to the conditions of its original production, but to the requirements implied in its reproduction within the context of prevailing economic conditions. When this rule is applied to commodity value under conditions of economic development, it implies a continuous alteration (generally a fall) in value. Marx does not, however, consider the implications of the application of the rule of 'socially necessary labor time' to fixed capital so far as its depreciation is concerned. To do so would have revealed essential difficulties in the calculation of the labor-value of com-

---

* This is especially the case for capital investments tied to fixed natural conditions, especially to investment in land. Indeed to the extent that the means of production are not produced, appreciation and depreciation are equally possible.

modities whose value includes a part corresponding to the consumption of fixed capital. The value contributed by the fixed capital to the product is determined neither by its original value nor by its current value, but by the change in value during the relevant period. It is this inherently dynamic component of the determination of the value of the commodity product which is lost in its reduction to a quantity of labor time. The quantity of value 'transferred' to the product within a given period varies with the rate at which the value of the fixed capital employed changes over that period. Since the determination of commodity value is governed by a rate of change of value, it is inherently irreducible to any fixed quantity of labor time. The determination of exchange-value in a sum of past and current labor time is excluded.*

The real determination of the contribution of the fixed capital to the value of the unit of product requires the full development of the concrete conditions bound up with the system of capitalist production taken as a whole.[6] Any immediate equation of the depreciated part of the fixed capital with a portion of the labor consumed in the production of that fixed capital only serves to falsely anticipate the real determination of commodity value and of the value of the capital investment.

It is of essential importance to the treatment of value that the exchange of commodities also take into account the quantitative relation which obtains between the capital invested and the necessities of the regeneration and expansion of that capital in the sale of the commodity products. While the renewal and expansion of the circulating capital are made possible when the price of the product exceeds by a sufficient margin the money expended in its acquisition, this does not hold for the fixed capital. The part of the receipts from the sale of the product which corresponds to the fixed capital consumed cannot be determined on the basis of the elementary considerations connected to the consumption of the circulating capital. It is impossible to estimate the contribution of the fixed capital to the value of the product on the basis simply of its

---

* In order to retain the 'labor theory of value' as a theory of the determination of exchange-value (either direct, as in the equation of labor time with exchange-value, or indirect, as in the transformation of labor-value into price) it would be necessary, in effect, to exclude fixed capital. This is the method pursued by classical political economy and by those economists working in the classical tradition.

productive consumption; therefore, it is impossible to reduce the valuation of the capital consumed in this way to conditions entailed in its own production process. In particular the reduction of the value of the capital to a quantity of past labor time is fundamentally inconsistent with the characteristic mode of circulation of the fixed capital in that it excludes the real process of its depreciation, replacing that process with a simple transfer of the labor costs of production of the fixed capital into the product. The value of the capital investment is not the determinant of its depreciation, and therefore of its contribution to the value of the product; but it is the depreciation of the investment which is the determinant of its value as so much capital investment. In this respect the fixed capital makes no determinate contribution to the value of the product, but determines its own depreciation in accordance with the forces which govern the development of the value of its commodity products.

For the production of commodities, it is necessary to employ a given quantity of labor-power and materials of labor together with the fixed capital investment taken *in toto*. Even where only a part of the value of the fixed capital reappears in the product within any given period, it is necessary that the whole of the plant and equipment be employed, therefore advanced to production, within each period and for the production of each individual unit of product. In this sense the fixed capital is consumed as a whole within the particular circuit, and its character as fixed capital is expressed in its repeated consumption from period to period.

For the fixed capital, the partial diminution of its value is connected to the consumption of the whole of that value within each cycle of its use. The contribution of the fixed capital to the total capital investment is, therefore, equal to the total value of the fixed capital at the commencement of the production period. This total value depends upon the original value of the equipment and upon its rates of depreciation. Where the value of the fixed capital at the outset of period i is K_f^i, the rate of depreciation during the period d^i is given by the relation:

$$d^i = \frac{K_f^i - K_f^{i+1}}{K_f^i}.$$

The total value of the fixed capital in period i is determined by its initial value and its rate(s) of depreciation:

$$K_f^t = K_f^o - \sum_{i=1}^{t} d^1 K_f^{i-1}. \qquad [1]$$

This total represents the investment of fixed capital during period t, or the quantity of fixed capital advanced to production in that period.

The value of the capital investment has a two-fold determination. The initial value of the fixed capital is given by its original purchase price. Since the fixed capital is acquired via exchange, it enters the circuit from outside. This determination of the value of the capital investment appears, then, to be wholly extrinsic to the circuit of the capital. The rule which governs the value of the capital investment, in this case, is:

$$K_f^o = \bar{K}_f^o. \qquad [2]$$

Once the acquisition of the fixed capital has been effected, however, the determination of its value ceases to remain fixed by this original condition. Indeed, the process of the productive consumption of the fixed capital is also the process of the reproduction of its value. This process is itself a determinant of the value of the capital investment so that the latter comes also to be determined within the circuit. If time period b represents the end of the productive life of the equipment so that:

$$K_f^b = 0 \qquad [3]$$

then it follows from conditions [1] and [3] that:*

$$K_f^o = \sum_{i=1}^{b} d^1 K_f^{i-1}. \qquad [4]$$

Thus, the determination of the value of the capital investment is the process of the reconciliation of two conditions ([2] and [4])

---

* This result holds in general for those commodities whose productive consumption entails a depreciation of their value. Where capital investment appreciates in value, that appreciation of value must be considered as, in effect, an element of profit and the re-evaluation of the investment may not lead to any equation of the sum of changes in its value with its original purchase price. In any case, equation [5] represents the relation abstractly and will normally be violated under the concrete circumstances of commodity production. It is significant, none the less, in clearly expressing the central opposition implied in the multiple valuation of the fixed capital.

given independently, one of which expresses the original mode of acquisition of the capital equipment and one of which represents its mode of consumption and re-evaluation. Where the rates of depreciation (d^i) are not given immediately in the original conditions which fix the purchase price of the equipment ($\overline{K}_f^o$), then this requirement is a substantive condition of the circuit and the equation:

$$\overline{K}_f^o = \sum_{i=1}^{b} d^i K_f^{i-1} \qquad [5]$$

is no mere tautology, but a condition which must be fulfilled within the circuit. Since the rates of depreciation are not given directly in the conditions of the acquisition of the equipment, it is equally false to consider the original purchase price to be determined by the discounting of the returns to its productive consumption, and to consider those returns to be determined by its original value and the depreciation already given in that valuation. Instead, the process of the circulation of capital must be itself the process within which condition [5] is actively pursued as a result to be achieved, and not as a result whose achievement is immediately given in the acquisition of the capital investment. Once the fixed capital investment is subsumed within the circuit of capital, its value, which is originally taken as an externally fixed condition, becomes a condition which is internalized. Thus, it is through the mechanism of the circuit that the value of the capital investment is produced by the activity of the capital itself.

3 Fixed and circulating capital

The consumption of the circulating capital is circumscribed by the period of production and the advance and return of the value of the materials and labor is synonymous with the single circuit of the capital. In this sense, the consumption of the value of the circulating capital transpires within the temporal confines of the period of circulation. This is not immediately the case for the fixed capital. So far as its depreciation is not given by its productive consumption that productive consumption does not mark out the periodic re-evaluation of the investment. Changes in the value of the fixed capital are not restricted to the periodic circulation of the capital but depend as much or more upon conditions existing within the system of capitals as a whole. To this extent the calculation of the periodic depreciation of the value of the fixed capital in relation to the period of production is essentially arbitrary. Indeed, the determination of the relevant period for the calculation of depreciation is largely a matter of external factors not implied in the logic of the circuit and of the cycle of particular periods of production (e.g. the periodic payment of taxes or dividends).

This same result holds for depreciation calculated per unit of product. The starting point for this calculation is the change in the value of the capital over a given period. When this change is opposed to the mass of commodity products of production during this same span of time it becomes possible to apportion the costs of fixed capital among the commodity products without thereby implying that the depreciation of the value is determined directly by the production of the commodity with which the proportional part of the depreciated value is associated.

In general, the circulating capital represents the advance and return of capital-value the movement of which is circumscribed by the length of the single circuit (fixed by the single production period). The fixed capital represents the advance and return of capital-value which is not circumscribed by the individual circuit and single period of production. The distinction with reference to circulation is, then, between those costs which may be fully retrieved within each cycle of the capital and those which are only fully retrieved over a sequence of connected production periods and circuits of the capital.*

IV The classical conception of fixed capital

The implied inconsistency of the notion of fixed capital with the classical and Marxian theories of value is not attributable to any

---

* This distinction is not to be equated with that between overhead and prime costs. The distinction between overhead and prime (or unit) costs rests upon the functional relation to the scale of production sustained by unit costs and not by overheads. While the costs of fixed capital are exclusively overhead costs, the costs of circulating capital include both prime costs and overhead costs so far as capital is expended upon labor and materials connected not to the production of the individual unit of product, but to the general conditions of the growth of the firm and of its market (e.g. to the development of new products).

differences in the level of analysis at which the problem is posed. The determination of the depreciation of the fixed capital in the portion of the labor-value consumed in the production of the unit of product is fundamentally inconsistent with the idea of fixed capital grasped on the most general and elementary level. The contribution of the means of production to the value of the product can only be given systematic consideration upon the basis both of the analysis of the circuit and the conception of the expansion process of the total capital. The concept of fixed capital immediately excludes any abstraction from the peculiarities of the mode of development of its value. Indeed, it is this distinctive mode of consumption of the value advanced as fixed capital which not only defines the fixed capital as such, but also establishes its conception as fundamentally inconsistent with any notion that the direct production process transfers to the product a quantum of value already fixed in the production of the means of production.*

The inability of economic theory to grasp the specificity of fixed capital is revealed most sharply in the continuing effort to reduce the valuation process of the fixed capital to that of circulating capital, thereby subsuming all of the component parts of the capital into the most elementary and undifferentiated conception of the circuit. This effort to obliterate the conceptual distinctions which develop in the analysis of circulation derives originally from the obliteration of the distinctions within the conception of commodity production. The peculiar productive role of the fixed capital is grounded in the universality of commodity production and of its objective. For the production of commodities and of capital, the qualitative distinction between the machinery and the other elements of the productive capital makes impossible any notion that the productive activity of the machine is reducible to

---

* The difficulties entailed in this conception are considered on a formal level by P. Sraffa in chapter 10 of *Production of Commodities by Means of Commodities* (Cambridge: Cambridge University Press, 1960). Sraffa only considers the problem, however, for a system which reproduces itself at a given level from period to period. Difficulties in the calculation of the labor-value of the fixed capital are all connected to the distribution of the value produced between the product and the means of production considered as also a result (or joint product) of its own productive consumption. The difficulties isolated in this way are only compounded when the problem of the distribution of the value of the fixed capital over the total product of its productive life is considered in the context of a growing system.

laboring. By contrast, when the fixed capital is presumed to stand for so much past labor, the productive function of the fixed capital is equated with laboring. This is the standpoint of classical political economy, for which labor is that category which grasps the totality of the process of commodity production. Where the fixed capital does labor, its productive consumption and that of direct labor are not qualitatively differentiable. Since the fixed capital labors in the present as the representative of past laboring, the contribution of the fixed capital to commodity production is nothing more than the temporal displacement of labor. The distinction between fixed and circulating capital is, accordingly, taken to be exclusively a matter of form and of degree. In classical political economy the object of the investigation of fixed capital is to establish the equation of fixed and circulating capital, thereby making all capital circulating capital. This conception obliterates the specificity of the fixed capital and violates essentially the conception of commodity production by eliminating all elements of production not given immediately in the idea of labor time. The peculiar force of capital, and of the labor which works as capital, is made into a quantitative intensification of laboring.

Smith defines circulating capital as capital which circulates and fixed capital as capital which does not.[7] The value of the circulating capital reappears in the product of the single production cycle while the value of the fixed capital remains for ever fixed. The fixed capital, in effect, receives a revenue but never any value which could replace that used up in its production. Since the fixed capital is not consumed in production, the value of the product contains no part corresponding to the depreciation of the equipment. Depreciation is effectively set at zero, and Smith resolves the problem of the contribution of the means of production to the valuation of the product by, as Marx puts it, eliminating the 'constant capital' altogether from the calculation.

Further on, in an effort to take into account the production of fixed capital, Smith considers fixed capital to derive originally from circulating capital. This makes the fixed capital directly reducible first to a sum of wages, and then to a quantity of labor time. In effect, the classical method requires either the complete elimination of fixed capital from the calculation of the valuation of commodities, or, what amounts to the same thing, the reduction of fixed to circulating capital. It is this reduction which makes possible the retention of the classical theory of value under conditions of capitalist commodity production.

It is this idea which Marx takes up, and seeks to formulate in a rigorous fashion. While Ricardo still tends to exclude depreciation of the value of the fixed capital, in effect making its productive life perpetual, Marx considers directly the renewal of the value of the fixed capital as the replacement of the labor-value which determines its original cost. Marx fails, however, to grasp the inner process of the reproduction of the value of the fixed capital because he adopts the classical presupposition that commodity production is ultimately reducible to the activity of the laborer. This makes the quantitative contribution of the fixed capital also one of labor, thereby undermining the qualitative distinction between labor-power and means of production which Marx is the first to clearly establish.

The reduction of fixed to circulating capital is also the objective of the effort to constitute the machine and its product as a single 'joint product' of the cycle of production. This identification of the means of production with its own product makes it possible to subsume the concept of fixed capital into that of circulating capital, and thereby to resurrect the method employed by classical political economy in the treatment of the circulation of the component parts of the capital.* Even where the allocation of the value of the fixed capital among its products in accordance with the principle of labor time must be denied, it remains possible to eliminate all qualitative difference between fixed and circulating capital and to consider their processes of valuation and circulation under a single rule.

The significance of the conception of fixed capital as a joint product lies in the explicit recognition that its valuation is not given in its immediate production, and that the transfer of its value to the product is not given technically in its immediate

---

* This makes it possible to

regard durable instruments of production as part of the annual intake of a process, on the same footing as such means of production (e.g. raw materials) as are entirely used up in the course of a year; while what is left of them at the end of the year will be treated as a portion of the annual joint product of the industry, of which the more conspicuous part consists of the marketable commodity that is the primary object of the process [P. Sraffa, *Production of Commodities by Means of Commodities*, p. 63].

productive consumption. Instead the valuation of fixed capital, and the development of its value from period to period, are made to depend upon the system of economic relations as a whole (the technical conditions of production and the overall rate or rates of profit). This method undermines the classical conception of the reduction of fixed capital to a given quantity of labor time. The determination of commodity value in general, and of the value of the capital investment, is made substantively an economic process irreducible to any simple technical condition. None the less, the method employed retains as its objective the determination of the value of fixed capital and its product upon the basis of an externally given rate of expansion of capital and productivity of labor. Thus, while the constitution of the fixed capital as a joint product of its own productive consumption excludes any reduction of its valuations to conditions given immediately in its own production (as was implied in the Marxian conception of the transfer of labor-value to the product), the idea that the fixed capital may be considered a joint product still provides a full determination of the valuation of commodities and of capital, based upon conditions of production and distribution which are fixed independently of the total process of the self-development of capital.

The valuation of commodities and of capital is determined by the distribution of income, as expressed in a rate of profit taken to be independently fixed, and by the technical conditions of production, presumed to be conceivable in static terms independent of the on-going growth process of the total capital. Thus the treatment of fixed capital as a joint product is peculiarly suited only to conditions of what Marx terms 'simple reproduction' (continuing production of a fixed system of commodities, at a fixed scale, and with a given technique). The idea is not extensible to conditions of expansion since the transformation of the conditions of production is always an intrinsic element of the expansion process. Where the growth process of capital is that process within which the conditions of production are themselves determined, that process cannot provide a valuation of commodities and capital predicated upon the givenness of the technical conditions.

It is, none the less, precisely this method of valuation predicated upon externally given conditions which provides the theoretical objective for that reduction of fixed to circulating capital which is characteristic of the classical and Marxian theories and equally of

the conception of fixed capital as a joint product of its own productive activity. The typically classical idea that fixed conditions
of production and distribution can be made to fully determine the
system of exchange relations while remaining themselves independent of the price system can only be extended to a conception
of circulation where the concept of fixed capital is identified with
that of circulating capital. This identification makes the valuation
of the fixed capital fully determined by conditions presumed to be
independent of the system of commodity exchange – the technical
conditions of production and the rate of profit. The valuation of
fixed capital is thereby made substantively independent of its mode
of existence as an element of capital. That valuation is considered
upon the basis of a conception of production and distribution
which is generalized to separate the valuation of commodities from
those dynamic conditions logically implied in the idea of the
production and circulation of capital and especially of the market
system as the system within which the full realization of capital is
accomplished.

The identification of the mode of valuation of fixed with circulating capital expresses the subsuming of fixed capital directly into
the most elementary notion of capital as self-expanding value. The
mobility of capital is thus made its single defining feature and the
necessity that movement take place only through its own periodic
interruption is evaded. This conception has the most telling implications at the level of the treatment of the competition and accumulation of capital. The elimination of the fixity of capital provides
the logical foundation for all traditional conceptions of the competition of capitals and of the growth process of capital as a whole.
Since each period of production is logically separable from the
ongoing sequence of productions so far as capital is concerned (in
that the capital-value can always be made fully independent of
whatever productive activity it happens to subsume within any
given period), the particularization of the unit of capital is restricted to the single production period. The logical fallacy in this
conception is to be found in its immediate identification of the re-
evaluation of the fixed capital investment from period to period
with its actual liquidation and circulation. The conditions necessary
for the latter are by no means implied in the calculation of the
depreciation of the capital investment. It is at this point that the
distinctive nature of fixed capital makes itself felt and that its

identification with the unit of production as substantively a unit of capital begins to be really effective. Where the marketability of depreciated equipment and its product are not directly identical, it is because they bear distinct relations to the ongoing process of the circulation of capital and must therefore be distinguished as opposed elements of that circuit.

It is in the nature of commodity production that the capital investment entail a fixing of capital which exceeds the period of production. Indeed, the measurement of the temporal fixing of the capital is not in terms of an undifferentiated sequence of substantively interchangeable production periods which are therefore in no way identifiable with the unit of capital, as in the notion of simple reproduction. On the contrary, the capitalist production of commodities involves necessarily a sequence of periods of production which form a single unified process subsumed into the identification of the unit of capital. With the continuous development of capital there is also continuous development of the production process so that the notion of capital subsumes a sequence of continuously changing production periods connected precisely by the force which expresses itself in the development from one to the next. It is this unifying force which is lost in the elimination of the concept of fixed capital implied in its identification, first, with its own product, and then with the circulating capital with which it is employed in production.

V The unit of capital

1 *Value advanced and value returned*

The total capital investment is made up of the sum of the value of the fixed capital and the value of that part of the circulating capital which must be paid out prior to the realization of the value of the product:

$$K^i = K_c^i + K_f^i.$$

The K_c^i is a function of the scale of production and the unit labor and material costs, while the K_f^i is a function of the original value of the fixed capital and its complex of rates of depreciation over its lifetime. The K_c^i and K_f^i are the component parts of the capital investment.

The production of commodities is the transformation of the capital investment into commodity capital, which makes possible the return of the investment in the money form. This return of the money capital reconstitutes the original capital investment in the form of a homogeneous sum of money. While this latter is a single sum of money, and appears as a homogeneous unit, it is itself intrinsically divided according to the law by which it must realize itself as a form of capital. The intrinsic divisions of the value returned are, however, by no means equivalent to the component parts of the capital investment.

The value returned at the finish of the circuit contains a part which corresponds to the renewal of the circulating capital consumed. This part differs quantitatively from the value of the circulating capital invested by the amount (equal to $W + M - Kc$) of the circulating costs not advanced out of capital. This latter, while not a component part of the capital investment, is a constituent element of the money capital acquired in the sale of the commodity products. Where the fixed capital has not exhausted its productive life, and the value returned covers the costs of circulating capital, the productive cycle may continue into the next period. Given the value (G) of the product of a given cycle of production and realization, the condition for the continuation of the circuit is:

$$G > W + M.$$

Where this condition holds, it follows that the value of the commodity capital divides into two parts, one of which makes possible the renewal of the cycle $(W + M)$, and one of which represents the margin (E) between the costs incurred for production within the single circuit and the value returned:

$$E = G - (W + M).$$

Assuming that $E > O$, then a basis for the reproduction of fixed capital has been established.

Where the value of the product exceeds the unit labor and materials costs, any of the following conditions may obtain: (1) The margin over unit costs may be such as to just make possible the replacement of the fixed capital, given the determination of its productive lifetime. In this case production is not the basis for the expansion of capital, and the money advanced as productive capital fails to act as such. Condition (1) is therefore inconsistent with the constitution of production upon a capitalistic basis. (2) The margin over costs, while sufficient to sustain the circulating capital, may be inadequate for the replacement of the fixed capital investment. In this case the original value of the capital investment ($\overline{K}_f^o$) exceeds the evaluation derived from its productive existence as capital. In effect the real value of the capital investment, established during its lifetime as the value which it reproduces, fails to sustain the value advanced as capital. In this case the circuit adopts the form of a diminishing spiral, whose eventual result is the extinction of the capital. Since the original investment fails to sustain itself within the circuit, it fails to exist as capital. This failure is expressed in the valuation of the capital investment which cannot be realized as capital because it is not even the equal of the value laid out in its acquisition. (3) Finally, the value returned may exceed unit costs by a margin which itself exceeds that required for the renewal of the fixed capital. This third case is the sole result consistent with the self-preservation and self-development of capital. The conditions which must be fulfilled in order that this result obtain are synonymous with the concrete conditions for the subsistence of capital within its circuit. The determinants of capitalist development are then bound up with the determination of the value of fixed capital, its renewal or reproduction and its expansion, as well as with the rate at which that replacement and increase of value are effected. This in turn depends essentially upon the margin developed between the costs of replacement of the circulating capital and the revenue returned from the sale of the product. The determination of this margin is therefore simultaneously the determination of the reproduction of the value of the fixed capital and the expansion of the value of the capital investment.

Within the circuit of capital it is the circulating capital, including labor-power, whose value is effectively fixed, and the fixed capital whose value is effectively variable. This does not imply an exclusive attribution of the surplus-value either to the productive force of the means of production or of the labor-power. On the contrary it is their unity which can alone account for the production of commodities and for the expansion of value. The difference between the valuation of the fixed and circulating capital is none the less essential to the conception of price determination and of the system of capitalist commodity production taken as a whole.

The circulating capital has a value which is effectively fixed outside of the circuit of the capital within which its consumption takes place. The fixed capital, by contrast, must find the conditions which govern its valuation both within and outside of the circuit of the capital within which it is consumed. The development of the value of the product is not indifferent to this peculiar feature of the fixed capital investment, and the relation which that fixed capital bears to the valuation of the product is qualitatively distinct from that of the circulating capital. The theoretical treatment of price is also the treatment of the manner in which the development of capital is a process of the valuation of fixed capital, and thereby also a process of the expansion of the total capital investment. It is the conception of fixed capital within the circuit which expresses most forcefully the necessity that the determination of the valuation of commodities be simultaneously the process of the self-expansion of capital-value.

2 *The capitalization of value*

The circuit of capital taken concretely differs from the circuit of capital taken in general by the explicit consideration of the complex of conditions required for continuing motion. These conditions are conditions of the circulation of the component parts of the capital, the complex of which constitutes the circulation of capital taken as a whole. The determination of this whole in terms of its constituent elements involves the analysis of (1) the different circuits of the component parts of the capital investment, and (2) the component parts of the capital-value returned with the realization of the value of the product. The difference between the costs of circulating capital and the value returned establishes a difference of quantity between the successive phases of the circuit. The component parts of the original capital (K_f and K_c) differ from the component parts of the value returned (W, M, and E) both quantitatively and qualitatively. The value invested in the subsequent phases of the circuit includes the value invested in the previous phases, together with an increment to that value. This new value becomes substantively capital by forming the basis for the process of its own expansion. This expansion of produced value is the process of its capitalization, its self-constitution as capital.

The problem of the capitalization of value cannot be resolved with reference to the margin, E, taken as a single sum. The margin divides into a part which corresponds to the replacement of the fixed capital investment, and a part which corresponds to the net product or surplus-value. This distinction expresses the further determination of the margin between unit costs and value beyond that already considered in the treatment of the depreciation of the fixed capital. Since depreciation cannot be determined independently of the determination of the value of the product, and especially of the development of that value over the lifetime of the equipment, it follows that the determination of the margin cannot proceed by addition to the costs of capital replacement, where those costs are given independently. Indeed, the reverse appears to be the case in that the depreciation of the equipment is itself dependent upon the determination of the value of the product in its relation to the circulating costs incurred in its production. Given the conditions which determine the value of the product and its movement,* the conditions for the determination of the depreciation costs are also established, and the margin over costs can be divided in accordance with the difference between replacement of capital and its increase. The surplus, or net product, generated in any given period is equal to:

$$R^1 = E^1 - d^1 K_f^{i-1}.$$

The condition for the expansion of the capital investment $(K_c + K_f)$ follows directly:

$$\sum_{i=1}^{b} [E^1 - d^1 K_f^{i-1}] > o.$$

The single circuit of capital is now the unity of the reproduction and expansion of value. There is, then, a differentiation of the value returned in accordance with the intrinsic logic of the circuit. Part of the value returned corresponds to the reproduction of the original value advanced, and part corresponds to what is sub-

---

* It is only possible to consider these conditions on the basis of the conception of capitalist production as a whole, therefore of the self-expansion of the system of particular capitals. The laws which govern this process of capital accumulation are simultaneously the laws which govern the process of the formation and development of prices and the valuation of the capital investment. These laws form the subject-matter of the second volume of the present work.

stantively new value. The new value is the product of the cycle, and indeed, is that result of the cycle directly attributable to it. This is the net product, the true object and product of the circuit, a sum which is not simply renewed or sustained within the cycle but directly generated within that cycle.

The produced value becomes substantively capital when it enters into the cycle as value advanced and becomes itself the original condition for the production of a net product. What represents new value, with respect to a single cycle of the capital, represents the original advance of capital for the next. For the conception of the circuit of capital, the element of an original advance of value not itself generated by capital is unnecessary.[8] As the circuit continues from period to period in its ever expanding spiral, the part of the value advanced which is not attributable to a produced surplus-value diminishes, until the point is reached at which the contribution of value not itself originating within the circuit goes to zero. For example, if a value of 100 is advanced at the origin of the cycle of the capital, and if it grows at a rate of 10 per cent, and if the whole of the new value is capitalized, then the value advanced into the second cycle is 110. Whereas originally 100 per cent of the value advanced is given outside of the circuit, in the next period that percentage of original value drops to 91 per cent. After ten periods, the portion of the capital advanced will have dropped to less than one half, and after twenty periods to less than one third. As the circuit continues, it ceases to be the simple process of the capitalization of value and becomes the complex process of the capitalization of capital.

The starting point of the circuit is not a sum of money which is yet to become capital, but a sum of money which is already intrinsically capital: value advanced as capital which was also originally produced as the increment to capital. At the same time, the constitution of the circuit entails the notion of an original advance of money which becomes something other than it is originally. Since it is only the surplus-value which is produced immediately within the present cycle of the capital, the cycle establishes an opposition of capital to its increment in which the increment is the part which fully functions as capital, while the original advance retains that aspect of existing for the particular cycle as a prior condition. In this respect the notion of the circuit of capital implies the conception of an original accumulation of capital, an original advance of a sum of value not itself produced as capital. So far as the circuit is simultaneously a preservation and expansion of capital, it always returns originally to a point at which the increment is produced by capital and the advance is not. The continual circular movement of capital has this as an original condition, even as that continuing circuit overcomes that original condition establishing its existence within the circuit as null.

It is within the conception of the circulation of capital that (1) its self-constitution is established as a continuing process which is (2) also a process of development away from dependence upon any extrinsic conditions. For the conception of the circuit, the vital element is the self-constitution of capital on a basis independent of any prior fixing of the conditions of its movement. The circuit is then both the process of the self-movement of capital, and the process by which it establishes itself as a self-movement. The circulation of capital, taken as a continuous process, establishes each of its moments as capital by situating those moments within a process of development which is endless, and which generates each of its own elements as the result of the movement of the whole.

3 The unit of capital

The complex of circuits of the component parts of the capital, taken in its entirety and subsumed under the process of the capitalization of value, is the life-cycle of capital. The unifying entity which connects the elements and phases of the cycle into a single total process is the unit of capital. This latter exists not as an inert object, a physically situated locus of a material production process, but as the concrete unity of the life process of capital. The mode of existence of capital is its growth and development. It is only within this process that the capital is able to realize its inner determination as capital. Just as the outcome of the growth process is capital, so also the inner law of that process is the law of capital's self-development. Capital is the original condition for expansion when it is considered as value advanced; capital is the result of the process when it exists as capitalized value; and capital is the process itself – the movement from advance to return.

Since capital reveals its inner nature only as a living process of growth and development, the true measure of the development of capital is the measure of its growth. This measure is the proportion of new capital to capital advanced, and expresses the adequacy of the value invested to the object of its self-constitution as capital. The circuit of capital traces out an expanding spiral. This spiral is capital's life process. The full determination of the circuit and of the life-cycle which it displays is the accumulation of capital, and it is only within the total process of the self-expansion of capital that its concrete self-determination can be accomplished.

Notes

Prologue

1 *Economic Studies: Contributions to the Critique of Economic Theory* (London: Routledge & Kegan Paul, 1977).
2 See particularly the *Theories of Surplus-value* (Moscow: Progress Publishers), vol. 1 n.d., vol. 2 1968, vol. 3 1971; and the *Grundrisse*, tr. M. Nicolaus (Harmondsworth: Penguin Books, 1973).
3 This connection has been pointed out by Ronald Meek in his *Studies in the Labor Theory of Value* (2nd edn, London: Lawrence & Wishart, 1973).
4 K. Marx, *Letters to Dr Kugelman* (New York: International Publishers, 1934) pp. 73–4, letter of 11 July 1868.
5 *Grundrisse*, tr. M. Nicolaus (Harmondsworth: Penguin Books, 1973) p. 105.
6 Ibid., p. 459.
7 P. Sraffa, *Production of Commodities by Means of Commodities* (Cambridge: Cambridge University Press, 1960).
8 See K. Marx, *Grundrisse*, pp. 100–2, and G. W. F. Hegel, *The Science of Logic*, tr. A. V. Miller (London: George Allen & Unwin, 1969) vol. 2, section 3, chapter 3.

Chapter 1: The object of economic science

1 J. J. Rousseau, *Discourse on the Origin and Foundations of Inequality*, ed. R. D. Masters (New York: St Martin's, 1964) pp. 155–6, 179–80.
2 G. W. F. Hegel, *Hegel's Philosophy of Right*, tr. T. M. Knox (London: Oxford University Press, 1952) p. 42.
3 Ibid., pp. 57–8.
4 Ibid., p. 58.

5 See D. Levine, *Economic Studies: Contributions to the Critique of Economic Theory* (London: Routledge & Kegan Paul, 1977) chapter 1.
6 See K. Marx, *Grundrisse*, tr. M. Nicolaus (Harmondsworth: Penguin Books, 1973) pp. 241–5.

Chapter 2: Commodity relations

1 See G. W. F. Hegel, *Hegel's Philosophy of Right*, tr. T. M. Knox (London: Oxford University Press, 1952) p. 127.
2 See D. Levine, *Economic Studies: Contributions to the Critique of Economic Theory* (London: Routledge & Kegan Paul, 1977) chapter 1.
3 *Ethica Nichomachea*, tr. W. D. Ross, *The Works of Aristotle*, vol. IX (London: Oxford University Press, 1915) p. 133.
4 Ibid.
5 *The Wealth of Nations* (New York: Modern Library, 1937) p. 30.
6 See D. Levine, *Economic Studies*, chapter 3.

Chapter 3: The circulation of commodities and money

1 See K. Marx, *Capital* (New York: International Publishers, 1967) vol. I, pp. 134–41.
2 James Steuart, *An Inquiry into the Principles of Political Economy* (Edinburgh: Oliver & Boyd, 1966) p. 46.
3 Adam Smith, *The Wealth of Nations* (New York: Modern Library, 1937) p. 30.
4 Ibid., p. 22.
5 K. Marx, *Grundrisse*, tr. M. Nicolaus (Harmondsworth: Penguin Books, 1973) p. 262.

Chapter 4: The circuit of capital

1 K. Marx, *Grundrisse*, tr. M. Nicolaus (Harmondsworth: Penguin Books, 1973) p. 270.
2 Ibid., pp. 269–74.
3 K. Marx, *Capital* (New York: International Publishers, 1967) vol. I, chapter V.

Chapter 5: Labor

1 K. Marx, *Capital* (New York: International Publishers, 1967) vol. I, chapter XIII.
2 Ibid., p. 326.
3 Ibid., pp. 339–42.

Chapter 6: The self-generative process of wealth

1 *The Works and Correspondence of David Ricardo*, ed. P. Sraffa (Cambridge: Cambridge University Press, 1951) vol. I, p. 12.

2 *Of Civil Government, Second Treatise* (Chicago: Henry Regenery Company, 1955) chapter 5.
3 *Discourse on the Origins and Foundations of Inequality*, especially part II.

Chapter 7: Social production

1 The developments considered briefly here are all subject to extended treatment, especially as regards their historical aspect, in K. Marx, *Capital* (New York: International Publishers, 1967) vol. I. The breaking up of the limitations of the handicraft form are described most vividly on pp. 484–6 of that work.
2 *The Wealth of Nations* (New York: Modern Library, 1937) p. 3.
3 For a descriptive account of this development see H. Braverman, *Labor and Monopoly Capital* (New York: Monthly Review Press, 1974) chapter 8.
4 For a comprehensive treatment of this question see K. Marx, *Capital*, vol. I, chapter XV.
5 See K. Marx, *Grundrisse*, tr. M. Nicolaus (Harmondsworth: Penguin Books, 1973) p. 489.
6 Ibid., p. 485.

Chapter 8: The circuit in general

1 This conception is considered in D. Levine, *Economic Studies: Contributions to the Critique of Economic Theory* (London: Routledge & Kegan Paul, 1977), especially chapters 4, 6 and 8.
2 Aristotle, *Politics* (tr. Benjamin Jowett) in *The Works of Aristotle*, ed. J. A. Smith and W. D. Ross (London: Oxford University Press, 1921) vol. X, p. 1257^a.
3 See K. Marx, *Capital* (New York: International Publishers, 1967) vol. II, p. 26.
4 This point is considered in chapter 9, below.
5 See K. Marx, *Capital*, vol. II, chapter 13.
6 Ibid., p. 152.
7 This relation will be considered in volume II of the present work.

Chapter 9: The component parts of the capital

1 See K. Marx, *Grundrisse*, tr. M. Nicolaus (Harmondsworth: Penguin Books, 1973) p. 620.
2 For a further discussion see D. Levine, *Economic Studies: Contributions to the Critique of Economic Theory* (London: Routledge & Kegan Paul, 1977) chapter 4.
3 D. Ricardo, *On the Principles of Political Economy and Taxation* in *The Works and Correspondence of David Ricardo,* ed. P. Sraffa (Cambridge: Cambridge University Press, 1951) vol. I, chapter XXXI.

4 This aspect of the problem is considered in D. Levine, *Accumulation and Technical Change in Marxian Economics* (Ph.D. dissertation, Yale University, 1973).
5 See also above, chapter 6.
6 K. Marx, *Capital* (New York: International Publishers, 1967), vol. II.
7 *The Wealth of Nations* (New York: Modern Library, 1937) pp. 262–6; see also K. Marx, *Capital*, vol. II, pp. 191–2.
8 K. Marx, *Capital*, vol. I, chapters 23–4.

Index

Abstract labor: not attained by artisan, 231–2; character of not grasped by Smith, 209–10; concept of, 163–7, 173; conception of impossible for Aristotle, 213n; connection of to mechanization, 221, 225; develops through division of labor, 169–70, 172–3; foreshadowed by work of slave, 233; implies equality of labors, 168; as necessary for social determination of production, 219, 221–4; requires separation of laborer from his labor-power, 223, 226–7, 229; sustained by force of laborer's personality, 174, 175–7, 222–3, 229; and useful labor, 183, 183n; *see also* Labor-power

Abstract person: concrete determination of by needs, 50–1, 59–60, 65–7; and connection of laboring to property, 204; constitution of, 42; located outside of society by social theory, 32–3; and Lockean idea of labor, 203; *see also* Individual; Individuality; Personality; Self-subsistent person

Advertising, 273, 275–6
Agriculture: *see* Production: agricultural
Allocation of resources, 10, 118, 121
Aristotle, 74, 221n, 231n
Assembly line, 266

Baran, P., 275n
Barter, 111–12, 143, 143n
Baverman, H., 167n, 180n, 224n, 257n

Cantillon, R., 71n
Capital: accumulation of, 25, 311, 316n, 319; not based on forcible appropriation, 134–5; as basis for full development of labor, 224–5; capitalization of, 317; circulating, 281–94, 284n, 305–6, 306n, 312–15; commodity capital, 252–3, 257–61, 262, 263, 270, 281, 286, 296, 313; component parts of, 278f, 280–1, 300, 315; conceived as limited by given needs, 125–7; conceived as naturally determined, 291; concept of, 121–2, 311; conception of in modern economic analysis, 121;

325

property, 50-1, 62; realization of, 106, 243-4; universality of, 214-15; and value, 66-7, 75-6, 112-13

Utility: defined, 62n-63n; *see also* Use-value

Value: appreciation in, 301, 301n, 304n; capitalization of, 257-60, 315-18; in classical political economy, 22, 36, 94, 146, 246-7, 306-7; as command over other commodities, 68, 72-5; as common substance underlying exchange, 69-71, 104-5; defined, 21-2, 66-7, 68, 71-2, 96, 105-6, 110; determination of, 22, 297-8, 301-2, 314; as determined independently of exchange, 94-5, 95n; development of concept of, 246-7; distinction between production and realization of, 146; distinguished from exchange-value, 69, 71, 75, 96; elementary form of, 76-80, 81-2, 84-6, 111, 122; equated with exchange-value, 80-1; equated with use-value in elementary form, 79, 81; in the equivalent form, 78-80; expanded form of, 82-4, 86; expansion of occurs within and outside of circulation, 149; expression of, 185, 192, 197, 244-5, 249f, 285, 287-8, 314-17; expression of requires interaction of use-values, 78; general form of, 84-6; as hoard of money, 116, 128; idea of excluded by Aristotle, 74; importance of equivalent exchange for concept of, 131-2; as indifferent to particularity, 67-72, 75-6, 81, 83-4, 114; Marx's theory of, 5-6, 69n, 76, 82, 85, 88n, 95n, 152n, 177n, 178n, 211-12, 293, 293n, 301-2, 306-7, 309; measure of, 90-6; in the

money form, 86-8, 88n; as a movement of commodities, 100, 104-5, 117-18, 123; as objectification of will, 48; as objective force preceding particular contracts, 41; preservation of, 117-18, 121, 197, 250-2, 263, 287; production of, 194-7, 261-262; and property, 40-1, 48-9, 199; as proportional relation of commodity to system of commodities, 110; realization of, 100-6, 108-9, 112, 122-3, 242-3, 244-5, 251, 252, 258-9, 261-2, 271-2; reduced to need by modern economics, 80-1; as relation to fixed needs, 126-7; as relation to the world of commodities, 83-6; relationship of to price, 6, 69n, 91-6, 95n; in the relative form, 78-80; Ricardian theory of, 3-4, 71n, 94-5, 95n, 199, 210-11, 247; self-expansion of, 125f, 127-9, 135-6, 142, 152-3, 255, 260, 285, 294, 311, 318-19; self-expansion of predicated on exchange, 136-7; within simple circulation of commodities, 119-21; Smithian theory of, 77, 80, 94, 146, 204-11, 205n, 247; as social substance, 95-6; starting point of theory of, 204; theory of prior to Smith, 41, 93-4, 199-202; and use-value, 66-7, 75-6, 112-13; *see also* Labor-commanded theory of value; Labor theory of value

Wage: cycle of payment of, 288-9, 294; determination of, 143n; as element of circulating capital, 284, 288-9; real, 293, 293n; relation of to means of production, 236; Ricardian determination of, 3-4; *see also* Abstract labor; Labor; Labor-power

Wages bill: determination of, 292-

293; equated with circulating capital, 290–1; as part of capital investment, 283, 291–2

Wealth: as command over all use-values, 72, 97; concept of, 21–2, 226; concrete determination of, 20–4; constituted through mutual dependence of needy persons, 48–50; constituted by value and use-value, 66; exists as circulation of commodities and money, 99, 106, 125; expansion of, 191, 236–7; as foundation of freedom, 54, 73, 113–14; illimitability of, 126–7, 226; limitation of in Lockean conception, 200–1; as means of production, 159–60, 182; as most elementary economic relation, 19; most elementary relations of, 24; preclassical and classical conceptions of, 129–30; production of, 191–6, 210, 224–6, 235–6; production of with unfree labor, 229–30; relationship of to money, 97–8; self-determination of, 13; as self-ordering totality, 16; Smithian conception of, 207–8; as social substance, 48–9; as useful property, 48–51, 66–7, 72–3

Wealth of Nations: connection of laboring to value in, 209; contribution of to economic theory, 211; treatment of value in, 204–5n; wealth in, 200

Winfield, R., 152n

Work, 8; pace of, 266–7, 268–9